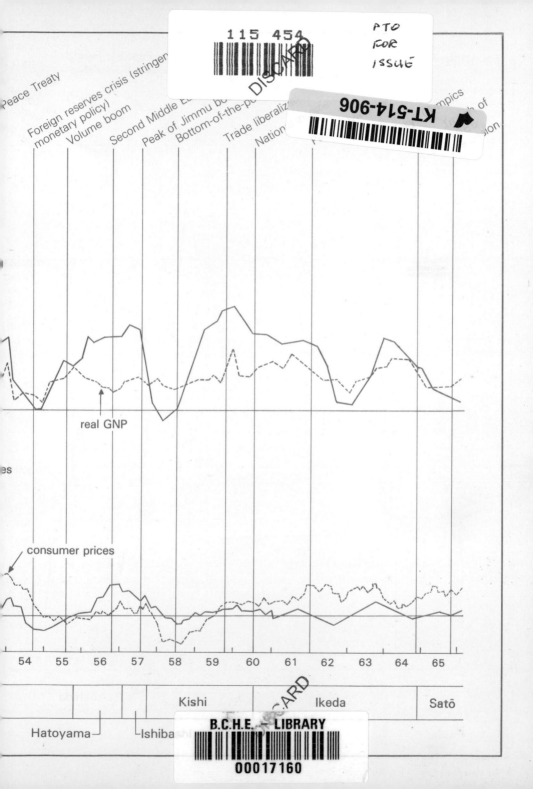

Peace Treaty

Foreign reserves crisis (stringent
monetary policy)
Volume boom

Second Middle Ea...

Peak of Jimmu b...
Bottom-of-the-po...

Trade liberaliz...

Nation...

...mpics

...h of

...ion

real GNP

...es

consumer prices

| 54 | 55 | 56 | 57 | 58 | 59 | 60 | 61 | 62 | 63 | 64 | 65 |

Kishi   Ikeda   Satō

Hatoyama   Ishibashi

JAPAN'S POSTWAR ECONOMY

JAPAN'S POSTWAR ECONOMY

An Insider's View of Its History and Its Future

Tatsurō Uchino

Translated by
Mark A. Harbison

KODANSHA INTERNATIONAL LTD.
Tokyo, New York and San Francisco

Note: Superscript numbers refer to the notes on pp. 251–78.

Originally published under the title *Sengo Nihon keizaishi* by Kodansha Ltd., 1978. Publication of this translation was assisted by a grant from the Japan Foundation.

Distributed in the United States by Kodansha International/ USA Ltd., through Harper & Row, Publishers, Inc., 10 East 53rd Street, New York, New York 10022. Published by Kodansha International Ltd., 12-21, Otowa 2-chome, Bunkyo-ku, Tokyo 112 and Kodansha International/USA Ltd., with offices at 10 East 53rd Street, New York, New York 10022 and The Hearst Building, 5 Third Street, Suite 430, San Francisco, California 94103.

Library of Congress Cataloging in Publication Data

Uchino, Tatsurō, 1925–
    Japan's postwar economy.
    Revised translation of: Sengo Nihon keizaishi.
    Includes index.
    1. Japan—Economic conditions—1945–   2. Japan—Economic policy—1945–   . I. Title.
HC462.9.U2613   1983   330.952'04   83–47621
IBSN 0–87011–595–2
ISBN 4–7700–1095–8 (in Japan)

CONTENTS

PREFACE

I have written this book because I feel that the present is an ideal time to reexamine Japan's postwar economic history and to reconsider a number of issues that are going to have an impact on the country and its economy in the future. Until the early 1960s, when postwar economic history spanned only ten to fifteen years, economic studies suffered from a lack of documentary materials. The decision-making processes of a number of major policies were still shrouded in secrecy. During this same period most Japanese were concentrating on rushing headlong into the future, anticipating the changes that were to transform the nation's society and culture. There was little time then to stop and look back over the course that had been taken since the war. This is symbolized by the fad for books aimed at white-collar employees that took as their theme management methods in firms characterized by the "do or die for the company" type of employee. The ideology of futurism, which advocated a disregard for the past and the single-minded pursuit of the future, was also in vogue then.

During the same period university courses in economic history declined in popularity. A curriculum in economics should give equal weight to theory, economic history, and case studies, but in the period of rapid growth the study of economic history was largely neglected. With few exceptions, students seemed to feel that all they needed were the theories and practical knowledge relevant to the economics of rapid growth, which had become a reality by the time they reached their college years.

In the meantime, scholars of modern Japanese history quietly continued their work of reexamining historical facts and commonly held theories concerning the war years and the postwar period. Their work began to appear around 1965, and the effects on postwar economic history have just begun to appear now. The United States government has only recently released previously classified documentary materials to the public, and scholars on both sides of the Pacific are now digging out the historical facts of the postwar period. At the same time, volumes of material that for various reasons had been kept secret by the Japanese government are also gradually coming into the open. More important, perhaps, is that the scope of the study of economic history has now expanded to span one whole generation. This is significant because one generation is a sufficiently long period for the filtering process of history to be effective and, thus, for the broad outlines of postwar economic history to emerge in high relief. All these recent developments have created a suitable background for taking a new look at the history of Japan's postwar economy.

I was fortunate to have been well placed to view the course of postwar economic policy during the nearly forty years of rapid changes since the war. After university, I joined the Economic Stabilization Board and then the Economic Planning Agency, positions that gave me ample opportunity to observe, analyze, and evaluate the flow of the postwar economy with some objectivity. I also participated in the preparation of more than fifteen white papers on the economy, either as a member of the research team or as its head. This experience threw me into contact with brilliant senior analysts and colleagues my own age, whose kind and thoughtful guidance played an incalculable role in shaping my own understanding of the postwar economy. It was under their influence that I gradually became accustomed to constantly looking over the long-term effects of changes in the economy or in economic policy. The drafting of white papers also provided excellent training for taking a broad, objective view of the economy. However, a number of problems cannot be dealt with sufficiently on the basis of a one-year study, and I often felt the limitations of such an approach in developing a more comprehensive evaluation of economic policies that had been conceived on the basis of a longer time span. It was while at the Economic Planning Agency that I began to feel that, given the opportunity, I would like to trace the entire development of the postwar economy. I have finally left the government to take a position at Sophia University in Tokyo, and this volume is the result of my research there.

In writing this book, I have tried to keep three points in mind. First, I attempted to grasp the flow of postwar economic history from an objective, neutral position. As I reread documentary and scholarly materials on the period, I was struck again by the paucity of works that deal with those years on the basis of objective historical fact and universally acceptable standards of accuracy. Rather, an overwhelming number of so-called works of research on the postwar Japanese economy are either projects sponsored by the government, and therefore oriented to the policy line of whichever administration happened to be in power, or completely dominated by the left-wing ideology fashionable among many academics and social critics. History does not belong either to the establishment or to those who fancy themselves to be antiestablishment.

Second, I have tried to give due consideration both to the major policies implemented during the period and to the major policy proposals that were not adopted or were abandoned in midstream. In many cases, the latter policies had enormous potential significance, and the fact that they were not adopted had a substantial impact on future events.

The influence of economic policy on the Japanese economy, and society as a whole, should not be underestimated. This is especially true of the postwar period, which has been characterized by substantial government intervention in the economy. The economic policies of the various cabinets in power during the period have not been uniformly effective. There have been successes and failures, wise policies and foolish ones, effective and ineffective responses to new problems. Indeed, in retrospect, the political culture of Japan, at least in terms of economic and social policy, has been characterized by intense debate over each new policy before and immediately after its implementation but little consciousness of the need to follow through with investigations of the effectiveness over the long run.

Third, while the focus of this book is on a general treatment of the main currents of postwar economic history, I have also included brief notes on political and social currents in postwar Japan, as well as an overview of shifts in public opinion. I hope that these will serve to refresh readers' memories of the major events of postwar economic history. At the same time, it is my belief that politics reflect changes in the economy and in society, which then affect and influence public opinion. An economic history that ignored the lives of ordinary people, their hopes and desires, would be completely without life or significance.

To avoid confusion, I should say something about my use of the word "postwar," both in the title and in my subsequent discussion. In the mass media, in a number of academic disciplines, and in government policy statements, it has become somewhat fashionable to say that "the postwar period is over." Such a statement attempts to distinguish the immediate postwar period of reconstruction from the high-speed economic growth of the 1960s and 1970s. My use of the term is not so complicated, and by "postwar" I simply mean the period from the end of World War II to the present. My own chronology of the postwar period is as follows.

1. The Immediate Postwar Period: August 1945 to the mid-1950s. During this period the economic level of every sector of the economy was below prewar levels.
2. The Korean War Period: 1950 to 1955. During this period the American policy shift, spurred by the outbreak of the Korean War, enabled Japan to achieve economic recovery and independence.
3. The Technology Revolution and the Mass Consumer Society: 1955 to 1959. It was during this period that the foundations for massive capital investment in new technologies and the development of a consumer society began to materialize.
4. High-Speed Economic Growth: the Early 1960s. This was the period of the so-called economic miracle, symbolized by the National Income-Doubling Plan, the Iwato boom, and the advent of the full employment economy.
5. Japan as an Economic Superpower: the Early 1960s to 1971. During this period rapid economic growth continued but was increasingly accompanied by new and unforeseen problems. At home, the heavy concentration of industrial facilities and the almost complete absence of any regulations resulted in the worsening problem of pollution. Internationally, Japan's growing balance of payments surpluses began to cause political problems that culminated in the "Nixon shock" and the revaluation of the yen in 1971.
6. The End of Rapid Growth: 1971 to 1983. During this period the entire global economy has been subjected to massive jolts. The collapse of the Smithsonian Agreement, inflation in Japan due to excess liquidity, the two "oil shocks," and rampant inflation occurred in quick succession. These problems, and Japan's solutions, have created a number of structural imbalances both in the domestic economy and in Japan's relations with other countries.

Finally, I have added a number of notes (*see* pp. 251–78), most of which attempt to relate Japan's postwar economic history to important international events or to major changes in the global economy. In some cases, I have included anecdotes or behind-the-scenes glimpses of the process of economic policy making, which may prove of some interest to readers.

INTRODUCTION

AUGUST 15, 1945

Japan's postwar economic history begins on August 15, 1945, with the radio broadcast by Emperor Hirohito announcing the end of World War II, acknowledging Japan's defeat, and accepting the terms of the Potsdam Declaration. It was also the beginning of the country's "modern era" (*gendai*), a term used by scholars, critics, and journalists to distinguish the postwar period from the period of modernization and Westernization (*kindai*) that began with the Meiji Restoration in 1868 and continued until Japan's defeat in 1945. Although these terms are not always used consistently, there is indeed an enormous historical gap between the two periods. The systematic demilitarization and democratization of Japan's social and economic structure after the war were accompanied by unprecedented changes in the mentality of the Japanese people that were occasioned by Japan's defeat.[1]

Making a New Start. With the end of the war, the way was open for launching a new economy, a modern economy without war. However, by the time defeat came, in August 1945, the country had been almost totally devastated. Its vast colonial empire was lost, its economic infrastructure was in a state of ruin, and its population was barely able to survive from day to day. The war had left its cruel marks on every aspect of life.

Aerial bombing by the United States, including the atomic bomb attacks on Hiroshima and Nagasaki, had reduced 119 major cities to rubble. The cities that survived the bombing can be counted on one hand: Kyoto, Nara, Kanazawa, Kurashiki, Yamaguchi. Approximately 2.2

Table 1. Damage to the National Wealth during World War II

(¥100 millions)

	Total damages	Proportion of damage	Remaining national wealth at end of war
Total national wealth assets	643	25%	1,889
Production goods	198	25	597
Industrial machinery	80	34	154
(Gas and electricity facilities)	16	11	133
Consumption goods	348	25	1,059
(Furniture and household effects)	175	21	634
Transportation facilities	96	29	233
(Ships)	74	81	18
Structures	222	25	682
(Dwellings and commercial shops)	103		
Forestlands, roads, historic properties	10		
Naval vessels, planes	404	100	
Totals	1,057	36	1,889

Notes: 1. Figures are based on wartime prices converted to current prices at end of war.

2. In the original report, damage to structures (buildings) was included in the categories of "production goods" and "consumption goods." In the present table, structures have been listed separately.

Source: Economic Stabilization Board, *Taiheiyō sensō ni yoru waga kuni no higai sōgō hōkokusho* (Comprehensive report on damage to Japan from the Pacific War), 1949.

Table 2. Damage to Residences during World War II

(1,000 structures)

	National totals	Urban areas
Total damage	2,362	2,264
Completely burned	2,188	2,119
Completely demolished	64	55
Partially burned	49	39
Partially demolished	61	51

million homes were lost, including those partially destroyed, and 9 million people were driven into the streets with only the clothes on their backs. Moreover, if the number of homes lost as a result of wartime confiscations and forced evacuations is added to this figure, the number of civilian dwellings had been reduced by 20 percent, from approximately 14 million before the war to 11.35 million.

Of course, the destruction resulting from the war was not limited to residential housing. As is clear from Table 2, cities were especially hard hit, and factories, roads, bridges, and port facilities (as well as ships docked in these facilities) were virtually wiped out. In a report entitled *Comprehensive Report on Damage to Japan from the Pacific War*, the Economic Stabilization Board, which was formed shortly after the end of the war, estimated that the total damage to the economy inflicted directly by the war amounted to ¥99.2 billion based on prices in 1945. At price levels in 1970, losses would have reached ¥12 trillion. Even if losses of military equipment, such as airplanes, ships, and weapons, is subtracted from this figure, damage to the economy amounted to ¥65.3 billion (¥8 trillion at 1970 prices). The rate of war losses to total national wealth in 1944 was as high as 35 percent, and to national wealth in nonmilitary sectors 25.4 percent. These figures represent staggering losses, almost equal to the entire gross national product in 1946. Indeed, at the time, it was thought that it would take more than ten years to make up these losses even if the economy followed a normal course of recovery and reconstruction. In human terms, the country lost at least 1.99 million military casualties and 690,000 civilians, a total of 2.68 million people.

Besides housing, the infrastructure sector most heavily hit by war damages was shipping. At the beginning of the war, Japan's shipping stood at 6.3 million tons, which was reduced to a mere 1.53 million tons by the end of the war. Moreover, much of the remaining shipping was comprised of vessels hastily constructed during the war years that were incapable of making long voyages. Faced with staggering shortages of food, raw materials, and commodities, Japan was unable even to import relief supplies from abroad on its own. Railways and hydroelectric facilities survived the war more or less intact, but they were by no means sufficient to meet the sudden and rapid increase of demand placed on them.

The war had also inflicted damages that cannot be expressed through statistics alone. A famous poem from the T'ang dynasty in China begins

> My country laid to ruins,
> Mountains and rivers remain. . . .

**Table 3. Sharp Declines in Production Capacity and
Consumption Levels in the Immediate Postwar Period**

(1934–36 = 100)

	1945	1946	1947
Real GNP*	..	62	65
Per capita GNP*	..	55	56
Real per capita personal consumption*	..	57	60
Real wages (manufacturing industries)	..	..	30
Production in mining and manufacturing	60	31	37
(Coal)	78	53	71
(Steel)	24	10	15
(Textiles)	7	7	10
Agricultural production	60	79	76
Volume of exports	..	..	7
Volume of imports	..	..	14
Total population	104	109	113
Wholesale prices (Tokyo)	350	1,630	4,820
Consumer prices (Tokyo)	..	5,000	10,910
Government bonds nominal value (year end) (Bank of Japan)	1,805	5,488	12,889

Notes: * indicates that index is based on fiscal year; other figures are for calendar
years.
.. indicates that data is not available.

In Japan in 1945, even the mountains and rivers had been laid to ruin. As the tides of war turned against Japan, the government neglected forestation projects for flood control and the repair and maintenance of water control facilities. Forests were stripped for timber, and reforestation virtually ignored. The total acreage under cultivation also dropped drastically due to labor shortages and the imposition of extraordinary labor levies for airfield construction. Remaining agricultural lands suffered huge declines in productivity due to overutilization and haphazard fertilization. The results of this neglect of the agriculture and forestry sectors of the economy were acutely felt in 1945, when harvests were disastrously low, and in 1946, when the country suffered from massive floods.

Japan had sustained crushing damages to its own economy during the war and, with defeat, it had found itself completely deprived of its former empire. The loss of Manchuria, China, and Southeast Asia reduced the territory of the Japanese empire to 56 percent of its peak during the war. As nearly 6 million demobilized soldiers and repatriated civilians flooded

Table 4. The Straitened Living Standards in the Immediate Postwar Period

(per capita commodities supplies)

	Unit	Prewar (av. for 1934–36)	1946	1947	1948	1949	1950
Rice	grams per capita	361	254	294	287	295	302
Wheat	〃	26	40	58	69	71	73
Sweet potatoes (*satsuma imo*)	〃	65	131	93	130	125	93
Potatoes	〃	11	35	41	41	42	43
Miso (bean paste)	〃	28	19	15	14	20	18
Soy sauce	〃	38	20	21	24	25	32
Sugar	〃	34	2	1	14.	13	9
Fish and shellfish	〃	40	26	27	27	32	40
Fruit	〃	56	19	24	33	36	42
Poultry and eggs	〃	6.3	1.0	1.1	1.2	1.8	2.3
Saké	〃	31	7	7	6	6	6
Clothing	pounds per capita	9.4	2.0	2.1	2.3	1.9	3.9
Leather shoes	pairs per 1,000 persons	56	27	33	33	36	28
Porcelain or pottery utensils	kilograms per capita	6.1	0.8	1.2	2.3	2.4	1.9
Charcoal	〃	22	12	16	16	15	15
Firewood	cubic feet	8	7	7	8	7	7
Soap	kilograms per capita	1.7	0.2	0.1	0.1	0.2	0.9
Lead pencils	number per capita	6.1	3.3	3.6	4.1	4.9	4.6
Newsprint	pounds per capita	9.2	2.9	2.4	2.8	3.0	3.4
Per capita commodities supplies index		100	57	64	67	71	80

Source: Economic White Paper, 1952.

into Japan from these lost territories, the cessation of military production threw another 4 million people out of work to make a total of 13.1 million unemployed at the end of the war. Even after making allowances for those who could be absorbed into the agricultural sector, the economy would have to create employment for approximately 10 million people. The loss of its empire, and the abrupt cessation of trade with countries in its former sphere of influence, revealed all too clearly how dependent Japan had been on imports of raw materials and agricultural products: rice, beans, iron ore, and anthracite from Korea; rice and sugar from Taiwan; timber, pulp, paper, and coal from the Sakhalin Islands; iron ore, coal, and soybeans from Manchuria; salt, iron ore, and coal from China. With the end of the war, Japan's access to these vital markets was completely cut off. This, together with the sudden increase in population, resulted in a demand for essential raw materials and basic daily necessities that bordered on hysteria.

The Japanese people rushed to welcome a long-awaited era of peace, but Japan itself had been thrown into a state of total ruin. The spirit of confusion and disillusionment with former values left the people with no clear vision of what the postwar world would bring. The government, which had dominated the country totally during the war years, was now in a political vacuum. Having accepted the terms of the Potsdam Declaration, it could only await the decisions of the Allied Occupation and was certainly in no position to outline a policy for the future. As shown in Tables 3 and 4, the gross national product (GNP) declined to only 60 percent of prewar levels (average for 1934–36), massive shortages of basic necessities reduced standards of living to unprecedented lows, and demand resulting from these shortages created a runaway inflation.[2,3]

Radical Reforms under the Occupation. Immediately after Japan's surrender, General Douglas MacArthur of the United States was appointed Supreme Commander for the Allied Powers (SCAP), and the Occupation Army began to disembark on Japanese territory on August 30, 1945. Japan was under foreign occupation for the first time in its history, and it was to last more than six years, until the signing of the San Francisco Peace Treaty in September 1951. Although the Occupation pursued a line of "indirect rule," no policies could be carried out without the direction, or the consent, of the General Headquarters of the Allied Forces (GHQ). The directions of GHQ, or SCAP, were, in fact, direct orders and, for all practical purposes, opposition to GHQ policies was impossible.

Moreover, GHQ enforced a rigid system of internal censorship so that the government was not free either to seek news from abroad or to appeal directly to public opinion for support of its own initiatives.

It has recently become clear that the Allied powers had discussed the plan of partitioning the country into four zones, following the example of the occupation of Germany. According to this proposal, Hokkaido and the northeastern region of Honshu (Tōhoku) would be controlled by the Soviet Union; Tokyo, Kyoto, and the intervening area would be controlled by the United States; southern Honshu and Kyushu would fall to England; and Shikoku to China. This plan failed to materialize due to deteriorating relations between the United States and the Soviet Union, and the Occupation was carried out exclusively by America, which adopted the system of "indirect rule," under which Occupation policies would be implemented by the Japanese government.

The Suzuki Cabinet, charged with the task of bringing an end to the war, was replaced at the end of the war by the short-lived Higashikuni Cabinet, and then by the Shidehara Cabinet (*see* Appendix). Shortly after the formation of the latter, MacArthur issued GHQ's order for the implementation of five basic democratization reforms (October 11, 1945). The basic points of GHQ's democratization program may be summarized as follows: 1) recognition of the right of women to participate in politics; 2) establishment of the right of workers to organize; 3) democratization of the educational system; 4) abolition of absolutist politics, including the abolition of all laws and state organs that restricted human rights; 5) promotion of economic democratization. From the point of view of contemporary Japanese politics, these demands seem quite obvious. However, under the Imperial Constitution, which had been in force since the Meiji period (1868–1912), they were nothing less than revolutionary, and there were severe limitations to their effective implementation. In fact, until the establishment of the new Constitution on May 3, 1946, the reforms proposed by GHQ were not effectively implemented, and they went through a series of fits and starts that were as much a result of GHQ's lack of knowledge of the people it had come to govern as direct Japanese opposition. After presenting its five demands for democratization, GHQ promptly issued a series of directives calling for a rapid succession of reforms in the economic system. The three pillars of GHQ's economic democratization policy were agricultural reform, democratization of labor, and dissolution of the *zaibatsu*, the huge financial combines that had dominated the economy before defeat.

Of these, it was agricultural reform, in the form of an extensive land reform, that the Japanese government took up first. Anticipating formal directives from GHQ, the government took the initiative, and in December 1945, pushed through the Diet a draft proposal that would have radically revised the wartime Agricultural Lands Adjustment Law (enacted in 1938). The revised law would have forced the sale of all agricultural land in the possession of resident landholders exceeding five hectares, the national average for individual landholdings. Moreover, all tenant lands were to be sold at low prices to former tenants with the government acting as the intermediary. In comparison to its behavior in implementing other democratization measures, the government attempted to play a much more active role in land reform, and the fact that it was able to do this may be explained by the recognition of contradictions in the landowner system for some time before the defeat.

However, the government's proposal (the first land reform proposal) did not go far enough for GHQ, and the program that was finally agreed upon called for an even more radical land reform. This second land reform was enacted in October 1946 in the form of two laws entitled the Revised Agricultural Lands Adjustment Law and the Special Measures Law for the Establishment of Owner-Cultivators. The land reform progressed at an extremely rapid pace from October 1946 to 1949, and resulted in the transfer to former tenants of 1.87 million hectares of cultivated land, or 81 percent of all tenant land, and 0.24 million hectares of pasturelands.

While the reform led to the decline of the former elite landowner class, it also meant that almost all the nation's farmers, most of whom had been tenants struggling under the burden of high rents in kind, were able to become landowners. However, due to its radical nature, the land reform also produced a highly dispersed, minutely fragmented pattern of land ownership that would place severe limits on the expansion of agricultural productivity for some time to come. Fortunately, the land reform did not extend to forestlands or wastelands, and the liberation of tenant farmers resulted in increases in agricultural production that helped to compensate for this problem. In general, it may be said that among the many nations that implemented land reform programs after World War II, Japan's land reform was an unparalleled success. It increased agricultural incomes, expanded domestic markets, and liberated the energies of a large number of former tenants, resulting in land improvements on a large scale and rapid increases in agricultural investment.

Labor reform, the second pillar of GHQ's economic democratization program, also proceeded rapidly with the enactment of three basic laws modeled on American labor legislation: the Trade Union Law (December 22, 1945); the Labor Standards Law (April 7, 1947); and the Labor Relations Adjustment Law (September 27, 1947). The Trade Union Law established, for the first time in Japan's history, the freedom of workers to organize trade unions and the right of assembly. The Labor Relations Adjustment Law established methods and procedures for dispute settlements and defined limits on strike behavior. The Labor Standards Law was a revolutionary advance in legislation protecting workers, which had lagged behind in Japan. It called for the elimination of feudalistic working conditions, prohibited forced labor, established the principles of the eight-hour work day and holiday systems, set limits on the employment of women and minors, and provided for compensation for work-related injury. Together, these laws established the legislative foundation for one of the most progressive labor relations systems in the world. In addition, the Employment Stabilization Law (November 30, 1947) and the Unemployment Insurance Law (December 1, 1947) established the institutional framework for the enhanced status and greater economic security of Japanese workers in the postwar period.

With the enactment of the Trade Union Law, there was a rapid increase in the number of organized workers. In the three months immediately after the enactment of the law, the number of union members increased from 380,000 to 3 million and by the end of 1948 had reached 6.7 million. The rapid increase in union activity sparked by this legislation, and the inexperience of both labor and management in handling wage disputes, created severe problems in the immediate postwar period, and the labor movement was harshly criticized for going too far. However, with the accumulation of actual experience, the labor movement quickly matured, and the demands of workers for an equal distribution of wealth, the normalization of labor–management relations, and the resulting increase in real wages have contributed enormously to the development of Japan's postwar economy.

The dissolution of the *zaibatsu* posed the most serious problems, and was carried out least successfully, of all the economic reforms. In *The Initial Postsurrender Policy for Japan*, published on September 22, 1945, GHQ was ordered to "direct the Japanese government to establish plans for the dissolution of the large industrial and financial combines that have controlled Japan's commerce and industry." Based on this, GHQ issued orders to the Japanese government, in the form of memoranda, pushing for a speedy implementation of measures to break up the *zaibatsu*. On November 2, 1945, the government ordered the freezing of the assets of fifteen of the largest *zaibatsu*, including Mitsui, Mitsubishi, Sumitomo, and Yasuda. In May 1946, the Holding Companies Liquidation Commission was established and, in September 1947, the commission ordered the dissolution of Mitsui Bussan and Mitsubishi Shōji. During the same period, GHQ carried out a purge of public officials who were considered militarists and of important figures in the financial world who were thought to have cooperated with the militarists in pursuing the war. The *zaibatsu* were broken up in this way, by severing their holding companies, the core of *zaibatsu* control, and by purging their leaders, including members of founding families.

Two laws enacted under the direction of GHQ pushed the attack against the *zaibatsu* and other large firms even further. The Antimonopoly Law, which is formally called the "Law Relating to the Prohibition of Private Monopoly and to Methods of Preserving Fair Trade," was enacted in April 1947. This law, which was based on the United States' Antitrust Law, established the Fair Trade Commission. In December 1947, the Diet passed the Law for the Elimination of Excessive Economic Concentration, which provided the legislative foundation for a radical democratization of the economy through the dissolution of any existing company that was considered monopolistic. Eventually, three hundred and twenty-five companies were designated for dissolution.

However, due largely to the reversal of U.S. policy with the deepening of the Cold War, this radical program for breaking up the *zaibatsu* and other large Japanese firms was never effectively implemented. Also, following the signing of the San Francisco Peace Treaty in September 1951, many of GHQ's policies were extensively modified, especially its program for the dissolution of *zaibatsu* and the economic democratization. The Antimonopoly Law was revised, former *zaibatsu* companies were allowed to resume the use of their prewar company names, and Mitsui and Mitsubishi were reorganized. This led to the charge that all the measures designed to break up the *zaibatsu* had ended in failure. However, such a criticism ignores the extent to which the postwar reforms were effective in destroying the foundations of the old *zaibatsu*, in which the heads of founding families held unquestioned authority through their control of stock and were able to impose a premodern system of management in which family ties were more important than managerial skill. The separation of capital from management wrought by the Occupation reforms started a "manager's revolution," in which skillful managers and new enterprises were able to compete freely whether or not they were associated with one of the traditional conglomerates. As we shall see in the following chapters, many of the old *zaibatsu* quickly reorganized in the postwar period and were joined by new conglomerates. However, the organization of these postwar "financial lineages," or *keiretsu*, is completely different from that of the prewar *zaibatsu*, both in terms of internal management and in the degree to which firms compete. To this extent, the attempt to break up the *zaibatsu* in the immediate postwar period must be credited with the transformation of the foundations of the Japanese economy.

An Evaluation of Early Occupation Policies. The Allied Occupation and the policies adopted by the United States in managing it played the leading role in the implementation of economic democratization policies and the destruction of Japan's semifeudal familial society. The new Constitution, drafted under the supervision of Occupation authorities, represented the climax of a vigorous program of demilitarization, elimination of the class system and special privileges, establishment of parliamentary democracy, and guaranteeing the rights of women. The radical social, political, and economic reforms that were carried out during the Occupation were of such a scale that they could not have been accomplished without Japan's total defeat. However, this by no means suggests that the Allied powers or the Occupation authorities designed and carried out these sweeping reforms on the basis of any sense of mission or feelings of friendship for the Japanese people. Certainly, the history of the Occupation of Japan by America does not support the naive belief of some Japanese leftists that the Occupation army was a "people's liberation army." The central aims of the Occupation's democratization program, and of its radical reforms, were the total disarming of Japan and the complete destruction of the economic and social structure that had made it possible for Japan to wage war. Early Occupation policy was directed principally to demilitarization and democratization, and an early directive from Washington to MacArthur clearly states, "You are not to assume any responsibility for the reconstruction or strengthening of the Japanese economy." Thus, even as the Occupation was ordering the implementation of democratization measures, Occupation authorities were drafting a reparations policy of such severity that it can only be interpreted as a policy to inflict punishment on Japan.

The implementation of this reparation policy began with the first reparations mission to Japan, headed by Ambassador Edwin W. Pauley. The Pauley Report became the basis for the Interim Reparations Program adopted by the Far Eastern Commission (officially the highest authority in establishing Occupation policies), which called for implementing the reparations program by removing existing plant and equipment from Japan. More than one thousand factories were designated for removal under this program. Pauley's Final Reparations Report, delivered in November 1946, was a shock to the Japanese and, had it been carried out, would have effectively returned Japan to the stage of an underdeveloped agricultural country. Moreover, a report prepared by the Brookings Institute recommended that the standard of living that should be allowed the Japanese people was that of 1930, before the Manchurian Incident. News of these developments produced great fear among the Japanese. The period before the Manchurian Incident in 1931, and particularly the year 1930, had been one of extreme hardship for farmers and workers. Was it impossible to set the targets for economic reconstruction at the 1934–36 levels, when living standards had been somewhat better? The Japanese economy and most of its industrial infrastructure had been destroyed by the war, and the reparations policy proposed by Pauley threatened to deprive the country of what little plant and equipment that still remained. It was impossible during this period to view the future of the 80 million Japanese people with anything but extreme pessimism. The Japanese were grateful for the restoration of peace and the economic democratization measures promoted by the Occupation. However, confronted with an economic crisis and increasing hardships in daily life, many people feared that the new democracy would not bear fruit. It is against this background that the postwar history of the Japanese economy begins.[4]

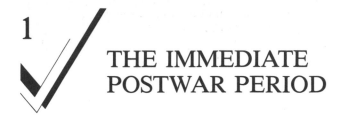

THE IMMEDIATE POSTWAR PERIOD

1. THE LONG ROAD TO RECONSTRUCTION

The "Bamboo Shoot Life." With the end of the war and the arrival of Occupation forces, the Japanese people quickly began to show signs of the vitality that had been submerged during the war years in the desperate struggle to survive the harsh economic conditions imposed by the government, and in the fear that they would perish in the defeat, which became more and more certain. On August 20, 1945, the blackout and curfew regulations—imposed as part of the defense against the intensive bombing that leveled most of Japan's major cities—were lifted; on August 22, radio weather forecasts were resumed; and on August 24, children who had been sent to rural areas to escape the bombing of major cities began to return to their families. In October, Japan's first postwar movie, *A Gentle Breeze*, was released, and its theme song (sung by Michiko Namiki), "The Apple Song," became the first postwar hit. Professional baseball reappeared on October 9. As the Occupation forces began to arrive, textbooks on English conversation topped the newly established best-sellers list.

However, prices of daily necessities began to rise from the day of Japan's defeat, and inflation continued to accelerate at a furious rate. Liberated from the fear and oppression of the war years, the Japanese people still had to confront the painful realities of daily life in a nation that had been physically and economically devastated. In fact, what emerged to supply immediate basic needs was an extensive black market, which sprouted throughout the country. Open-air markets flourished on bombed-out lots around train and streetcar stations or near busy streets, where people were

Figure 1. Black Market Prices in the Immediate Postwar Period
(compared to official prices)

Source: National Policy Agency Report,
end of October 1945.

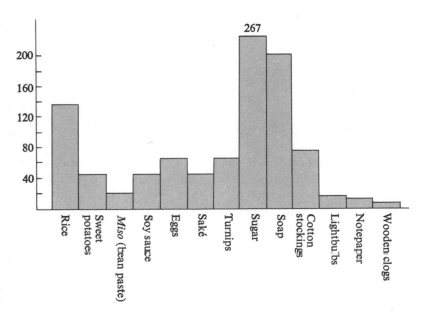

able to obtain products that had not been available during the war years. Everything from such foodstuffs as rice balls, potatoes, cabbage, and dried fish to clothing, blankets, gloves, cooking utensils, and other essentials could be obtained at these markets, as well as luxury items such as cigarettes, lighters, fountain pens, clocks, and leather shoes. At portable stalls, a sweet bean soup called *shiruko* or a suspicious-looking "squid" stew was available and, of course, a variety of cheap grain alcohol was offered as well.

It is estimated that the total number of open-air markets and portable stalls involved in black market operations reached over 60,000 during the immediate postwar period. They were largely supported by the illegal diversion of military supplies in the form of secret hoards brought home by demobilized soldiers and by black market factories. These factories had been established originally to produce military supplies, but even

Figure 2. Inflation in the Immediate Postwar Period (1934–36=1)

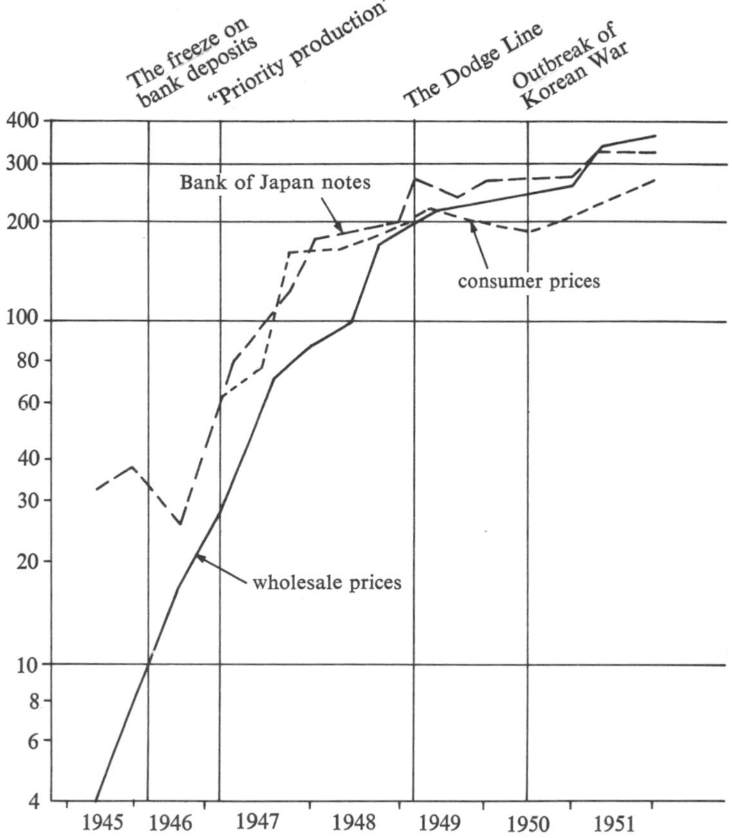

Note: All prices are for Tokyo.

during the war years their owners and managers turned increasingly to the production of articles for everyday use that could be diverted to the black market in order to support their employees. In addition to these sources of supplies, the fact that the black market became a center for barter insured its spectacular growth.

As inflation worsened at an alarming rate, even the salaries of the lucky few with steady employment could not keep pace, and many less fortunate had lost their jobs with the defeat. The Japanese people had no choice but to maintain a tightrope existence by trading heirlooms, such as costly kimono, treasured antiques, and other possessions for daily necessities. This process of giving up precious belongings one by one for barter on the black market or in exchange for food from farms suggested the image of peeling the layers off a bamboo shoot. A popular slang expression of the postwar period, the "bamboo shoot life" (*takenoko seikatsu*), evokes the squalor of everyday living and the prevailing consciousness that life was extremely tenuous. Such phrases as "selling things off" or "the household vegetable plot," which referred to the furtive practice of planting vegetable gardens in burned-out lots near one's home, also became common slang expressions. Thus, while urban dwellers lacked the means to produce food and other necessities for themselves and were forced to endure hunger and destitution, a large class of black market brokers and corrupt farmers emerged to reap enormous profits by taking advantage of their plight.

The worsening food supply situation provides an extreme example of the basic contradictions in the Japanese economy and the unfairness of the existing distribution systems. In 1945 Japan experienced its worst crop failure since 1935, with an official rice harvest of only 5.8 million tons, a mere 60 percent of the average annual harvest since the earlier crop failure. The poor harvest was due to damage to crops from early frost and typhoons in the fall, as well as to the continued neglect of fertilization, and it made an already grave situation critical. There were widely publicized predictions of massive starvation unless at least 4.5 million tons of rice could be imported as relief from abroad. In fact, however, the country managed to get through the following year with only 0.7 million tons of imported rice.

Clearly, both the government and the press had wildly exaggerated the seriousness of the food crisis. On the other hand, it is also clear that the gap between official forecasts and actual outcome was partially the result of the postwar breakdown of the economic order. With defeat went a decline in the government's authority and ability to enforce economic controls, and it was no longer possible to force farmers to maintain regular shipments of foodstuffs. Not only was the government unable to suppress black marketeering but it was also unable to search out illegal food hoards and channel them to the official rationing system.

If the food supply situation is viewed only in the context of the official rationing system, shortages had indeed reached crisis proportions. The daily per capita quota of staple foods in 1946 was two hundred and ninety-seven grams, less than one bowl of steamed rice per meal. Moreover, while quotas were established for white rice, in actual practice nearly 30 percent of these rations was composed of substitutes, such as potatoes, soybeans, and bean curd. The per capita intake in these terms was only one thousand two hundred calories daily, about half prewar levels. And worse, the government was unable to guarantee food supplies even at these levels. During the preharvest summer months of 1945, there were rationing delays of up to ten days, and eventually cases of curtailed rationing. It was during this period that "hand over the rice" demonstrations began to flare up.

Against this background, black market prices for basic consumer commodities rocketed thirty to sixty times higher than official prices, the controlled prices under the rationing system. Of course, price increases for staple foodstuffs were most dramatic, with the rate for white rice outstripping increases in the official price by one hundred and thirty to one hundred and fifty times, which naturally reflects the "panic buying" of available supplies. However, the food situation was by no means the only cause of rampant inflation during this period. By far the most important factor in this hyper-inflation was the huge increase of currency in circulation.

Hyper-Inflation and the Bank Deposits Freeze. A Bank of Japan survey estimated that black market prices in Tokyo had risen 30 percent between September and December of 1945, and had doubled by February 1946. At the same time, the value of redeemable Bank of Japan notes jumped 40 percent between April 15 and April 30, 1945, from ¥30.3 billion to ¥43.5 billion in only two weeks. By the end of February 1946, the value of Bank of Japan notes in circulation had reached ¥59.9 billion, or doubled within a period of only six months. This situation created a vicious cycle: black market prices surged upward in the wake of rapid increases in currency issues, and the spiraling black market prices forced the upward revision of official prices.

The hyper-inflation resulting from this interaction of prices and currency supply was similar in severity to the inflation in Germany immediately after World War I. In short, the root of the hyper-inflation lay in the existence of a huge gap between the availability of money and that of supplies. The origins of this phenomenon may be traced to the government's financial policies during and immediately after the war. Successive wartime governments had dealt with the need to procure colossal sums for military funding by increasing government bond issues through borrowing from the Bank of Japan and through forcing bonds on the civilian population. Income obtained in this manner did not emerge as effective demand during the war because of economic controls but enormous purchasing potential had accumulated in the civilian economy by the end of the war. The release of this latent purchasing power onto the market at the end of the war coincided with the economy's inability to supply consumer commodities, and these two factors alone were more than sufficient to trigger rapid inflation. Moreover, additional factors leading to further increases in currency issue appeared in rapid succession.

First, large government outlays for military expenses were made in the four months immediately following defeat. These expenses included demobilization allowances for Japanese troops as well as war indemnities for businesses that had been ordered to engage in military production. The huge deficit incurred by these outlays was totally covered by the issue of government bonds accepted by the Bank of Japan. In the three and a half months between the end of the war and the order of General Headquarters (GHQ) to suspend indemnity payments in November 1945, the Special Account for Provisional Military Expenses disbursed ¥26.5 billion, a higher figure than for any period during the war.

Second, there was a sudden increase in loans to private businesses nationwide by commercial banks, which, in turn, relied on heavy borrowing from the Bank of Japan. These loans were intended for the acquisition and transportation of raw materials to firms that were shifting from military to civilian operations, and for the payment of special compensations to factory workers for the loss in real wages due to inflation. In both cases, the extension of financing to private businesses was considered a patriotic obligation.

A third factor exerting pressure on the money supply was the movement that developed among businesses and individuals to withdraw savings from financial institutions, eventually producing the extraordinary phenomenon of overdrawing across the country. The background of this movement is complex. For the average person, the withdrawal of bank deposits was just one fact of the "bamboo shoot life," necessitated by the spiraling prices of basic commodities. In October 1945, foreign news reports began to trickle into the country, predicting that property and war profits tax levies were imminent; these rumors provoked a flood of bank deposit withdrawals and conversions of cash to consumer products as people sought to avoid the new taxes.

Deficit spending by the government and the massive withdrawals from financial institutions caused excessive demand in the form of tremendous purchasing power in the domestic economy. Even more pressure was applied on already short supplies as individuals and businesses rushed to convert cash to consumables.

In addition to all these factors, the presence of American Occupation forces may be cited as a fourth factor. The responsibility for financing emergency supplies of goods and services for the Occupation forces was assigned to the Japanese government, and it is undeniable that disbursements to meet these expenses became an extra factor in the government's deficit financing and the worsening supply situation.

For a short time after the end of the war, opinion was divided on the nature of this inflation as well as on policies to deal with it. Professor Hyōe Ōuchi of Tokyo University warned that inflation was advancing at a catastrophic rate, a view shared by Keizō Shibusawa, the minister of finance in the Shidehara Cabinet. In a now famous speech on NHK radio, Shibusawa called for daring measures to check inflation, including the cancellation of indemnity payments. On the other hand, Tanzan Ishibashi, soon to become minister of finance in the first Yoshida Cabinet (May 1946–May 1947), took an optimistic view of the situation. Ishibashi, a Keynesian, reasoned along the following lines.

Since military spending had ended abruptly with Japan's defeat, fiscal outlays should be reduced as a matter of course. Moreover, supplies that previously had been diverted to meet military demand could now be returned to the domestic production sector. The economy was suffering from both unemployment of labor and underutilization of production capacity, and prices were rising while production was stagnating. This was by no means a true inflation, which, in the Keynesian sense, meant rising prices under full employment and full capacity utilization. Therefore, any attempt to deal with rising prices by adopting deflationary policies would risk creating financial panic and further reductions in production and living standards. In view of this, sound policies for the reconstruction of the economy lay precisely in the direction of deficit fiscal spending and further increases in the money supply. Furthermore, to increase production, economic controls should be eliminated and extensive liberalization implemented. This latter theory of the postwar economy received wide support from the business community, which repeatedly called for an early end to economic controls.

Despite the support for Ishibashi's optimistic view, Shibusawa persisted in his efforts to dampen inflationary pressures. He announced the cancellation of war indemnities, and on several occasions placed moratoriums on cash withdrawals. In fact, economic conditions were by no means as favorable as Ishibashi's analysis suggested, and from November 1945 there was a sudden awakening within the government to the seriousness of the crisis. By this time, members of the various cabinet ministries were meeting in secret to discuss measures for dealing with the economic crisis (these included the Ministry of Finance, the Ministry of Agriculture and Forestry, the Ministry of Commerce and Industry, the Ministry of Home Affairs, the Ministry of Public Welfare, and the Cabinet Councillor's Room).

The principle points of the policy proposals advanced during these meetings became clear early in 1946, and may be summarized as follows.

1. The ministries proposed immediate implementation of new fiscal and monetary policies, including a freeze on bank deposits and a survey of private assets in preparation for the imposition of a property tax as well as a new yen currency issue.

2. A new official price system with rice and coal as the key commodities was to be established.

3. They proposed to stabilize the rationing system through the enforcement of stricter measures, the strengthening of enforcement agencies to uncover illegal supply routes, and the appeal to General Headquarters for imports of relief supplies.

4. Measures were to be implemented for the government to buy up and distribute commodities that had been illegally diverted in the immediate postwar period, hoarded commodities, and goods purchased on a speculative basis.

5. Relief and compensation were to be planned for the unemployed and those placed in straitened circumstances at the end of the war.

These proposals were worked into a general policy called the "Emergency Economic Crisis Policy," which was announced on February 16, 1946, with the approval of GHQ. On the following day five ordinances were promulgated for its implemetation: the Emergency Monetary Measures Ordinance; the Bank of Japan Notes Deposit Ordinance; the Extraordinary Assets Investigation Ordinance; the Emergency Hoarded Commodities Measures Ordinance; and the Emergency Foodstuffs Measures Ordinance. On March 3, 1946, the Commodity Price Control Ordinance was promulgated as an additional measure. Most of these were ineffective. Only the extreme Emergency Monetary Measures Ordinance, which froze all deposits in financial institutions and forced the exchange of old yen currency for new yen had a substantial effect in curbing inflation.

The purpose of the freeze on bank deposits was to contain inflation by reducing the money supply, which had stimulated excess demand in the form of extraordinary purchasing power. This measure stipulated that all old yen notes would cease to be recognized as legal tender as of March 2, 1946, and that they should be deposited in frozen accounts by March 7. During the intervening period no more than ¥300 for household heads and ¥100 for each additional family member could be withdrawn in new yen notes. All remaining assets were placed in frozen new yen accounts. Subsequently, withdrawals by families without monthly incomes were limited to the same levels. Wage and salary earners could be paid up to ¥500 monthly in new yen, with the remainder paid into the frozen accounts. These measures gave rise to a new slang expression, "the five hundred yen life."

A glance at black market prices at the time attests to the straitened circumstances of "the five hundred yen life." The price for 1.5 kilograms of rice was ¥68, for 3.75 kilograms of white potatoes, ¥50, and for the same amount of sweet potatoes, ¥46. However, despite the hardships entailed, these measures were successful in reducing the Bank of Japan note issue by ¥50 billion. While the effect of this reduction was temporary, it did bring inflation to a momentary standstill and enabled the government to reinstitute price controls, which had been almost completely ineffective since the end of the war. During this period GHQ finally began to realize the seriousness of the economic crisis and permitted imports of relief food supplies, which, although inadequate, marked a major shift in Occupation policies. For the first time since the end of the war, Occupation policies began to assume more concern for Japan's economic rehabilitation.

The Economic Stabilization Board and the Priority Production Concept. Since the very beginning of Occupation rule, GHQ had been critical of the Japanese government's halfhearted, inefficient administration, citing a series of stopgap measures that had ended in failure. The government's miscalculation of the scale of the food crisis had done little to assuage feelings of mistrust toward its administration. With the initiation of emergency financial policies in March 1946, the government intended to establish a central administrative organ within the cabinet to oversee the implementation of the new policies. However, GHQ viewed this move as insufficient and called for a strong, politically independent commission of specialists entrusted with the task of enforcing these comprehensive economic policies. Moreover, GHQ disapproved of the government's attempts to rehabilitate the private economic controls groups that had existed during the war on the grounds that such groups violated the principle of antitrust and insisted on the institution of a separate, independent body to administer the new economic controls. It was through these negotiations with GHQ that the government established the Economic Stabilization Board and the various public corporations responsible for economic controls (including the Commodity Supply Control Corporation and the Price Adjustment Corporation).

The Economic Stabilization Board was established in August 1946, in the administration of the first Yoshida Cabinet, with the responsibility of formulating major national economic policies and overseeing the reconstruction of the economy. In addition, it was entrusted with supervising the nationwide network of new economic controls. The prestige of the newly established board was considerable, headed as it was by the prime minister in the position of president and a director general with the rank of minister of state. Moreover, the board had the power to issue orders to public prosecutors and to the police in matters relating to the Economic Controls Ordinance, as well as authority over the financing of all public corporations. It was the most powerful economic planning agency in the entire postwar history of Japan, and, in conjunction with its authority within the Japanese government, soon came to play the central role in negotiations between the government and GHQ on economic policy.

At about the same time that plans were being made for its establishment came the implementation of a series of drastic measures that were to have long-term effects on the Japanese economic and social systems. First, a graduated tax was levied on personal assets, the rumored property tax. All assets in excess of ¥100,000 were taxed on a graduated scale, up to 90 percent on assets over ¥15 million. The government's decision to implement this property tax was accompanied by GHQ's decision to institute a policy discontinuing indemnity payments to private corporations. The harsh property tax brought about the immediate collapse of the old nobility and the landholder class, whose wealth and social position had enabled them to dominate Japanese society up to that time. It was during this period that Osamu Dazai wrote his famous novel *The Setting Sun*, containing a vivid description of the social changes wrought by the decline of the privileged classes.

The sudden suspension of indemnity payments amounted to a tremendous blow to private enterprises. The directives issued by GHQ noted that the government had already made substantial indemnity payments and called for an immediate 100 percent war profits tax on all such payments, amounting essentially to a confiscation of these assets. Proposals by GHQ for the cancellation of indemnity payments had met with stiff opposition from both Ishibashi, the minister of finance, and Yoshida, but the decisions taken by GHQ in August 1946 were enforced nonetheless. The risks were substantial. Indeed, had the suspension of indemnity payments been allowed to proceed as directed by GHQ, the probability of financial panic was overwhelming. A large number of major private enterprises held enormous credit accounts of wartime claims against the government. If these firms were suddenly deprived of their claims, they would be forced into bankruptcy, as would the banks and other financial institutions that had advanced them credit on the basis of such claims. This would mean, in turn, that individuals with savings deposits would suffer enormous losses, which could easily lead to chaos and even to violent uprisings.

In order to avert a catastrophe, the government enacted the Company Accounts Emergency Measures Ordinance and the Financial Institutions Emergency Accounting Measures Ordinance on August 15, 1946, to help companies consolidate their assets and reserves and go into liquidation. In addition, the Industrial Bank of Japan, which later was to become the Reconstruction Finance Bank (also called the "Reconversion Finance Bank" in GHQ documents), began supplying reconstruction funds to private businesses through its Reconstruction Finance Department. It soon became clear that further measures were necessary and, in mid-October 1946, the War Indemnity Special Measures Law, the Enterprise Rehabilitation and Reorganization Law, and the Financial Institutions Rehabilitation Law were promulgated. The rapid implementation of these measures reflects the crisis mentality that prevailed among economic policy makers after GHQ's decision to discontinue indemnity payments. Indeed, it seemed that the Japanese economy had been driven to the brink of disaster. Even the positive effects of the earlier emergency policies could not be sustained, and it was feared that, unless rapid progress was made toward reconstruction, the economy would collapse.

The money supply, which had been temporarily brought under control by the freezing of bank deposits, grew by leaps and bounds, reaching levels, in September 1946, that surpassed those of the period before the freeze. Inflation again resumed at a rapid pace. The new yen, issued under the emergency measures, accumulated in farm villages or in the pockets of black market brokers, while the household budgets of the urban population became more stringent. At the same time, production indexes for the mining and manufacturing industries, which had shown a superficial upward trend, began to reveal a pronounced downward shift toward reduced production based largely on remanufacturing. The slight production rise had been the result of the resumption of domestic production with supplies released by the military and the stocks of raw material on hand. As these stocks were depleted, even these reduced levels of production were no longer possible, and there was considerable danger that the entire economy would be thrown into small-scale production based on remanufacturing.

The most serious bottleneck in the rehabilitation of these sectors was the shortage of coal, the basic energy source. Besides the demobilization and dispersal of Korean and Taiwanese forced laborers, who had comprised the bulk of the labor supply, the coal mining industry itself was short of the basic raw materials necessary for greater production. The effects of the coal shortage rippled through the entire economy as stockpiles were depleted in one industry after another, thus creating new bottlenecks. The steel industry was affected almost immediately and quickly forced to curtail operations. The chemical fertilizers industry, so essential to stimulating food supplies, was affected by both shortages of coal, its principle energy source, and of steel, needed for repairs of plant and equipment facilities. Railway transportation declined because of the coal shortage, and this decrease created another bottleneck in the supply of raw materials to industry, thereby throwing the whole economy into a critical situation.

Confronted with an imminent economic crisis, it was clear that no ordinary economic policies could save the situation. A positive and highly innovative policy was urgently called for. As the government debated a number of old and new policies, Professor Hiromi Arisawa of Tokyo University proposed a general economic policy, which he called the "Priority Production Concept," to Prime Minister Yoshida. The implementation of this policy became the most important task for the newly formed Economic Stabilization Board.

Essentially, the Priority Production Concept was an attempt to reverse the vicious cycle between the coal and steel industries that had led to massive bottlenecks. All economic policies would concentrate on increasing coal production; the coal would then be thrown into the steel industry to stimulate steel production; and the steel would then be thrown back into the coal industry. Existing shortages of coal in these two industries would be filled by imported crude oil until increases could be channeled gradually to other basic industries to promote overall economic recovery.

To achieve this, controlled commodities were allocated on a priority basis to the coal and steel industries, and the Reconstruction Finance Bank was established under the Financial Institutions Capital Financing Regulation to channel funds into the priority industries (until 1947 the bank had existed as the Industrial Bank of Japan within the Reconstruction Finance Department). Prime Minister Yoshida appealed to MacArthur for emergency imports of crude oil, anthracite, steel, rubber, and trailer tractors. At the same time, he requested approximately 2 million tons of emergency relief food. Although agricultural production improved to some extent in 1947, the government still could not maintain food rationing at the officially sanctioned level of thirty-five grams of rice per day without outside assistance.[1]

2. THE CRISIS OF INFLATION

The Emergency Economic Policy and the First Economic White Paper. In 1947 the attitude of the Occupation authorities toward Japan's economic crisis was mixed. On the one hand, GHQ was forced to recognize the seriousness of the situation; on the other, GHQ, which had almost completed its sweeping demilitarization and democratization programs, was now clearly impatient with the Japanese government's inability to take even the first steps toward formulating a policy for economic reconstruction. In a memorandum dated March 22, 1947, MacArthur agreed to the government's request for emergency imports of all the industrial commodities except steel. In the same memorandum, however, he directed the government to adopt, on its own responsibility, firm policies for promoting reconstruction in every sphere, calling for the expansion and strengthening of the Economic Stabilization Board.

On the basis of these recommendations, a radical reorganization of the Economic Stabilization Board was carried out in May, with the appointment of four new deputy directors, the creation of ten bureaus and forty-eight sections within the board, and an increase in staff from three hundred and sixteen to two thousand. Such an increase was unprecedented, and would be unthinkable in Japan's bureaucratic system today. In short, staff increases were accomplished by transferring all planning, and the staff involved, from the various ministries concerned with economic policy to the Economic Stabilization Board, a major reform of the entire economic planning system.

The expansion and strengthening of the Economic Stabilization Board coincided with important changes in the domestic political situation. The first general election under the new constitution (announced March 6, 1947) was held on April 25, 1947, capturing the attention of the entire nation. The Socialist, Democratic, and Liberal parties won almost equal numbers of votes, but the Socialists emerged with the largest number of seats in the Diet. Forming a coalition with the Democratic Party and the tiny People's Cooperative Party, Tetsu Katayama, the Socialist Party leader, formed the Katayama Cabinet (June 1947–March 1948).

Beginning with the selection of Hiroo Wada as director general, appointments to the Economic Stabilization Board produced an unprecedented line-up of qualified officials drawn not only from the government but from academia and private industry as well. Individuals from the private sector were appointed to positions at the deputy director general and bureau chief levels, while outstanding officials from government ministries were placed in important positions at the deputy bureau chief level and below. Representative of this select group were Shigeto Tsuru, chairman of the General Regulation Committee (the highest position in overseeing policy formulation and conducting negotiations with GHQ), Shigeo Nagano (deputy director general), Sōichirō Ōhara (deputy director of the Price Board), Takayuki Yamamoto (secretary general), Hidezō Inaba (deputy secretary general), Osamu Shimomura (Price Policies Section chief), Kazushi Ōkawa (Household Budget Expenses section chief), and Saburō Ōkita (Economic Surveys section chief).

On June 11, shortly after the inauguration of the Katayama Cabinet, the Economic Stabilization Board announced a new comprehensive economic policy titled the "Emergency Economic Policy." The eight points of the new policy may be outlined as follows.

1. Guarantee of Food Supplies. Delays in food rations would be curbed by improving the supply system, curtailing the flow of food supplies into black market channels, and prohibiting the operation of eating and drinking establishments. These measures would be coupled with further appeals to GHQ for emergency food imports.

2. Establishment of an Effective Commodities Distribution System. Effective rationing controls would be implemented, measures for eliminating hoarding would be strengthened, and the movement of

black market commodities would be suppressed by stronger controls on transportation.

3. Overall Reform of the Wage and Price Systems. Real wages would be improved by basing all official prices on wages and by increasing commodities supplies distributed through official rationing channels.

4. Elimination of Inflationary Pressures Resulting from Money Supply Expansion. The government would adhere to the principle of balanced fiscal budgets, taxes would be raised on black market profits and inflationderived profits, and stricter controls would be imposed on the lending activities of financial institutions.

5. Increased Production and Improved Productivity. Plans for stimulating industry would be drawn up with emphasis on coal and steel production and the rehabilitation of the transportation system. A long-range plan for economic reconstruction would also be made.

6. Social Insurance and Employment Guarantees. Plans would be made for improving working conditions and facilities, expanding housing construction for workers, and increasing employment opportunities. In addition, unemployment insurance and unemployment compensation programs would be implemented.

7. Expansion of Exports. A rational export policy would be formulated with emphasis on the improvement of all industrial and infrastructure systems that would support Japan's reentry into the world trading community.

8. Development of a New Administrative Structure. This would enhance the effects of economic recovery and give due respect to the skills and status of workers.

Taken singly, not one of these policies seems to contain anything particularly new. However, in the sense that the Emergency Economic Policy was a comprehensive, consistent set of policies, and in its recognition of the severity of the crisis, it may be said to have had quite a different quality compared to previous plans. Moreover, on July 4, 1947, the Economic Stabilization Board published Japan's first Economic White Paper, titled *A Report on Actual Conditions in the Economy*. The purpose of this first White Paper was to analyze the economic situation as a premise for the Emergency Economic Policy, to present the theoretical basis for the new policies, and to appeal to the population for understanding and cooperation. Because of the central role played in its preparation by Shigeto Tsuru, it was also called the "Tsuru White Paper."

The White Paper portrayed the economic crisis in uncompromising terms. In the two years since the end of the war, raw materials stockpiles and industrial assets that could be utilized in making up for sizable deficits in the three major sectors of the economy had been almost used up. The people, in order to carry on living, had no choice but to rely on the black market, but the "bamboo shoot life" had continued for so long that families were beginning to run out of personal belongings that could be bartered. Moreover, while major legitimate industries were suffering huge losses, a substantial part of the commercial sector was reaping large profits by engaging in black market transactions. Due to the nationwide trend toward reduced production based on remanufacturing, the deterioration of cities, farmlands, and industrial facilities as well as decreasing nutrition standards of the population continued unabated. Therefore, the road to recovery would have to be preceded by a temporary austerity.

The White Paper was severely criticized by the Communist Party, which charged that the government was attempting to shirk its responsibility and impose hardship upon the people. The Liberal Party, which had been in power before the Socialist victory, took issue with the statement that the current economic crisis was a result of the failure of governments of the previous two years to set up economic stabilization policies. However, to the extent that this White Paper was an attempt to break down the traditional "don't tell them anything" attitude that had characterized economic policies in the past and to present to the people statistics and analyses that would clarify the true state of the economy, it was welcomed by the public and by progressive economists. Moreover, when Director General Wada of the Economic Stabilization Board presented it in the Diet, it was decided that such publications should be made regularly once or twice a year.

The first Economic White Paper also represented a milestone in the postwar democratization of the bureaucracy, which up to then had not been conducive to the training of economists for it had been dominated by an elite group of officials with legal training, and the status of specialists in other fields had been extremely low. With the reorganization of the Economic Stabilization Board and the introduction of economic white papers, the first steps were taken toward a larger role and a higher status for economists within the bureaucracy, as well as toward a greater voice for academics in influencing economic policy.[2,3]

The Fight against Inflation. As we have seen, dramatic changes in the policy-making process were effected by the Katayama Cabinet. However, the basic economic policy had been inherited from the previous Yoshida Cabinet. The central pillar of this policy was the Priority Production Concept, which had received the support of GHQ. By implementing the concept as policy, economic planners hoped to set the economy on the track to expanded production and recovery. At the same time, the most pressing problem was how to implement the overall reform of the wage and price systems called for in the Emergency Economic Policy (*see* p. 38). The basic policy for effecting this reform was to reestablish an ordered distribution system by ensuring that as large a supply of commodities as possible was routed through official rationing channels, thus checking the expansion of the black market resulting from the inefficient and unfair rationing system.

However, as black market prices were as high as ten times official prices in urban areas, in order to persuade producers to return to official rationing channels, it was necessary to raise official prices so that they could make a profit. It was also essential to respond to strong demands for wage increases as inflation continued to accelerate. If wages were raised too much, however, there was the danger that a wage-price spiral would push inflation even higher because low production and low labor productivity were the essential factors influencing inflation. Confronted with this situation, the Economic Stabilization Board published a new wage and price policy on July 5, 1947, shortly after announcing the Emergency Economic Policy. The core of this new policy was "stabilization belt" prices for basic commodities and a basic wage of ¥1,800 per month. The goals and provisions of the new policy may be more fully outlined as follows.

1. The prices of basic commodities, or "stabilization belt" commodities (coal, coke, pig iron, steel, lead, ammonium sulphate, caustic soda, soda ash, etc.), were to be stabilized at sixty-five times prewar levels (the average prices of 1934–36). The government would pay adjustment subsidies to producers whose costs exceeded these levels.

2. A parity system was established for the agricultural and marine products industries in which government subsidies would be paid according to the price increase rate for essential production materials.

3. The monthly salaries of government employees were set at ¥1,800, and private business was encouraged to follow this standard. This

Table 5.   A Breakdown of U.S. Relief Imports

($1 million)

	1945	1946	1947	1948	1949	1950	1951
Total	6	167	350	325	468	281	120
Food supplies (total)	4 (12)	142 (528)	241 (799)	228 (780)	239 (1,742)	90 (778)	53 (424)
Wheat	1.3	52	82	82	172	73	41
Wheat flour		12	25	34	2		
Canned goods		51	7				
Rice	2					5	
Industrial raw materials	2 (67)	25 (706)	109 (1,147)	97 (1,456)	229 (2,080)	191 (1,802)	67 (380)
Oil	2	13	21	35	44	23	5
Coal				4	8		
Fertilizer		11	61	34	37	17	
Raw cotton					62	124	55

Note: Figures in parentheses are for volumes (wheat: 1,000 tons; oil: 1,000 KL).
Source: Foreign Ministry, "Materials Related to Debt Liability toward the U.S."

basic wage standard was only 27.8 times prewar levels, but it was based on estimates that minimum household budgets could be maintained at this level with increased rationing quotas, and that an inflationary wage-price spiral could be prevented.

With the implementation of the new wage and price system, black market prices did begin to slow down. Moreover, the Priority Production Policy was effective, and production in the manufacturing industries began to record slow but steady increases. The Katayama Cabinet succeeded in meeting its goals for production increases in priority industries, and the effectiveness of the policy was particularly marked in the coal and steel industries. Delays and suspensions of food rations were eliminated as imports from the United States (food supplies financed by the Government Account for Relief in Occupied Areas, or GARIOA) and emergency food supplies from GHQ–related agencies (Licensed Agencies for Relief of Asia, LARA) were channeled into the rationing system. In August 1947, GHQ authorized a resumption of limited trade, and the economy finally moved in a favorable direction, albeit slowly.

Despite the favorable trends outlined above, enormous problems still confronted economic planners, and inflationary pressures in the economy proved deeply rooted. In early August 1947, Director General Wada of the Economic Stabilization Board reported optimistically to the Diet that deficits in household budgets would continue through October, but that rice rations from that year's harvest and lower black market prices would enable urban households to balance their budgets by November. The conditions, however, for such a forecast were simply not present. The new wage and price system had been instituted as policy, but several months were required before official prices could be set for the thousands of commodities that fell under the price control system. During this period, the currency supply increased much more than expected, and ultimately it was impossible to curb the upward trend of black market prices. Wada's ill-advised forecast of balanced household budgets by November resulted in a political fiasco for the Katayama Cabinet, which was forced to assume responsibility.

As is true of most radical economic policies, the new wage and price policies themselves created another set of problems that had much to do with the failure to halt inflation. Price adjustment subsidies were tied to official prices and could not be increased no matter how long the delays were in increasing official prices in response to inflation and wage increases. Moreover, many producers still found it necessary to procure at least part of their supplies at black market prices, thus suffering losses when they distributed the commodities through the official rationing system, despite the subsidies. The government attempted to make good these losses by providing loans through the Reconstruction Finance Bank in the form of operating capital (in fact, deficit financing), which, in turn, were covered by outlays from the national budget. In effect, the Reconstruction Finance Bank was extending loans to private enterprises and financing these loans by borrowing from the Bank of Japan, greatly increasing the amount of currency circulating. Moreover, massive loans for plant and equipment investment were made by the Reconstruction Finance Bank, which were financed by issuing Reconstruction Finance Bank bonds accepted by the Bank of Japan, further increasing the currency issue and triggering the Reconstruction Bank inflation. The high cost of implementing the new wage and price control system also increased the government's deficit, constituting an additional source of inflationary pressure. For example, price adjustment subsidies accounted for 20 percent of total government expenditure in 1947, and 24 percent in 1948.

As we have seen, the economic policies of the Katayama Cabinet, which had been instituted with a view to curbing inflation by increasing production through the priority production system, and the elimination of the black market by expanding the rationing system, came up against deeply rooted inflationary pressures in the economy and, in some cases, produced transitional inflationary pressures of their own. This reflects the critical nature of the situation, as well as the fact that, comprehensive as it was, the policy still attempted to deal with Japan's economic crisis on a piecemeal basis. Nevertheless, while shortages of supplies persisted, the attempt to expand production had been largely successful and the inflationary gap between supply and demand was being steadily reduced.

In fact, the effectiveness of these policies did not become clear until the Katayama Cabinet had been replaced by the Ashida Cabinet (March–October 1948). In 1948, as increases in production exceeded government forecasts and the pace of inflation began to slow, the policies established by the Economic Stabilization Board under the Katayama Cabinet began to bear fruit. This was not because the economic policies of the Ashida Cabinet were more effective but because of the one-year lag that exists between the implementation of economic policies and their effect on the economy. The substantial improvement of the economic situation under the Ashida Cabinet should be understood in this light. The economic policies of the Katayama Cabinet have been highly criticized up to the present. Such criticism ignores the interval between policy and effect and, considering that the Katayama Cabinet was in power for only nine months and held only 58 percent of the seats in the Diet (including those of the two other parties in the coalition), its economic policies were exceptionally effective. This was due in large measure to its reorganization of the Economic Stabilization Board and the degree to which it allowed the board to function as an independent body for economic planning.

First Steps toward Recovery: Secret Currency Reform Proposals. As the economy began to show the first signs of recovery, the problem of developing new policies for the anticipated period of reconstruction assumed concrete dimensions. Particularly pressing were new policies to deal with inflation, a fixed exchange rate, and the setting up of targets for reconstruction. In view of this, a secret committee of seven members, with Shigeto Tsuru as chairman, was established within the Economic Stabilization Board on August 14, 1947, not long after the publication of the first Economic White Paper. This committee was responsible for investigating and developing proposals for an anti-inflationary currency reform policy and foreign exchange policies that would enable Japan to compete effectively after its reentry into the world trading community—in short, a fixed exchange rate. The committee was also empowered to consider any other policies that would enhance the effect of the new foreign exchange policy in promoting the country's competitiveness.

The following proposals, which were the result of the committee's work, were circulated within the government during the latter half of December. They were: 1) a currency deflation, which would check inflation by eliminating the excess demand resulting from the swollen money supply; 2) a fixed exchange rate eliminating the complicated system of exchange rates for each item of trade.

While the first of these proposals called for a devaluation of the legal denomination of the yen to 10 percent of its current level, it also included a revolutionary income redistribution measure aimed at ameliorating inequities after the long period of inflation. In principle, a forced exchange of old yen for new yen at the rate of ten to one would be implemented but would be enforced selectively depending on the type of deposit concerned. Current accounts would be devalued to 20 percent of their current levels, while general deposits would retain 40 percent and time deposits all of their current values. Thus, the types of accounts most likely to be held by black market brokers or farmers who benefited from inflation would be hardest hit, while ordinary wage earners would suffer relatively little. The next problem was timing. The Emergency Monetary Measures of 1946 had failed to produce more than a temporary deflationary effect because they had been implemented before production recovered. On the basis of this experience, the committee recommended that the radical yen devaluation outlined above should be enacted in March or April 1948, after a solid basis for recovery in industrial production had been established.

These sweeping proposals had reached the discussion stage between the Economic Stabilization Board and GHQ when the long-standing conflict between the left and right wings of the Socialist Party erupted in March 1948 over the issue of living allowances for government employees, forcing the Katayama Cabinet to resign. This resulted in the resignations of Shigeto Tsuru and Hiroo Wada, the principle architects of the new policies. In any case, the new government of Shigeru Yoshida was not likely to support such radical measures. Indeed, outside a select group, the fact that this kind of planning was going on remained a closely guarded secret for some time thereafter. It is quite likely that the yen devaluation in the committee's deflationary proposal would have encountered stiff opposition had the Katayama Cabinet remained in power, but it is worth noting that the inevitability of a drastic deflationary policy and the need for a fixed exchange rate were recognized by planners within the Japanese government before such policies were forced on it by GHQ a year later under the Dodge Plan.

The Dodge Plan itself reflected a major shift in Occupation policy, which occurred at about the same time as the resignation of the Katayama Cabinet and the inauguration of the Ashida Cabinet in March 1948. Behind this shift of policy was an intensification of the Cold War, occasioned by the repeated successes of the communist revolution in China. Not only were relations between the United States and the Soviet Union deteriorating but England was also suffering a reduced international role due to the destruction of its economy during the war and the gradual loss of its colonial empire. Moreover, the success of the Communist Party in China undermined Chiang Kai-shek's position as leader of a powerful U.S. ally in Asia. Against this background, GHQ's attitude toward Japan rapidly shifted from the harsh, punitive spirit of the Pauley Report to one that emphasized Japan's central role in the recovery and development of Asia. New American policies began to call for active efforts to hasten reconstruction as Japan was the only industrialized country in the region and a potential bulwark against communism. The harsh reparations advocated by Pauley, particularly those calling for the dismantling of industrial facilities, were now seen as measures that would increase the burden on American taxpayers and slow down the recovery of America's only potential ally in Asia. This reversal of GHQ's policy was marked by a conspicuous relaxation of reparations policies and deconcentration measures, as well as by substantial increases in economic aid, which up to that time had been supplied only as relief at levels only sufficient to prevent mass starvation and disease.

Japan's access to news from outside concerning the new international situation was extremely limited under the Occupation. However, even before the shift in GHQ's policy was recognized, economic planning for reconstruction was being conducted on the premise that the basic goal of new economic plans should be to optimize negotiations with GHQ, and thus with the U.S. government. By fall 1947, the first draft of the Economic Rehabilitation Plan, which was completed and submitted to GHQ in early 1948, was being prepared under the supervision of Hidezō Inaba. A five-year plan that envisioned a return to prewar (1930–34) standards of living by 1952, it was the first long-term plan (or medium-term for that matter) formulated by the Japanese government after the war.

The basic framework of the Economic Rehabilitation Plan included a set of specific targets for improvements in domestic economic performance and an outline of requests for changes in American policy to be negotiated with GHQ. In the case of the domestic economy, the plan called for increases in mining and manufacturing production to levels 30 percent higher than prewar levels (or more than three times the projected levels for 1948), increases of more than nine times the 1947 levels in exports, and of more than three times the 1947 levels in imports. At this rate, Japan could achieve economic independence by 1952. However, a basic premise of these targets was that, during the transitional period before they could be achieved, Japan would have to rely on extensive economic aid from the United States for imports of basic industrial materials and foreign commodities to provide daily necessities for its people. The plan therefore called for GHQ to raise the levels of permitted industrial production limits, to increase economic aid, and to curtail the removal of industrial plant and equipment that was being carried out under the Advance Transfer Program as part of the reparations plan devised by Pauley. The main points of the Economic Rehabilitation Plan were accepted by GHQ, in part because GHQ had already begun to shift its own policy. Shortly after receiving Inaba's first draft plan, GHQ formulated its Five-Year Plan for the Economic Independence of Japan, and the concepts underlying this plan clearly reveal the significance of Inaba's proposals in the negotiations between Japan and GHQ.

While this important economic planning was being undertaken in the bureaucracy, particularly by the Economic Stabilization Board, the domestic political situation was changing dramatically. On March 10, 1948, the Socialist Katayama Cabinet was replaced by the shaky coalition government of Hitoshi Ashida. The Ashida Cabinet was formed by a coalition of Ashida's Democratic Party, Takeo Miki's People's Cooperative Party, and the right wing of the Socialist Party. Both the left wing of the Socialist Party and Yoshida's Liberal Party refused to cooperate with the new government. If anything, Ashida attached even more importance to relations with GHQ than his predecessors and pinned high hopes on increases in American aid and the introduction of foreign capital, so much so that his cabinet was nicknamed the "Foreign Capital Cabinet." To that extent, he was anxious to formulate an economic reconstruction plan of his own that would enhance negotiations with GHQ while appealing to public opinion.

In fact, despite encouragement from GHQ, the Ashida Cabinet was virtually powerless to take any initiatives in economic policy. While GHQ called on the government to check the accelerating wage-price spiral by instituting an anti-inflationary policy, including a drastic balanced budget policy, the cabinet was simply too weak to act on these recommendations. Without the support of left-wing socialists, it faced strong opposition from the labor movement, and new labor unrest erupted at the first signs of any new deflationary policy. Moreover, the government was plagued by the Shōwa Electric scandal, which finally brought down the cabinet in October 1948. Ashida himself was accused of accepting bribes in connection with massive loans to the Shōwa Electric Company by the Reconstruction Finance Bank. Ultimately, the most notable developments of the eight-month Ashida Cabinet were the result of actions by GHQ. The Strike Reparations Report, published by GHQ on March 21, called for large-scale reductions in reparations. Moreover, in May, the Elimination of Excessive Economic Concentration Commission, headed by New York shipbuilder Roy Campbell, was sent to Japan and, after extensive inspections of corporate records, it recommended major reductions in the number of firms designated for liquidation.

The second Yoshida Cabinet was established to make preparations for a general election after the fall of the Ashida Cabinet in October 1948. In the election, held in January 1949, the Socialist and the Democratic parties suffered heavy losses, and Yoshida's Liberal Party emerged with an overwhelming majority in both houses of the Diet. Thus, the third Yoshida Cabinet, which would rule the country until the beginning of 1955, assumed responsibility for devising an economic program that would put an end to runaway inflation while getting the country on the track toward economic recovery, the two problems that had plagued successive governments since the end of the war.[4,5,6]

The Dodge Line. Even during the three months of the second Yoshida Cabinet, there was increased pressure from Washington to take decisive action on the Economic Rehabilitation Plan. While the ultimate objectives of GHQ were the rapid rehabilitation of the Japanese economy and the establishment of a fixed exchange rate, the immediate problem confronting both Japan and GHQ was to devise an effective anti-inflationary policy. On December 18, 1948, the State Department and the Department of the Army published a joint declaration titled the "Nine-Point Economic Stabilization Plan for Japan" and ordered MacArthur to take immediate steps to implement it. The plan may be summarized as follows.

1. To achieve a balanced budget at the earliest possible date by a stringent curtailment of government spending and an increase in revenue;

2. To accelerate and strengthen tax collection, including criminal prosecution of tax evaders;

3. To stringently reduce the extension of credit by financial institutions;

4. To establish an effective program to achieve wage stability;

5. To strengthen and, if necessary, expand the coverage of existing price controls;

6. To improve the operation of foreign trade and exchange controls;

7. To improve the effectiveness of the existing system of materials allocation and rationing with a view to maximizing the expansion of exports;

8. To expand the production of all key raw materials and manufactured products;

9. To improve the efficiency of the food supply system.

In February 1949, Joseph Dodge, a Detroit banker who had played a key role in the postwar currency reform in Germany, was sent to Japan as ambassador with the authority to implement the new plan. Immediately upon his arrival, Dodge presented his diagnosis of the country's economic problems in a famous press conference with Japanese reporters. According to Dodge, the Japanese economy was like a person walking on stilts. One of the stilts was U.S. aid and the other was the Reconstruction Finance Bank and various institutions that were providing hidden subsidies to industry. Arguing that the stilts had become too high and the economy was in danger of toppling over and falling on its head, Dodge said that the stilts had to be removed and the economy must learn to walk on its own two feet. His prescription for dealing with these problems, which was presented to the Japanese government as a list of directives concerning the fiscal budget for 1949, consisted of five basic elements.

1. An Overbalanced Budget. While calling for complete balance in the budgets for each year, the Dodge Plan actually produced fiscal surpluses by compelling the government to redeem the major portion of government bonds issued up to that time. Long-term government bonds had already been prohibited under the Finance Act of 1947, but the government had been covering its large deficits by issuing short-term bonds and rolling them over. The Dodge Plan

forced the government to redeem these bonds as quickly as possible, even above the legally established rate, and thus was a full-scale deflationary budget policy.

2. The Reduction and Elimination of Subsidies. All price subsidies, subsidies guaranteeing protection against losses, and other subsidies paid from the government's general or special accounts were to be reduced and abolished as quickly as possible.

3. Suspension of New Loans from the Reconstruction Finance Bank. All new lending from the above-mentioned bank would be suspended, and the government would redeem as quickly as possible all Reconstruction Finance Bank bonds issued from the general account.

4. A Fixed Exchange Rate and Elimination of Hidden Trade Subsidies. A fixed exchange rate for the yen would be established immediately, and all hidden subsidies paid by the government for export and import trade through its Special Account for Trade Funds would be abolished.

5. Establishment of the Counterpart Fund Special Account. The Counterpart Fund Special Account would be funded by the sale of American relief supplies in Japan and would take the place of the Special Account for Trade Funds as well as the subsidies eliminated by the second item of Dodge's policies. In other words, funds from the Counterpart Fund Special Account would be supplied to key industries for plant and equipment investment, and to exporting and importing industries for acquiring foreign capital.

These policies provided the framework for Dodge's economic policy for Japan, which is still famous in Japan under the name given it by Professor Ōuchi of the University of Tokyo—the "Dodge Line." Debate continues as to whether the inflation could have been brought under control without it. The Dodge Line was a truly drastic deflationary policy, calling for life or death surgery on the Japanese economy through the overbalanced budget policy and the immediate adoption of a fixed yen exchange rate, thereby exposing the Japanese economy to international competition. It compelled the new Liberal Party cabinet to make drastic revisions in a budget proposal that had already been drafted, and it is unlikely that the Japanese government would have been able to implement the policy without the back up of GHQ. In fact, the Dodge Line was forced on Japan and, for all its success in curbing inflation, it threw the economy into a crisis.

Besides widespread anxiety concerning the overall impact of deflationary fiscal policies, the most pressing question was at what level GHQ would set the fixed exchange rate between the yen and the dollar. The determination of the exchange rate would be the most important factor influencing not only the international competitiveness of every sector of the economy but also the levels at which targets could be set for Japan's economic independence. The fiscal budget for 1949 was based on a rate of ¥330 to the dollar (including projected expenditures for price supports and trade subsidies), and it was widely believed that this would be the appropriate exchange rate. In fact, on April 25, 1949, the rate was set at ¥360 to the dollar, which made the yen cheaper than had been expected. It has become clear only recently that the decision to set the exchange rate at this level was made on strong recommendations from Washington, and not on the initiative of GHQ.

Work on the Economic Rehabilitation Plan had continued from early 1948, when Hidezō Inaba submitted the first draft plan to the Katayama Cabinet, through the Ashida Cabinet to the second Yoshida Cabinet. The second draft plan, which had been drafted and submitted to Yoshida in May 1949, received the support of GHQ, and the Occupation authorities awaited its publication eagerly. However, Yoshida, who as prime minister also had authority over the Economic Stabilization Board, disowned the plan, and it was never adopted as official government policy. It is true that the second draft of the Economic Rehabilitation Plan did not deal sufficiently with the problem of how to provide the necessary capital for plant and equipment investment under the restrictions imposed by the Dodge Line or the problem of reorganizing economic control institutions, which was the reason advanced at the time for rejecting the new proposal.

More than anything else, however, what killed the Economic Rehabilitation Plan was the fact that Yoshida himself did not like economic plans or economic controls. He believed that long-term, planned administration of the economy was synonymous with socialism and opposed to the principles of a free economy. According to many accounts, Yoshida "could not distinquish a Ministry of Commerce and Industry bureaucrat from an insect," and he was highly critical of the so-called controls faction within GHQ, a group of young "New Dealers" in favor of a planned economy and economic controls. Rejecting the Economic Rehabilitation Plan, which emphasized expanded production through the priority production system, Yoshida welcomed Joseph Dodge and the Dodge Line. Dodge exercised his authority to put the lid on the controls faction within GHQ, and his stringent deflationary fiscal policy appealed to Yoshida as one that would pave the way for the development of a free market economy in Japan. Moreover, Yoshida's own background as a bureaucrat in the Ministry of Foreign Affairs, as well as the positions of his closest advisers, led him to agree with Dodge that the best medicine for the economy was exposure to international competition.

In any case, the drastic cure imposed by the Dodge Line was extremely effective in achieving its principle objective of curbing the chronic inflation of the immediate postwar period. Issues of new currency by the Bank of Japan, which had increased by more than five times in 1946, more than nine times in 1947, and more than four times in 1948, actually declined 0.4 percent in 1949. The real price index, which included both official and black market prices, began to level off in 1949, and the index for consumer products declined 10 percent. In fact, black market prices declined by as much as 30 percent, and for all practical purposes the black market, which had dominated a major segment of the economy since the war years, was about to disappear as a major economic force. At the same time, rationing and price controls were relaxed, then abolished, one after the other, beginning with the abolition of price controls on vegetables in April 1949, marking the reestablishment of a free market after nine years of rationing and price controls. For the general public, liberation from rationing and price controls was the most welcome and the most immediate accomplishment of the Dodge Line. It was also during this year that beer halls began to reopen and bananas were sold for the first time since the end of the war.

On the other hand, the Dodge Line policies threw business into the so-called stabilization panic. In the face of a decrease in inflation, a reduced money supply, and improved tax collection measures, businesses were strapped for capital. Dodge's draconian measures had also succeeded too well in reducing effective demand so that businesses were saddled with mounting inventories. Massive unemployment was also an inevitable result of the Dodge Line. Indeed, Yasuyuki Maeda has called the Dodge Line a program of "rationalization through unemployment" (*kubikiri gōrika*), and "administrative rationalization" under its stringent policies resulted in employee dismissals on a large scale: the Japan National Railways fired nearly 100,000 workers, and the Post Office and the Telegraph and Telephone Corporation dropped approximately 220,000 workers from their payrolls.

Bankruptcies and rationalization programs in private industry added to the unemployment figures, and the shrinking black market produced a new type of "latent unemployed." Not only were workers who had been employed in black market operations now officially unemployed, but the black market itself ceased to be an effective labor market into which surplus labor could be absorbed. The same thing was true of the so-called bubble companies, which had sprung into existence because of the black market, or because of the high profits to be made in a period of rapid inflation, and disappeared just as quickly when inflation was brought under control. Labor disputes increased both in number and intensity, and riots made headlines one after the other. Moreover, the newspapers were filled with articles on the suicides of presidents of small and medium-size businesses, as well as suicides of entire families. On July 5, 1949, the body of Sadanori Shimoyama, president of the Japan National Railways, was discovered on the tracks of a JNR line. This was the precursor to a series of disturbing incidents, including the case of a runaway train at Mitaka Station on July 15, three days after the JNR authorities announced a second series of measures to dismiss 60,000 employees. While the true nature of these incidents is not fully understood even today, there is no doubt that they reflected the panic caused by the Dodge Line, and 1949 remains in the memories of many Japanese as the darkest year in the nation's postwar history.

At the same time that the domestic economy was in the grips of this stabilization panic, private industry attempted to launch an export drive on the strength of the newly established exchange rate. However, on September 19, 1949, just five months after the yen exchange rate had been established, England carried out its first postwar devaluation of sterling and was quickly followed by all the countries in the so-called sterling zone, many of them countries in South and Southeast Asia. The devaluation erased the advantages anticipated from the ¥360 exchange rate, dampening prospects for a rapid increase in exports.

While the Dodge Line had certainly brought inflation to an end, it had achieved this at the cost of almost completely undermining the policy of priority production, which had enabled the country to take the first steps toward economic recovery. Moreover, the devaluation of the pound by 30.5 percent against the dollar meant that Japanese products were overpriced in their principle export markets. The winter of 1949 proved to be the harshest since the end of the war, and the threat of revolution came perilously close. Against this background, the Bank of Japan warned that deflation had gone too far, and on its own initiative, instituted a policy of disinflation. With the tacit approval of GHQ's Economic Scientific Section the controls faction—the Bank of Japan implemented a policy that would channel the fiscal surpluses created by the Dodge Line back into the economy.

This policy, envisioned as a measure to neutralize the tight money policies of the Dodge Line, was to be implemented by mobilizing financial institutions to bail out failing private businesses. The capital for this massive lending program was to be provided by Bank of Japan loans and by buying up bonds held by financial institutions. In short, this policy was the predecessor of the so-called overloan phenomenon, in which increases in commercial bank lending exceed increases in deposits, and foreshadowed the strengthening of the control over commercial financial institutions by the Bank of Japan, both of which characterize the postwar economy. Unfortunately, GHQ issued specific orders stopping this new policy in early 1950, and with this the Japanese economy was driven literally to the brink of collapse. Moreover, at Dodge's insistence, the government's budget for 1950 continued the stringent overbalanced budget policy of the previous year.

As minister of finance, Hayato Ikeda (prime minister from July 1960–October 1964) was sent to Washington in April 1950 to conduct secret negotiations with the U.S. government concerning the possibility of concluding a peace treaty and to meet with Dodge in an attempt to negotiate a relaxation of GHQ's deflationary policy. Ikeda's meeting with Dodge ended in failure, and it appeared that hopes for the reconstruction of the Japanese economy would be permanently frustrated. A continuation of the Dodge Line under prevailing economic conditions could only result in more bankruptices, more unemployment, and a stagnant economy at levels far below those before the war. Dodge's refusal to reconsider his policies promised only a continuation of hardships and deprivation far into the future. This outlook was altered completely by events taking place outside Japan, events that would culminate in the outbreak of the Korean War.[7,8,9]

2 THE KOREAN WAR AND THE SAN FRANCISCO PEACE TREATY

1. AN UNEXPECTED SHOT IN THE ARM

The Korean War and Special Procurements. In early 1950, Japan was still under the Occupation and the Dodge Line continued to dominate economic policy. However, when war broke out in Korea on June 25, 1950, the situation changed completely. The Korean War not only triggered immense changes in the economic situation but was also to have an influence on the future of postwar Japan that was nothing less than prodigious.

In the early days of the conflict, the North Korean army, in a show of strength, occupied Seoul, the South Korean capital, on June 28. The United States immediately committed itself to the defense of South Korea and, with United Nations sanction, quickly formed the United Nations forces. On July 8, the American Eighth Army in Japan, led by General MacArthur as supreme commander of the United Nations forces, launched a counterattack to halt the southward advance of North Korea. By now the Occupation forces in Japan had been steadily reduced from a peak of fifteen divisions—comprising about 400,000 troops in October 1945—to only four divisions, or barely over 80,000, at the outbreak of the war. This was judged to be insufficient to prosecute the war and MacArthur ordered the Japanese government to establish a police reserve force of 75,000 (the National Police Reserve, later to become the Self-Defense Forces) and to increase the Maritime Safety Police to 8,000, an order resulting in the enactment of the National Police Reserve Law on August 10.

On September 15, UN forces recaptured Seoul, and by October 1 had advanced to the thirty-eighth parallel. On October 7, the UN General

55

Assembly approved a resolution allowing MacArthur to advance into North Korea, and on October 20, UN forces entered P'yŏngyang, the capital. In retaliation, the Chinese People's Liberation Army entered Korea in overwhelming numbers and, in November, joined up with North Korean forces in a counteroffensive, forcing UN forces into a disorderly retreat. On December 16, 1950, President Truman declared a state of national emergency, and it was at this point that the war reached its most dangerous dimensions. By spring of 1951, however, UN forces had again advanced to the thirty-eighth parallel and, until the armistice signed at P'anmunjŏm on July 27, 1953, both sides fought a holding action there. In the intervening period, on April 11, 1951, General MacArthur, the architect of the Japanese Occupation, had been stripped of his posts as supreme commander of the Allied forces and as supreme commander of the United Nations forces. As is well known, MacArthur had, in open opposition to Truman's policy, advocated expanding the war into China, even at the risk of total nuclear war with China and the U.S.S.R.

Most economic historians emphasize the enormous influence of the Korean War on Japan's economy at this crucial stage, and it is certainly true that the war triggered an unexpected boom just at the point when the economy was suffering the full impact of the stabilization panic created by the Dodge Line. The Korean War boom proved to be an unexpected shot in the arm and made it possible for Japan to make a complete economic recovery almost at a single stroke. However, there were two other important aspects of the war that are sometimes overlooked. First, Japan's cooperation with the United States during the war placed it squarely in the Western camp at a time when the international situation was increasingly colored by worsening East–West relations and the beginnings of the Cold War. Second, the Korean War, and Japan's role in it, hastened the end of the Occupation and the signing of the San Francisco Peace Treaty. The rapid improvement of Japan's economy, as well as the shift in American policy toward making Japan a bulwark against communism, helped speed up the negotiations that led to the peace treaty in September 1951.[1]

The economic boom resulting from the Korean War was the largest and the most important in Japan's postwar economic history. It was triggered by the special procurements income that derived from U.S. army expenditures and by the sudden rise in exports that accompanied the expansion of world trade after June 1950.

Special procurements, or special Korean War demand, may be defined in two ways. Defined narrowly, the term refers to the enormous orders for goods and services for the UN forces in Korea placed with Japan in a very short time by the commander of the Eighth Army and by the supplies department of the American army in Japan. This was largely due to the fact that Japan was the industrialized country nearest the war zone and, therefore, the best source of emergency supplies. Even when considered in this narrow sense, foreign currency income from special procurements reached about $1 billion during the three years of the Korean War, about 70 percent and 30 percent for materials and services, respectively.

During the first half of the war, demand for commodities was comprised largely of military supplies such as sandbags, army blankets, cloth, trucks, gas tanks for planes, ammunition, and barbed wire. However, with the start of truce negotiations, this demand shifted to supplies for the reconstruction of South Korea. The demand for services was composed of labor and facilities for the repair of trucks, tanks, and aircraft, the construction and staffing of base installations, and communication and transportation services.

The broad definition of special procurements includes this direct procurement by the UN forces and the yen expenditure of military personnel stationed in Japan as well as staff of foreign organizations such as relief and aid programs. In the period from 1950 through 1955, special procurements taken in this broad sense are estimated to have reached $2.4 billion to $3.6 billion. If this figure is compared to the total amount of U.S. relief aid to Japan up to June 1951, when aid was suspended—approximately $3 billion—the impact of the special procurements demand is clear. The temporary foreign currency income from special procurements amounted to 60 percent to 70 percent of exports, raising the balance of payments ceiling at a single stroke.

The special procurements boom was accompanied by a remarkable increase in exports. With the outbreak of the war, international trade was freed from the worldwide recession of 1949, showing an increase of $19 billion, or 34 percent, from 1950 through 1951. The rapid expansion of national defense budgets, the buying up and stockpiling of basic materials, and the resulting boom in speculative buying by private enterprises transferred the buyer's market of 1949 into a seller's market, constituting the background for Japan's rapid export expansion. From the first half to the second half of 1950, the value of Japanese exports clearing customs increased 55 percent, with total volume increasing by 35 percent. Surplus inventories, which are estimated to have reached ¥100 billion to ¥150

**Figure 3.   Shift of Dependence on U.S.
from Relief Aid to Special Procurements**

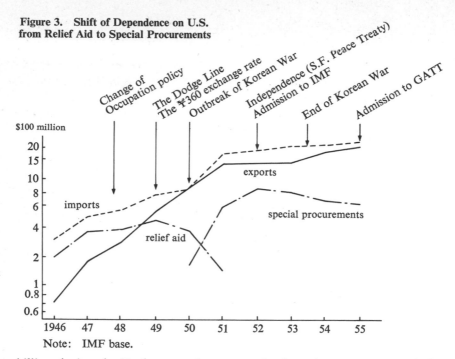

Note: IMF base.

billion during the Dodge recession, were wiped out in a one-year period, and industrial production levels shot up at unprecedented rates.

By October 1950, the mining and manufacturing index had surpassed prewar levels (calculated on 1934–36 averages), and real gross national product reached prewar levels by 1951, thereby achieving complete economic recovery in a little over one year. Due largely to dollar income from special procurements, foreign currency reserves also increased. The Special Foreign Exchange Account, which had been transferred to Japanese government control at the end of 1949 with a balance of only $200 million, increased four-and-a-half times to $940 million by the end of 1951, an enormous sum at that time. This increase was an important result of the special procurements for it raised the ceiling of Japan's import capability, thereby pushing up its GNP.[2]

The Japanese Economy during the Korean War Boom. The economic boom triggered by the Korean War and the accompanying expansion in world trade had an immediate impact on the financial world. As is usually the case with a boom, a large portion of global trade expansion was actually accounted for by price inflation. The total volume of exports increased by

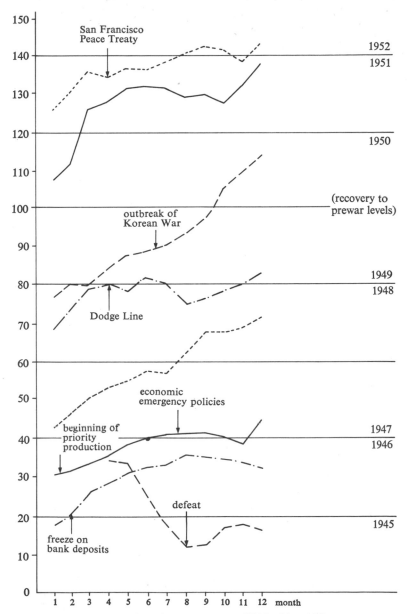

Figure 4.　The Recovery of Mining and Manufacturing Production

San Francisco
Peace Treaty

1952
1951

1950

(recovery to
prewar levels)

outbreak of
Korean War

1949
1948

Dodge Line

economic
emergency policies

beginning of
priority
production

1947
1946

defeat

1945

freeze on
bank deposits

month

Note:　Economic Deliberation Agency Indexes (1934−36 = 100)

only 10 percent internationally, and most of the increase was due to a 23 percent rise in average unit export price. In Japan wholesale prices, which had stood still during the Dodge recession, increased 52 percent in the one-year period following the outbreak of war. Of course, products that were in high demand due to special procurements and import and export trade—including metals, textiles, machinery, and construction material—led the field in wholesale price advances and were the prime movers in the price inflation. The influence of special procurements and export expansion on the reoccurrence of inflation may be explained by a number of factors.

1. The abrupt and extreme concentration in a short period of time of special procurements demand, together with the sudden increase in exports, created an extremely tight situation in overall demand.
2. Special procurements orders, made in Japan during a period of extreme international tension, resembled wartime emergency orders and, therefore, price was a secondary consideration to speediness of delivery, creating the attitude that products could be sold at any price.
3. While the Special Foreign Exchange Account was receiving un-precedented amounts of foreign currency in payments from foreign sources, its yen payments to domestic producers were also excessively high, resulting in inflationary pressures caused by the sudden increase in money supply.
4. As the international situation intensified, countries throughout the world scrambled to buy up stockpiles of basic materials while hoarding their own supplies. These two factors served to push up the average prices of basic raw materials by more than 70 percent, with key raw materials registering gains of over 100 percent.
5. The sudden expansion of world trade created a sudden shortage of shipping and a corresponding increase in international freight charges. This increase in shipping costs added to import costs, exerting inflationary pressure on the prices of imported commodities that spread to domestic prices.

As a result of the boom, Japanese companies began to post high profit margins for the first time since the end of the war, laying the groundwork for an increase in equity capital accumulation. According to a survey by the Mitsubishi Economic Research Institute, the profit rate on the available capital of major enterprises increased from 2.2 percent in the first half of 1950, to 4.1 percent in the second half of 1950, and to 7.9 percent in the first half of 1951 (compared to 6.2 percent in the first half of 1937). Reflecting improved business prospects, the stock market also enjoyed its first postwar boom and the Dow Jones average on the Tokyo Stock Exchange rose 81 percent, from ¥91.9 at the outbreak of the Korean War to ¥166 by the end of December 1951. In financial circles, pundits spoke of the thread boom and the metal boom, referring to the fact that textiles and metals—for which both special procurements and export demand were high—led the stock market advance. Japanese textiles were in such demand in Southeast Asia that buyers could be found at any price: Japanese textiles soon reclaimed their prewar position as the leader in world exports.

Steel exports increased from 30,000 tons per month at the beginning of 1950 to 100,000 tons in December 1950, raising the year's steel exports to 800,000 tons, a development that sent the price of steel materials soaring. Large profits were not limited to textiles and steel, and a boom in the automobile industry—which had been revitalized by orders for trucks worth nearly $13 million from the U.S. army and the U.S. Economic Cooperation Administration between July 1950 and February 1951—sparked a general boom in the machinery industry. Somewhat later, with the beginning of U.S. foreign aid to South and Southeast Asia, there was a boom in ammonium sulphate, paper, and sugar, the so-called white boom. Moreover, the economic boom did not only affect large firms involved in basic industries but permeated to small and medium-size companies as well, occasioning an overall improvement in production and profitability.

The Korean War boom also brought about a dramatic improvement in the situation of labor, which suffered from "rationalization" under the Dodge Line. Besides these price increases, the improvement of corporate profitability was enhanced by a marked gain in capital and labor productivity that was the result of improved plant and facilities utilization ratios and longer working hours. In the early stages of the boom, when effects of the stabilization panic were still felt, large firms attempted to fill their labor requirements through longer working hours and overtime, increasing the use of subcontractors, and acquiring temporary workers. As the boom continued, however, these measures proved inadequate, and companies began to draw up ambitions plans to hire new lifetime employees. Partly as a result of this the real wages of workers in manufacturing industries, including overtime allowances and bonuses, posted record gains in 1950, nearly 30 percent over average real wages in 1949.

These changes in the private sector were accompanied by a radical shift in government policy, reflecting the change in both the internal economic situation and the international environment. Economic policy under the Dodge Line had been dominated by Dodge's belief that Japan should achieve economic independence by halting inflation. Hence, the basic thrust of policy had been toward dampening domestic demand by stringent fiscal and monetary policies. With the outbreak of the Korean War, the dominant theme of economic policy discussions became Japan–America economic cooperation, and the highest priority was now placed on stimulating the productive capacity of the Japanese economy to the highest possible levels. This was based on the view that Japan, as a member of the Western camp, should attempt to respond to the United States' needs for emergency supplies and contribute to the development of South and Southeast Asia.

The biggest obstacle to this policy was the ceiling placed on economic expansion by the availability of raw materials imports. At the peak of the war, there was considerable anxiety that the worldwide scramble for basic raw materials would severely limit Japan's ability to secure imports. This led the Special Foreign Exchange Account to expand allocations to private industry and to extend preferential long-term financing to importers. However, by spring 1951, the war began to wind down, special procurements orders declined sharply and the international situation began to grow calmer. Nevertheless, the government's policy shift remained, and what was left of the Dodge Line was quickly dismantled.

The overbalanced budget and the rapid redemption of outstanding government bond issues were already policies of the past, and the budget revision of 1950 and the draft budget proposal for 1951 clearly signaled a general move toward expansive fiscal policies. Moreover, the establishment of the Export-Import Bank of Japan on December 15, 1950, was clearly designed to circumvent Dodge's ban on long-term loans from the Reconstruction Finance Bank. While the bank's capital of ¥15 billion was supplied in part from U.S.–aid counterpart funds, the remaining capital came from general account budget allocations, and these expenditures marked the end of conservative fiscal administration. Indeed, while Dodge continued to participate in drafting budgets until 1952, both the Occupation and Dodge's influence on economic policy were gradually coming to an end.

2. THE SAN FRANCISCO PEACE TREATY

By 1951 movements toward restoring Japan's independence and peace negotiations with its former enemies began to materialize with the gradual shift of authority from GHQ to the Japanese government. On September 8, 1951, the San Francisco Peace Conference was convened and forty-seven countries signed the San Francisco Peace Treaty. On April 28, 1952, with ratification by all signatories the peace treaty came into effect, and the signing of the U.S.–Japan Security Treaty in May 1952 marked the restoration of Japan's independence. The latter agreement left American military bases inside the country and extended a number of special privileges to the United States. (It continues to be a major subject of social and political conflict up to the present.) With U.S. sponsorship, Japan was admitted to the International Monetary Fund (IMF) and the International Bank for Reconstruction and Development (the World Bank) on May 29, 1952, opening the way for Japan to rejoin the international economic community. It should be noted, however, that participants in the San Francisco Peace Conference did not include all of Japan's former enemies, and a number of years elapsed before normal diplomatic relations were restored, especially with communist and socialist governments.[3]

Revision of Occupation Reforms. The Occupation, which had lasted for more than six years, came to an end with the San Francisco Peace Treaty, but GHQ had begun transferring its controlling and supervisory powers to the Japanese government as early as 1949, and this trend accelerated with the appointment of General Matthew B. Ridgway as supreme commander in April 1951. With independence in early 1952, changes of all kinds were made in the policies implemented during the Occupation, although the basic principles of Occupation reforms had already become deeply rooted in Japan's political culture. The most heated debates during this period concerned Japan's future and ranged around defense; the purge of leading government officials and business leaders carried out under the Occupation; the American-style compulsory education system of six years of elementary and three years of secondary schooling (the so-called six-three system); revisions to the Antimonopoly Law; and administrative reform. However, the Occupation reforms were extremely popular, and revision of the peace constitution continues to be virtually impossible even today (as seen by the problems encountered by the Nakasone Cabinet in its attempts to increase defense expenditures). Qualitatively, these revisions were not as large as many commentators have suggested.

In some areas, however, the revision of Occupation policies was extremely significant. The revision of the Purge of Public Officials Law in

1951 resulted in the depurging of approximately 170,000 persons who had been purged by the Occupation. More significant perhaps to Japan's post-war economy were the revisions to the Occupation's Antimonopoly Law, which is formally called the "Law Relating to the Prohibition of Private Monopoly and to Methods of Preserving Fair Trade," of April 14, 1947.

The Antimonopoly Law had a checkered career even before the end of the Occupation, and GHQ itself authorized the first formal amendment in June 1949, relaxing restrictions on stock retentions and interlocking directorships. The second revision of the Antimonopoly Law in 1953, drafted during the truce recession after the Korean War boom, was designed to promote exports and hasten recovery. The most important revisions may be summarized as follows.

1. The authorization of depression cartels and rationalization cartels;
2. Termination of liquidations of firms under the Elimination of Excessive Economic Concentration Law;
3. Sanctions of retail price maintenance contracts.

The consequence of these revisions was the fostering of new "financial lineages," or *keiretsu*, as successors to the *zaibatsu*, and a general softening of the Occupation-sponsored Antimonopoly Law. Moreover, the Japanese government announced the conclusion of *zaibatsu* dissolution on July 1951, and the Holding Companies Liquidation Commission was disbanded. With independence and revision of the Antimonopoly Law, former *zaibatsu* firms were allowed to use their old trademarks, symbolizing the reorganization of the prewar *zaibatsu* into new *keiretsu*, as they came to be called. For example, Mitsui Bussan and Mitsubishi Shōji, which had been broken up into two hundred and twenty and one hundred and forty companies, respectively, under the *Zaibatsu* Dissolution Law, were quickly reorganized, although their respective banks now played the leading role in the conglomerates.

Other *zaibatsu*-related firms soon followed this lead, and their reorganization into *keiretsu* established a unique pattern of cooperative arrangements that would play an extremely important role in Japan's subsequent economic development. Based on cross-shareholding between banks and affiliated enterprises, the *keiretsu* typically includes a big bank, several industrial firms, and a general trading company. The big six *keiretsu* that came into being at this time were those based on the Fuji, Sanwa, Dai-Ichi, Mitsui, Mitsubishi, and Sumitomo banks. The crucial difference between the postwar *keiretsu* and the old *zaibatsu* is that family-controlled holding companies were replaced by the big banks as the nuclei of the *keiretsu*, eliminating many of the semifeudal business practices characteristic of the *zaibatsu*.

Capital Accumulation and the Role of Economic Policy. Besides revisions of the Antimonopoly Law, the government also began to hammer out new economic policies firmly committing the country to economic development. Even before the San Francisco Peace Conference, the theme of discussions had shifted to economic expansion and strengthening the foundations for development. The main subject of these debates was the problem of capital accumulation. The Korean War boom had enabled the country to recover from the recession imposed by the Dodge Line and to achieve economic reconstruction. This windfall, however, had also exposed the basic structural weakness of the economy. Economic reconstruction during the Korean War boom had been accomplished by concentrating investment capital on increased supplies of raw materials, thus increasing the productivity of plant and equipment facilities that had survived World War II. By the early 1950s, these facilities were badly outmoded by international standards, which had risen quickly as technology developed in the war was introduced into industry, and Japanese industries were characterized by comparatively low capital intensiveness and a reliance on cheap labor. Industrial rationalization under the Dodge Line had meant personnel rationalization through layoffs. It was now clear that new policies would have to be developed if Japan were to achieve complete economic independence and sustained growth. The problem for economic planners was capital accumulation in a poor, capital-starved society. Where was the investment capital needed for the modernization of Japanese industry to be found?

The result of this debate was the policies and institutions of high growth that led to the economic miracle, although no one at the time anticipated how effective the new set of policies would be. In March 1952, the Enterprises Rationalization Promotion Law was enacted, and amendments to the Special Tax Measures Law established various new exemptions and set up a system of reserve funds to assist developing industries. The new tax exemptions included up to 50 percent exemption of a firm's income earned from exports, a special depreciation system for designated investments for industrial rationalization, deductions for royalties paid for foreign technology, and many others. The reserve funds system provided for tax exemption or tax deferment on a whole set of newly authorized corporation reserve funds. The best known of these is the retirement reserve fund for lump-sum payments to employees when they retire. Others include the price fluctuations reserve fund, the reserve fund for export losses, and a number of others. Collectively, the new tax policies were called the "capital accumulation tax system," and they effectively dismantled the system recommended by the Shoup mission in 1949. Nevertheless, the new tax system, and particularly the special depreciation system, played a major role in the modernization of Japanese industry in the period of rapid economic growth, for which it set the stage. Certainly, these new policies were essential at this stage for the promotion of capital investment and export expansion. It is true, however, that the preferential application of the new policies resulted in strengthening existing privileged positions and in making industrial policy much more rigid.

A second set of new policies was designed to mobilize the government's own capital to promote capital accumulation and rapid economic development. The Japan Development Bank had been established in March 1951, with an initial capital of ¥10 billion from the Counterpart Fund Special Account, and assumed the assets of that fund until the end of the Occupation. With the end of the Occupation, the government gave the bank authority to issue its own bonds and to borrow funds from the government's investment budget. The investment budget itself was based on the Fiscal Investment and Loan Plan, established in July 1952, by combining postal savings accounts into one large investment pool. During the same period came the establishment of the Export-Import Bank (previously the Export Bank of Japan), the Housing Loan Corporation, the Smaller Business Finance Corporation, and the Agriculture, Forestry, and Fishery Finance Corporation. Besides providing government financing to promote modernization in basic industries, new industries, small and medium-size businesses, and agriculture, the new government banks were designed to provide a steady flow of government funding for social overhead investment, which had fallen off drastically under the Occupation. This would, of course, improve the environment for industry by hastening the modernization of the economic infrastructure.

War Reparations and Repayment of U.S. Relief Aid. The signing of the San Francisco Peace Treaty immediately necessitated settlement of the long-standing problems of war reparations and repayment of U.S. aid. The United States, however, had begun to renounce its right to reparations even before the peace conference and, as a result, many of the signatories renounced their rights to demand reparations from Japan. Southeast Asia, on the other hand, which had sustained especially severe war damages, insisted on reparations, and provisions were made in the treaty for Japan to negotiate with each of these governments. The Philippines, Indonesia, Burma, and South Vietnam demanded reparations totalling $30 billion and, after months of difficult negotiations, the following settlements were concluded.

> The Philippines: $550 million in reparations to be paid over a ten-year period beginning in 1956;
> Indonesia: $223 million in reparations to be paid over a twelve-year period beginning in 1958;
> Burma: $340 million in reparations and outright economic cooperation aid to be paid over a ten-year period beginning in 1955;
> South Vietnam: $390 million in reparations to be paid over a five-year period beginning in 1960.

Outright economic cooperation aid agreements were also concluded with a number of the countries that eventually waived their rights to reparations, including South Korea, Laos, Cambodia, Singapore, and Micronesia. Total war reparations during the twenty-one years up to July 1976, when all payments were finally concluded, amounted to about $1.6 billion, or a little more than ¥5,000 per capita for the Japanese population. Seen in this light, the economic burden imposed on Japan by direct war reparations was relatively light; however, if the wealth left in former colonies and in various countries, to which Japan renounced all rights in the peace treaty, is counted as being in effect reparations payments, the actual figure rises to $20 to $30 billion.

Given the U.S. stance on reparations, negotiations proceeded relatively smoothly and, with the exception of a few installations still under U.S. army control under the terms of the U.S.–Japan Security Treaty, the old munitions facilities that had been designated for confiscation as reparations were returned to their original owners a few days before the treaty. The problem of negotiating the repayment of U.S. relief aid to Japan followed a much more difficult course, and a final settlement was not reached until 1962. Problems centered on how much of U.S. aid, particularly that supplied under the GARIOA (Government Account for Relief in Occupied Areas), should be considered a debt liability repayable by Japan. The final settlement in 1962 set the figure at $490 million, to be paid over a fifteen-year period with annual interest of 2.5 percent. Japan's share of the burden for defense expenditures was also established under the new security pact: in the budget for 1952, Japan appropriated funds to cover approximately half the expenses of U.S. forces stationed in Japan and to provide all the funds for the leases of base facilities for the U.S. army. It was also agreed under this pact that periodic adjustments would be made for Japan's share of the defense burden as the nation increased its own defense capabilities.

3. FROM INDEPENDENCE WITHOUT AID TO INDEPENDENCE WITHOUT SPECIAL PROCUREMENTS

The basic weakness of the economy was revealed most clearly by the truce recession following the beginning of truce negotiations in Korea in spring 1951. The domestic boom that accompanied the Korean War peaked after the first seven or eight months of the conflict, and the business-cycle adjustment caused by the reduction in demand for special procurements and exports threw the economy into a temporary recession. In spring 1951, the U.S. government called a halt to the policy of buying up strategic materials, and other countries followed suit as the relaxation of international tensions slowed worldwide military build-ups. The general trading companies were particularly hard hit and there were a large number of bankruptcies when these companies, which had participated in the worldwide scramble for basic commodities, suffered huge losses with the plunge in the price of soybeans, leather, and rubber, the three new products in which they had invested heavily. The textile industry was also thrown into a panic by massive cancellations of orders by Indonesia.

It was against this background that the government began to hammer out new economic policies even before the end of the Occupation. Financing was extended to large enterprises, primarily to general trading companies in the newly forming *keiretsu*, as well as inventory loans to cover the sharp drop in prices of soybeans, leather, and rubber. Moreover, on February 25, 1952, the Ministry of International Trade and Industry (MITI) evaded the Antimonopoly Law to carry out its first "administrative guidance," by informally advising the ten big cotton spinners to reduce production by 40 percent and assigning production quotas to each firm. It was also at this time that the first moves were made by MITI to encourage "recession cartels" in the industries hardest hit by the recession. Cartels were eventually formed in the rolled steel, steel wire, tire, chemical resins, soda, oil, and sugar industries, all of them organized with administrative guidance from MITI. However, even during the truce recession, the tempo of economic expansion did not weaken that much as a whole. Special procurements demand had also stimulated a rapid increase in domestic demand, and firms were anxious to increase plant and equipment investment. Moreover, after the signing of the San Francisco Peace Treaty, the government adopted a series of agressive fiscal and monetary policies to encourage business.

The First Postwar Plant and Equipment Investment Boom. In retrospect, it is clear that this period foreshadowed the sustained growth of investment in new technology to modernize industry, leading to Japan's rapid economic growth era from 1955 to 1965. The effects of these new policies to promote capital accumulation may be seen in a number of major industries. Coal and steel had been the leading stars of the Priority Production Policy only a few years earlier, but with the end of government subsidies in 1952, their prices on international markets rose rapidly, revealing the basic weakness of these two key industries. Given the significance of the role assigned the two industries, they were crucial to the plans calling for a shift in the economic structure toward heavy industrialization. If these plans were to be realized, and if the domestic economy as a whole was to become competitive internationally, the problem of high prices for Japanese steel and coal would have to be solved.

Moreover, the close relationship between the two industries meant that, in order to reduce the price of steel to international levels, the price of coal in the domestic market would have to be reduced by half, from $13 per ton to $7 per ton. The coal industry attempted to respond to this by importing advanced mining technology from Germany, and government planners cooperated with the industry to draft the Coal Shaft Development Plan, which aimed at achieving structural modernization by closing down inefficient mines and exploiting new coal sources. Unfortunately, however, these efforts were doomed from the beginning because of the poor quality of Japan's coal deposits, and the industry was never able to reduce costs sufficiently to become competitive internationally. It declined steadily during the early 1950s and, in any case, coal was soon to be replaced by oil in the global energy revolution that accompanied the discovery of large new oil reserves in the Middle East.

In contrast to the failure of the coal industry, the achievement of the steel industry's structural modernization was conspicuous. Steel companies were anxious to overcome their weak international position and in

1952 launched the industry's First Rationalization Plan. Originally a three-year plan, it was extended to five years, during which total investment in plant and equipment reached ¥120 billion, representing yearly averages more than ten times higher than investment levels before the plan. The plan focused on introducing new technology in the hot rolled steel sector, and particularly on importing continuous rolling equipment (strip mills) to replace the outmoded pullover method. With the enormous investment in new technology, and the subsequent production increases and cost reductions made possible by automation, high speed operations, and economies of scale, the industry increased its production capacity by as much as one thousand times.

The success of the steel industry also reflects the effectiveness of the government's commitment to improving the economic infrastructure. Under the Enterprises Rationalization Promotion Law, for example, the government launched the revolutionary Keiyō industrial belt and *kombinato*, a huge industrial park built in Chiba Prefecture on land reclaimed from Tokyo Bay. The Kawasaki Steel Company, a new entry, received 3 million square meters of this land and, in 1953, opened the most modern integrated steel facility in the world at that time. Not only was the facility located near a new, modern harbor but the production line was also one continuous process from dockside delivery of raw materials to blast furnace to steel production to rolling. The success of the project resulted in furious competition among established steel producers (Yawata, Fuji, and Nippon Kōkan) to launch modernization projects of their own.

These developments were not confined to the coal and steel industries, as four industries—coal, steel, electric power, and shipbuilding—had been designated key industries in the government's new plans to promote rationalization and modernization. The Electric Power Development Promotion Law, promulgated in 1952, transformed the electric power industry, which had been hard pressed to satisfy existing demand. The most dramatic result of the new law was the Sakuma Dam, which introduced the most modern hydroelectric power plant technology of the time as well as large-scale civil engineering and construction equipment. This project was launched in 1953. In the same year, Japan received its first loan from the World Bank to finance contracts to import thermal-generating plant technology for new plants constructed by the Kansai, Chūbu, and Kyushu Electric Power companies. In the shipbuilding industries, increased production and modernization were hastened with the introduction of new automatic welding and block construction technology to replace the old labor-intensive construction methods prevalent in major shipyards.

The movement toward modernization also became firmly rooted in other industries during this period, in many cases industries that would become the leaders of rapid economic growth after 1955. The chemical fertilizer industry had been nurtured up to this time by a system of government subsidies, including an arrangement under which the government supported prices by buying up and distributing supplies through the semi-governmental agricultural cooperatives system. When this program of price supports and distribution controls was discontinued after independence, the industry began to suffer from overproduction as export demand declined when its prices rose above international levels. This sparked a rise in plant and equipment investment as the industry attempted to modernize. Petroleum gas and natural gas quickly replaced coal as the principle energy source, and new technologies were introduced to diversify and lower the costs of the industry's products. For example, it was during this period that new technologies were introduced for producing urea and super phosphates.

The synthetic fibers, electrical machinery, and automobile industries also underwent rapid modernization, both by cooperating with foreign makers and by developing new technologies independently. In the synthetic fibers industry, Tōyō Rayon entered into a technical cooperation agreement with Du Pont to purchase nylon technology, while Kurashiki Rayon developed in-house technology for the production of vinylon (vinyl chloride).

Modernization of the electrical machinery industry was stimulated by the Electric Power Development Plan of 1952 and the first television broadcasts in the same year. Plant and equipment investment rose rapidly as firms in the industry rushed to import new technology. Competition was volatile, with smaller firms such as Hayakawa (Sharp) and General (Yaō) rising to challenge Matsushita and Tōshiba. Sony, a new entry into the industry, developed the first domestically produced transistors in 1953.

The automobile industry, revitalized by the special procurements demand for trucks, took advantage of this income to invest heavily in new technology for the domestic production of automobiles. Toyota launched a five-year plant and equipment modernization plan to develop its own passenger car, while Nissan, Isuzu, and Hino entered into technical cooperation agreements with Austin, Hillman of the Rootes Group, and Renault, respectively, to assemble foreign automobiles in their own facilities. These moves toward technological modernization and increased

Figure 5. Recovery of Personal Consumption to Prewar Levels

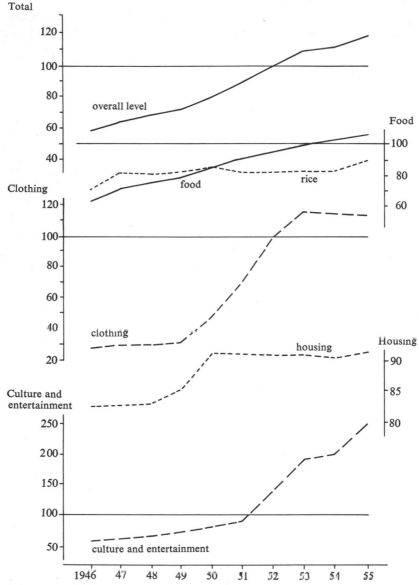

Note: Supply of goods and services in terms of volume per capita
        (average for 1934–36=100)

Source: Economic White Papers, 1955 and 1956.

plant and equipment investment had barely got started, but they foreshadowed the huge rise in plant and equipment investment that characterized the ten-year period after 1955.

The growth of plant and equipment investment also sparked the first postwar boom in the construction industry, especially in big buildings. The Shinmaru Building, halted during the war by restrictions on building materials supplies, was completed in 1952, and Tokyo's Nikkatsu International Hall (presently the Hibiya Park Building) was completed at about the same time, the largest and most modern in Tokyo at that time. The Seibu Department Store built a huge new complex with a floor space of eleven thousand square meters, and Hankyū and Daimaru, Osaka department stores, also built new complexes in Tokyo.

The First Postwar Consumption Boom. The most remarkable feature of economic activity during this period was the revival of personal consumption to prewar levels and its subsequent rise to even higher levels. This consumption boom occurred in 1952–53, the first of only two periods in which personal consumption has played a significant role in the development of the postwar economy. The second, of course, was from 1959–60 when the "consumer revolution," as it came to be called, created the mass consumption society. Real per capita consumption levels (adjusted for inflation) rose 16 percent in 1952 and 13 percent in 1953. As indicated in Figure 5, the increases for 1953 raised consumption indexes above prewar levels (1934–36).

Both qualitatively and quantitatively, the most conspicuous improvement was in the availability of inexpensive clothing. At the end of the war the textiles and apparel industries were in deep decline, their recovery retarded by production quotas established under MITI's administrative guidance and by the practice of promoting exports at the expense of the domestic market. With this "social dumping," as the practice was called by foreign competitors, white-collar workers had grown accustomed to wearing shirts with frayed collars and sleeping between tattered and patched sheets. During the consumption boom, this aspect of daily life became a thing of the past as the elimination of domestic controls and the decline in exports led the industry to shift its attention to the domestic market. The prices of textiles and clothing, which had been the highest in the domestic consumer market, dropped rapidly to levels that consumers could afford.

Food consumption also regained prewar levels during the period and, as early as 1951, newspapers began to proclaim the end of shortages under such headlines as SAYONARA "BAMBOO SHOOT LIFE." The consumption of white rice had reached 80 percent of prewar levels (297 grams per day in 1952, compared to 361 grams before the war); consumption of·wheat tripled from 26 grams to 80 grams per day in 1952, reflecting the shift of dietary habits to bread and noodles, as well as a high reliance on food imports at this time. Sweet potatoes lost their importance as a staple substitute and consumption dropped by more than half from the 1948 peak.

The most striking aspect of the consumption boom was the rapid increase in durable goods consumption. While the overall rate of popularization was still quite low, refrigerators, sewing machines, radios, cameras, and fluorescent lamps began to appear in more and more homes. Moreover, increases in expenditures for newsprint reflected the revival and growth of the publishing industry. The improvement in living standards may not have been as dramatic as in the subsequent consumer revolution, but the availability of affordable clothing, the possibility of dining out, and the dream of being able to purchase new products for the home gave Japanese people the opportunity to enjoy a feeling of liberation in a free economy for the first time since the beginning of World War II. The consumption boom was not simply due to the general prosperity that accompanied the Korean War boom; the democratization reforms of the immediate postwar years were beginning to show their effects as domestic markets expanded. Agricultural reform had drastically reduced the number of tenant farmers, and more food was produced by independent cultivators. In urban areas, democratization of labor–management relations, particularly in large firms, resulted in a fairer distribution of the profits from the Korean War boom, and wages, as well as the number of employees in secondary industries, rose as the boom progressed. The consumption boom was paralleled by increases in personal savings, and total savings deposits posted surpluses in 1950 for the first time since the immediate postwar period.

The consumption boom did not bring a solution to the problem of housing shortages, particularly in large cities. The availability of housing was still far below prewar levels, and much that was available was cramped and poorly constructed. Indeed, a large number of people were still living in temporary barracks contructed by GHQ immediately after the war. The boom also produced a number of undesirable results. Bars and other entertainment facilities (strip shows, music halls, and *pachinko* parlors) were packed every night, and expense account spending guaranteed that prices in such establishments would soar. Spending for imported luxury items reached $70 million to $80 million a year.

Negative Effects of the Korean War Boom. There is no question that the economic situation had improved considerably in terms of living standards, corporate profits, and industrial production. However, the large part played by special procurements in the reconstruction of the economy meant that the economy had assumed a special, and highly unstable, structure that made Japan extremely dependent on the United States. The Economic White Paper of 1953 vehemently attacked this distorted structure.

> The level of Japan's economy has been raised by the existence of special procurements. However, the fact that the economic structure has been so distorted that it cannot function without depending on special procurements must be considered a "sin" of special procurements.

The reasoning of the White Paper may be summarized as follows. Special procurements demand, which by its nature should have produced only a temporary source of income, continued far longer than expected. In 1952 and 1953, the level of special procurements still remained as high as $800 million a year, giving the economy the false appearance of having achieved a higher degree of independence than expected. In some sectors of industry, this had even led to the naive expectation that expanded investment and high profits could be maintained by new special procurements in the future, generated by U.S. military expenditures and foreign aid to Southeast Asia. Not only had special procurements enabled Japan to cover its balance of payments deficits after the termination of U.S. aid, but the resulting foreign currency income had been absorbed by increasing domestic demand, therefore creating even higher levels of demand. If this increase in foreign currency income had been in the form of relief aid, its function would have been limited to guaranteeing supplies of basic commodities and covering the resulting balance of payments deficits, and would not have resulted in the expansion of income.

In the case of special procurements, a powerful snowball effect was launched in which income from special procurements induced consumption demand and demand for investment capital. Therefore, when special procurements orders were reduced or eliminated, it would be extremely difficult to achieve a normal balance of international payments. Japan's tilt toward the United States would become even more pronounced, and there was the possibility that the country would be locked permanently into a dependent relationship.

Special procurements demand had also forced up domestic prices, and Japanese products were relatively expensive on international markets. This was particularly true in the heavy and chemicals industries, in which Japanese prices were 20 to 30 percent higher than those of foreign competitors. Without special procurements, producers would have reduced prices and attempted to increase exports. In fact, the volume of exports in 1952 and 1953 was somewhat lower than in 1951, and there had been virtually no increase between 1952 and 1953. While exports amounted to approximately $1.3 billion a year during the three-year period, special procurements had reached $800 to $900 million in the same period, maintaining a general balance in international payments as well as in supply and demand. Therefore, there was little incentive for producers to take the necessary steps to reduce prices in order to increase exports.

Two other factors also influenced the stagnation of exports. First, the 1949 Chinese Communist Revolution had closed Chinese markets, eliminating a raw materials source on which Japan had been dependent for more than 20 percent of its imports. This resulted in a drastic rise in import costs as producers were forced to procure raw materials from foreign markets that were much further away. Second, Japan's principle export commodity was still textiles during this period, and the increasing capacity of underdeveloped countries, particularly of Southeast Asia, to produce their own textiles made any increase in textile export extremely difficult. Precisely because this was so, firms in heavy industry, which had become Japan's Achilles heel in international markets, would have to stop relying on special procurements demand and take concerted steps to improve their competitiveness and, thus, their export performance. This could only be accomplished by eliminating the price disadvantage resulting from their failure to modernize.

This critique of the economic situation became the basis for the fiscal budget of 1953, the first budget drafted by the Japanese government. Politicians were also calling for a shift to expansive fiscal policies, and the government's budget draft called for large spending increases. In addition, these increases were accompanied by a ¥100 billion tax cut, which was to be covered by a government bond issue. Since the original draft called for deficit spending, it was criticized in many quarters as inflationary. However, the scale of spending rose with each subsequent revision. The first revision was necessitated by the delay in drafting the budget until August because of the dissolution of the cabinet and the general elections. The second budget revision increased spending to implement agricultural relief measures when heavy frost led to a disastrous harvest. Fiscal spending in 1953 finally reached levels exceeding ¥1 trillion.

The Foreign Currency Crisis and the Yoshida Deflation. The problem of independence without special procurements was settled much more quickly than anyone had expected. With the death of Stalin, international tensions relaxed, and expectations of new special procurements and a special relationship of economic cooperation with the United States came to nothing. Moreover, the government's aggressive expansionist economic policies were badly shaken by a sudden, large balance of payments deficit, forcing the government to take emergency steps to dampen domestic demand. With the rapid worsening of the international payments situation beginning in fall 1953, the government was faced with a payments deficit of nearly $400 million by the end of the year, despite the $800 million income from special procurements. At the same time, foreign currency reserves, which had amounted to $2.14 billion in November 1953, dropped to $0.6 billion by June 1954. Japan was thus faced with its first foreign currency crisis since admission into the IMF in August 1953 and had to take advantage of its new status by drawing IMF loans three times in a single year. These loans amounted to £22.3 million, or $62 million, which were to finance Japanese imports from those Southeast Asian countries in Britain's sphere of influence.

Two special factors contributed to the crisis. First, 1953 had been disastrous for agriculture, with spring frost, typhoons in the summer, and an early frost in the fall. The rice crop declined by 20 percent from the previous year and the buckwheat crop by 6 percent, increasing foreign currency allocations for essential food imports by $200 million. Second, the worldwide downward trend in business and trade had seriously weakened sterling, and import restrictions imposed by countries in the sterling zone worsened the stagnant position of Japanese exports. It was this phenomenon that was the cause for the large loans from the IMF. However, the foreign currency crisis basically resulted from the overly high domestic demand for imports. Given this excessive demand, domestic prices for imported products under the ¥360 fixed exchange rate continued to rise even though their prices on international markets were declining. Aware that high profits were guaranteed no matter how much they imported, general trading companies scrambled to import. Moreover, a number of them increased import purchases on a speculative basis because of an anticipated reduction in foreign currency allocations by MITI.

In the face of this crisis, and to restrain internal demand, the government hammered out fiscal and monetary policies that served to support economic policy long after they were adopted. Beginning in September 1954, the Bank of Japan limited borrowing by city banks (the twelve national banks to which the Bank of Japan extends loan privileges) through the unique system of "window guidance." This measure limited loan increases by each bank on a month-to-month basis, with punitive interest rates for exceeding them. It was effective because of the system of "overloaning," or indirect financing, in which the firms in a financial *keiretsu* overborrow from its city bank and this city bank, in turn, overborrows from the Bank of Japan to guarantee the loans, making the city banks extremely vulnerable to window guidance. At the same time, the measures for preferential import financing were abolished. These measures, which had been established to promote emergency imports during the Korean War boom, included a special foreign currency loan accounts system and special financing arrangements for import transactions by the Export-Import Bank. Prime Minister Yoshida took the lead in reducing government spending to ¥1 trillion (the actual budget for 1954 was ¥999.5 billion), applying the brakes to expansive fiscal policies that had raised budgets every year since the end of the Dodge Line. In particular, the new budget for 1954 reduced the Fiscal Investment and Loan Plan budget by 20 percent, and the budgets for public works by about 10 percent.

The policies adopted in 1954 have come to be called the "Yoshida deflation" and, because the effects of the resulting recession were concentrated in that year, the recession has also been called the "1954 recession." The 1954 policies are especially important because they became the precedents for the "stop-go" measures that have characterized monetary and fiscal policies in Japan ever since. These measures may be seen as short-term cyclical adjustment policies in which domestic demand is suppressed whenever deficits arise in the international trade balance and are immediately relaxed as soon as the balance improves. The policies themselves were conceived as a last-ditch effort to stave off an imminent foreign exchange crisis, but they were surprisingly effective. The trade balance began to improve in June 1954, and the recession bottomed out three months later. The direct curtailment of exports by reduced foreign currency allocations and import credits was particularly effective in this period, when Japan had yet to achieve "Article 8 status," or advanced nation status, in the IMF, and its effectiveness was helped by the stringent monetary policies to curb domestic demand.

The monetary policies, however, were not undertaken without high cost. The rapid decline in domestic demand was reflected in sharp decreases in inventory investment and in plant and equipment investment, accompanied by production reductions in such key industries as steel and machinery. Bankruptcies threatened such large firms as Amagasaki Steel, which was saved only by a merger with Kobe Steel, and Nippon Yakin Kōgyō and Komatsu Seisaku-sho were bailed out by a consortium of city banks. Ōji Paper, Mitsui Miike Machinery, and Nissan suffered some of the longest strikes in postwar labor relations. These labor problems stemmed in large part from the fact that many firms attempted to weather the recession by carrying out large-scale rationalization programs, cutting back on the number of temporary workers and subcontractors. This increased the number of unemployed to 600,000, even higher than the 400,000 figure under the Dodge Line.

The economic turmoil of 1954 was matched by political instability, symbolized by the temporary split in the Liberal Party as conservative politicians groped for an agreement that would lead to a coalition of conservative forces. The Liberal Party government of Yoshida was replaced by the Democratic Party government of Ichirō Hatoyama as its followers scrambled to mend fences in the first moves toward the formation of the Liberal Democratic Party (LDP) in November 1955. The Hatoyama Cabinet proclaimed its Six-Year General Economic Plan (later to become the Five-Year Plan for Economic Independence) as the cornerstone of domestic policy, and the reestablishment of ties with the Soviet Union as its foreign policy goal, but it failed to alter the policies of the Yoshida deflation.[4]

The Economic White Paper of 1955. More than anything else, recovery from the recession created by the Yoshida deflation was led by exports, as well as the worldwide upturn in business conditions. The economies of Europe had very early on experienced business downturns following the post–Korean War recession and, by mid-1953, had already begun to recover, led by a revival of plant and equipment investment. The recession had hit the United States somewhat later than Europe, but still before its impact on Japan, and the American economy had begun to recover by fall 1954. Therefore, Japan was able to recover relatively quickly, with sharp increases in exports and a rapid improvement in trade leading the recovery as Japan took advantage of the early recovery of its trading partners and the resulting expansion of international trade.

The original aim of the Yoshida deflation had been to stave off the foreign currency crisis by suppressing domestic demand and thereby reducing imports in order to achieve an international trade balance at lower levels of total foreign trade. In 1955, as exports began to rise rapidly with worldwide recovery, Japan was actually able to achieve a balance of international trade at much higher levels of total foreign trade than before. Exports for 1955 were nearly 60 percent higher than for 1953, representing a total that would enable the country to maintain its balance of international payments even without special procurements income and with relatively high levels of exports. Moreover, as a result of the Yoshida deflation, even the largest firms in key export industries had been forced to streamline operations, resulting in cost reductions that lowered the price of exports. Export prices, which had been artificially inflated by special procurements demand, declined 12 percent in the period 1953–55, and the double price structure, whereby export prices were higher than domestic prices, was finally eliminated.

Domestically, both wholesale and consumer prices declined significantly, particularly for agricultural products. The poor harvest of 1954 was followed by a bountiful crop in 1955, with a rice harvest of 12.4 million tons (30 percent higher than the previous year's and 17 percent higher than the 1933 harvest, the largest prewar rice crop). This increased supply and lower price of foodstuffs significantly reduced the burden of importing food supplies, making 1955 and 1956 the best years for consumers since the end of the war. These two years also marked the transition between the period of reconstruction of the immediate postwar years and the new period of economic development that was to follow. For the first time since the war, the overloan phenomenon, which had been growing up to the beginning of the Yoshida deflation, was replaced by a financial situation in which the supply of credit was greater than the demand for it. Despite increased exports considerable excess capacity remained as a result of the Yoshida deflation, and industrial firms were more inclined to use export income to repay existing loans than to increase plant and equipment investment.

The boom that followed this economic recovery was hailed in the Economic White Paper of 1955 as a "volume boom" (*sūryō keiki*), although this designation fails to capture its unique quality. The characteristics of the volume boom may be summarized as follows.

1. The boom was accompanied by a surprisingly high surplus in the international payments balance.
2. It was not accompanied by a significant rise in prices.
3. It was accompanied by a reduction in corporate borrowing.

This type of volume boom is a rare occurrence in Japan's economic history, both before and after the war. For example, what was called a volume boom in the 1969–72 period was characterized by the following.

1. A large surplus in the balance of international payments;
2. A huge increase in demand for speculative venture capital as a result of excess liquidity;
3. Rapid price increases.

What created the volume boom in 1955 and 1956 was the existence of excess plant and equipment capacity, the fact that the economy was in less than full employment, and the fact that there was little pressure on prices. This was a highly unusual situation and, as such, was doomed to be short-lived. As we shall see, the volume boom was quickly replaced by the Jimmu boom (*see* Chapter 3), a plant and equipment investment boom that was completely different in character. The only true volume boom in the postwar history of the Japanese economy had a lifespan of only about one year.

The Yoshida deflation proved extremely effective in its short-term goal of curbing domestic demand, and the unexpected volume boom in its aftermath insured that the basic principles of economic policy developed at this time would remain as pillars of monetary and fiscal policy. In fact, however, it was an eleventh-hour policy launched only after the failure of fiscal policies enacted in 1953, which were intended to suppress demand but turned out to be highly expansionary, leading to an international payments and foreign currency crises. Moreover, because it was a "stop-go" monetary policy that attempted to suppress demand by sheer force, it has been criticized for worsening economic fluctuations. However, it must be remembered that the economy was still being buffeted by both the positive and the negative effects of the Dodge Line, and that the Korean War boom had reactivated inflationary pressures that had existed since the end of the war. By 1954, it was clear that the economy could not longer depend on special procurements demand and the problem of domestic inflation could not be ignored.

In the sense that Yoshida's policies signaled the end of a complacent attitude toward inflation and established a firm basis for the policies of the subsequent period of high economic growth, they must be considered extremely significant. According to *The Yoshida Memoirs*, the two most important reasons behind these policies were: 1) the World Bank and a number of other international financial institutions refused to extend foreign currency credit to Japan unless inflation was brought under control; and 2) the foreign currency crisis had made it impossible to increase Japan's defense capabilities and, therefore, to petition the United States for a reduction in troop strength in Japan. Moreover, it is undeniable that the impetus given by these policies to the modernization of Japanese industry, leading to the elimination of the noncompetitiveness of the heavy and chemicals industries in international markets, was a major factor in Japan's long-term economic development.

3 THE TAKE-OFF TOWARD MODERNIZATION

1. THE TECHNOLOGY REVOLUTION

The Economic White Paper of 1956. The year 1955 marks the beginning of the ten-year period of rapid change that transformed every aspect of social, political, and economic life. In the fall of 1955, the two leading conservative parties, the liberals and the democrats, united to form the Liberal Democratic Party (LDP), which has ruled the country ever since, and the left and right wings of the Socialist Party joined to form a more or less unified opposition. In spring 1956, Yoshio Nakano, a leading literary critic, announced that "the immediate postwar period is over," and called on Japanese intellectuals to free themselves from the illusion that they could cling forever to the ideals of the Occupation period. His sentiments were echoed in the Economic White Paper of 1956, the tenth since the first Tsuru White Paper: "It is no longer postwar. We now confront a completely different situation. The period of economic growth through reconstruction is over. Future economic growth must be supported by modernization." The Economic White Paper used such terms as "technology revolution" (innovation) and "modernization" (transformation), and they had such appeal that they soon became catchphrases among businessmen and the general public.

The factual background to these statements is suggested by the statistics presented in Tables 6 and 7. By 1955, most of the key economic indicators had already risen higher than prewar levels. Real GNP had accomplished this by 1951, and per capita GNP by 1955. Real per capita consumption returned to prewar levels in 1953, although differences in the distribution of income meant that personal consumption in urban areas lagged behind

Table 6. Years in which Major Economic Indicators Passed Prewar Levels

	Indexes for 1955 (av. for 1934–36=100)	Year indicators passed prewar levels	Year indicators doubled prewar levels
*Real GNP	136	1951	1960
Industrial production	158	1951	1957
Agricultural production	148	1949	1967
Volume of exports	75	1959	1964
Volume of imports	94	1957	1961
*Real GNP per capita	105	1955	1960
*Personal consumption expenditures per capita	114	1953	1965
Industrial production per capita	122	1953	1960
Agricultural production per capita	115	1952	—

Notes: 1. * indicates that figures are for fiscal years; others are for calendar years.
2. Forestry and marine production are not included in indexes for agricultural production.

Table 7. Changes in the Composition of Exports

(%)

	Prewar (av. for 1934–36)	1955	1965	1970	1975
Heavy industrial products and chemicals		38.0	62.0	72.4	83.4
Metals		19.2	20.3	19.7	22.5
(Steel)	2.4	12.9	15.3	14.7	18.2
Machinery	2.8	13.7	35.2	46.3	23.1
(Ships)	0.1	3.9	8.8	7.3	10.8
Chemicals		5.1	6.5	6.4	7.0
Light industrial products		52.0	31.8	23.2	13.0
(Textile products)	57.4	37.3	18.7	12.5	6.7
(Others)		14.7	13.1	10.7	6.3
Food products	8.4	13.3	4.1	3.4	1.4
Raw materials		6.8	1.5	1.0	1.0
Total value of exports ($100 millions)	6.9	20.1	84.5	193.2	557.5

Source: Ministry of Finance, *Gaikoku bōeki gaikyō* (General survey of foreign trade).

prewar levels until 1954. This was because the Occupation-sponsored agricultural reform had had the effect of narrowing the disparity between urban and rural consumption, which had been heavily weighted in favor of urban dwellers before the war. On the other hand, a number of key economic indicators supports the conclusion that the Economic White Paper of 1956 was more a manifesto for the future than an objective analysis of the situation. The nationwide housing shortage, which stood at 4.2 million residences immediately after the war, had been reduced by only 1.5 million, leaving a 2.7 million shortage in 1956, and the number of people living in temporary barracks was still high. The total volume of foreign trade was especially slow to show signs of recovery and, by 1955, exports had reached only 75 percent of prewar levels.

This phenomenon was by no means the result of the economy's increased ability to supply domestic demand and a corresponding decline in the need to increase exports for the necessary foreign currency to cover imports. Rather, the potential demand for imports was still high, and essential imports were being curtailed precisely because exports, and therefore foreign currency income, continued to lag behind due to the structural weaknesses of principle export industries. Ten years after the end of the war, light industries, including textiles, plywood, miscellaneous items, and foodstuffs, continued to comprise about 65 percent of total exports. Textiles, still the most important export industry, had poorer prospects now that developing counties had their own textile industries, not only satisfying their demand but also challenging Japan in its foreign markets. At the same time, with the exception of shipbuilding, the heavy and chemicals industries, upon which economic planners had staked their hopes for the future, still proved to be weak because of insufficient modernization for international competition.

At this time Japan had reached the stage when it was essential to discard old ways of thinking about the economy, which took the recovery of prewar economic levels as the yardstick of performance and saddled planners with the fatalistic view that Japan was doomed to be a poor country. The Economic White Paper's catchphrase, "It is no longer postwar," was widely proclaimed in the press as a celebration of accomplishments since the end of the war. In fact, it was an assertion of the necessity to modernize the economy with a view to the future. Now that growth through the process of recovery had come to an end, it was essential to stop relying on the idea that growth could be sustained by simply increasing production. To the extent that economic planners in the government and in the private sector failed to consider the quality of life, the total economic structure, and the infrastructure at this new stage of development, the economy would certainly weaken.

In order to avoid such a scenario, it was necessary to join the worldwide movement toward industrial modernization, stimulating the latent power of the economy, which would then rise of its own accord if high goals were set for growth. The key force of modernization would be the technology revolution, which was already proceeding at an unimaginable pace in Europe and in America. Therefore, as the White Paper asserted, the most important task for economic planners was to devise policies that would facilitate modernization and hasten the technology revolution in Japan— in short, to catch up with the West. Moreover, the revolution envisioned by the White Paper would not only include industry, communications, and transportation, but also entail a sweeping transformation of the entire society. In private industry, it called for the development of new industries and new products, the transformation of input–output performance, automation, the development of new markets, and an overhaul of the distribution system. It foresaw a revolution in personal consumption and vast changes in consumer habits. In its discussion of the labor market, it called for a shift of labor from primary and light industries to high productivity sectors, as well as a reduction of disparities in incomes between workers in large and small companies.

The "Semideveloped Country." While those responsible for drafting the White Paper were proclaiming the end of the postwar period of recovery, the view of Japan from abroad was quite different. In 1955, Japan was viewed as a third-rate, or, perhaps, a second-and-a-half-rate country. The label "the semideveloped country," reflects Japan as ranking somewhere between Europe and America and the underdeveloped countries of the Third World. Japan's real GNP reached $24 billion in 1955, only one-fifteenth the GNP of the United States and about half that of West Germany. Its per capita income of $220 made it thirty-fifth among countries of the free world. With 40 percent of the work force employed in primary industry, Japan was by no means an advanced industrialized nation.

Moreover, as has been noted, the structure of Japanese exports made the country highly dependent on light industries such as textiles and toys for foreign currency income, and, particularly in the West, Japan had a bad image as a cheap labor economy that relied on social dumping. Because of the high price of its heavy industrial and chemicals products, it was extremely difficult for private enterprises in these sectors to expand exports unless there was an unusual increase in international demand. The repeated experience of losing out to Western competitors in bids for contracts made Japanese producers appear as "marginal suppliers." Even in 1955, plant and equipment in heavy industries was characterized by a heavy reliance on skilled labor and a high percentage of old and outmoded equipment.

At the same time that Japan was being called a "cheap labor" economy and accused of social dumping by Western competitors, policy planners in Japan were wrestling with the problem of unemployment, which had become an important policy issue. While the number of completely unemployed persons listed in official government statistics was extremely low (hardly ever rising above 2 percent), this simply reflected the fact that a large number of workers were marginally employed for extremely low wages and under poor working conditions. At the time, these underemployed workers were referred to as the "latent unemployed," and, indeed, objective observers of the labor market in 1955 were hard pressed to refute the social dumping charges.

Another problem lay in the concept of "dual structure," which refers to the Japanese phenomenon of a highly privileged group of workers employed by large firms in modern industries and a large work force employed in smaller subcontracting firms, premodern cottage industries, agriculture, and household industries. Even in modern industries, there is a "dual structure," in which the privileges of lifetime employment and seniority-based wage increases are extended to new junior or senior high school graduates, while "temporary workers," who may, in fact, have worked for the same firm for many years, receive less pay and are subject to layoffs. In 1955, Hiromi Arisawa, the inventor of priority production and the government's leading academic adviser, stated that, "The dual class structure of Japanese society persists despite the reforms of the immediate postwar period." The Economic White Paper of 1957 was the first official document to address the dual structure of the labor force, arguing that aggressive economic expansion was essential to its elimination and to the modernization of the labor force. This was by no means empty rhetoric. The population of young workers had swollen as a result of the postwar baby boom and, by the latter half of the 1950s, economic planners were confronted with the need to find jobs for 800,000 new school graduates per year. It was feared that failure to take positive measures to reduce the gaps between wages and working conditions in new and premodern in-

Figure 6. Comparison of the Actual Growth of Real GNP
to Targets Set in National Economic Plans

¥1 trillion

1. Five-Year Plan for Economic Independence (5.0)
2. New Long-Term Economic Plan (6.5)
3. National Income-Doubling Plan (7.2)
4. Medium-Term Economic Plan (8.1)
5. Economic and Social Development Plan (8.2)
6. New Economic and Social Development Plan (10.6)

Real GNP

Notes: 1. Figures in parentheses are projected growth rates targeted by each plan.
2. Real GNP figures are based on 1970 prices.

dustries, principally by an aggressive industrial development policy, would result in making the dual structure a permanent feature of the postwar economy.

The Economic White Paper of 1957 also reflected the formulation of new premises for economic policy, and a consciousness among policy makers that Japan was about to embark on a new course of economic development. The Five-Year Plan for Economic Independence, which was the result of revisions to the proposed Six-Year General Economic Plan, after much discussion and research in the Economic Deliberation Council, was published at the end of 1955, the first economic plan enacted by a cabinet decision. This plan was further revised in December 1957 and retitled the "New Long-Term Economic Plan." Each of these plans called for full employment and economic independence as the basic goals of economic policy. Moreover, they signaled a new determination to manage economic policy on the basis of a medium-range vision rather than eleventh-hour countermeasures to cope with short-term fluctuations.

However, the growth rates of real GNP targeted by these plans were based largely on trial and error projections, and both the Five-Year Plan for Economic Independence and the New Long-Term Economic Plan set goals that were overfulfilled by the actual performance of the economy. The reasons the economic planners failed to accurately project the growth rate of the economy are complex, but ultimately they can be traced to simple underestimation of the scope of the technology revolution. While planners were aware that a 7 percent growth rate was optimal for full employment and for elimination of the dual structure, they feared that such a high growth rate would result in an overincrease in imports, making it impossible to maintain the country's balance of international payments. In short, they projected a balance of payments ceiling that was much too low in comparison with the projected full employment ceiling. Imports of technology and other capital investment necessary for industrial modernization were accomplished at a lower cost than expected and, therefore, the capital investment coefficient (the amount of investment necessary for a one-unit increase in production) in modernizing industries remained relatively low. This had the effect of increasing the rate of economic growth far above the goals set in the plans.[1]

The Explosion of Investment for Modernization. Japan's technology revolution also proceeded at a much faster pace than predicted by either the white papers or the economic plans of the early years of the ten-year period of rapid growth. The revolution was led by the spectacular growth in private plant and equipment that began in 1956 and 1957, which permitted the entire economy to step into a new period of postwar modernization. Plant and equipment investment, which had begun as a tiny trickle in 1952 and 1953, quickly swelled, and the technological transformation of the materials and processing industries was accompanied by the sudden rise of new industries and new products.

The steel industry led the materials manufacturing sector in launching comprehensive large-scale plant and equipment investment plans for modernization. After the spectacular success of its First Rationalization Plan (1950–51), the industry launched its Second Rationalization Plan for 1955–60. During the five years of the plan, the industry enlarged blast furnaces, introduced new LD converters, and enlarged its continuous rolling facilities, creating huge new steel complexes equipped with fully integrated technology. The economies of scale produced by combining the most advanced imported technology in large integrated plants had been demonstrated by

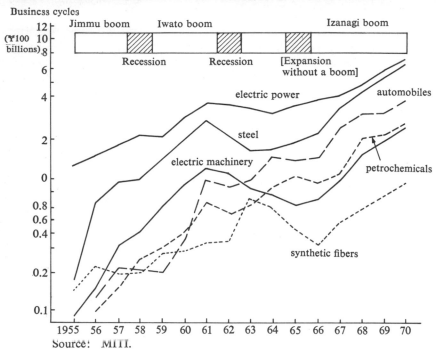

Figure 7. Plant and Equipment Investment in Rapidly Modernizing Industries

the Kawasaki plant in Chiba Prefecture, and new plants were constructed by Yawata Steel, Kobe Steel, and Nippon Kōkan. The introduction of LD converters was particularly innovative, reducing the industry's reliance on scrap steel and lowering installation and energy costs. Improvements in the technology and the scale of continuous rolling equipment not only increased production but also enhanced quality, reducing the dependence of related industries on imports of high-quality steel. The ripple effect of technology advances in the steel industry was especially remarkable in the automobile industry, which was now able to secure domestic supplies of such special steel products as high-grade art metal sheet that had previously been imported from the United States.

The star of the new industries was the high-polymer chemicals industry. Synthetic fibers and plastics developed quickly as new technologies were introduced, and the synthetic rubber industry began to show the first signs of its future potential. After the successful commercialization of nylon and vinylon, the industry quickly expanded its plant and equipment investment to include the introduction of polyester and polyacrylic technology. The plastics industry followed up its successful commercialization of vinyl chloride resins by introducing a wide range of new technologies, including those for urea, melamine, meta-acrylic resins, and silicone. The rapid popularization of synthetic detergents was particularly striking. In conjunction with the commercialization of the high-polymer chemicals industry, the petrochemicals industry rapidly developed as the most important supplier of basic materials for the new industry.

MITI maintained strict administrative guidance over the various development plans of the firms involved, and in 1955 launched its own First-Period Plan for the Petrochemicals Industry (1955–60), designed to prevent excessive competition in the industry by limiting the number of new entries. The new five-year plan emphasized the development of polyethylene and polystyrene production by introducing naptha-cracking technology. Huge new naptha-cracking facilities were constructed by Nippon Petrochemicals, Mitsubishi Yuka, Mitsui Petrochemicals, and Sumitomo Chemicals. The restrictions against new entries were relaxed under the Second-Period Plan for the Petrochemicals Industry (1960–65), and five new petrochemical complexes were established by newcomers to the industry. Despite MITI's strict administrative guidance, the industry was unique in the postwar period in the sense that it received very little government protection from imports and developed in an atmosphere of liberalization.

As is well known, the industry that developed superior levels of modernization fastest by international standards was shipbuilding. By 1956, orders for new ships, principally oil tankers, had propelled Japan to the position of the largest shipbuilder in the world, and Mitsubishi's Nagasaki facility was the largest single shipyard. In a very short period of time, shipbuilding was transformed from an infant industry dependent on orders from the government, or from private domestic shipping companies acting under administrative guidance, to one of the country's most important exporting industries.

During this period the potential of the automobile industry was still viewed pessimistically. Nevertheless, in spring 1955, MITI announced its "people's car" (minicar) concept, and Toyota and Nissan began to invest heavily in automation. During the same year, Toyota began sales of its Toyopet Crown, the first passenger car produced entirely in Japan.

While total plant and equipment investment was not as great as in the materials industry, the pace of technological innovation was most remarkable in the home appliances industry, which benefited from developments in the electronics industry. In every way Matsushita Electric (Panasonic) was the leader, and the pace of Matsushita's introduction and commercialization of new products was amazing. In 1955, the company announced a five-year plan to increase sales by 30 percent a year, from ¥22 billion in 1955 to ¥80 billion by the end of the plan, and to increase its work force by 10 percent a year to 18,000. Besides expanding its number of specialized electronics factories, the company launched plans to build a series of new automated electrical appliance factories that employed the most advanced technology available. The results were impressive, as the following summary suggests. In 1956, the company introduced automatic electric rice cookers, vacuum cleaners, electric juicers, and electric blankets. In 1957, transistor radios, ultrabright fluorescent lights, and gas stoves with electric pilots were produced, followed in 1958 by stereos, tape recorders, air conditioners, gas heaters, sewing machines, and mercury lamps. In 1959, electric clothes driers and garbage disposals appeared, and in 1960 color televisions and transistorized televisions. Matsushita's success in implementing its modernization plan provided a stimulus for the entire industry, and its daring new management techniques presented a challenge to other firms in the industry, sparking off intense competition in new products.

The energy industry was transformed as both established and new industries attempted to adapt to the pace of modernization set by the manufacturing industries. Following the success of new hydroelectric power technologies in the construction of Sakuma Dam, even larger and more modern facilities were constructed as new dam projects were launched by the government. Nevertheless, the myth of abundant hydroelectric energy resources was quickly dispelled by the inability of the industry to meet the surge in demand from the manufacturing sector. The shift from the traditional reliance on hydroelectric power first, with steam-powered electric power making up the difference, to a policy that recognized the preeminence of steam-powered electric generators became clear in the Five-Year Plan for the Electric Power Industry adopted at the end of 1956. At the same time, the shift from a reliance on coal as the primary energy source for steam-powered generators to oil reflected the worldwide trend toward making oil the basis of industrial development.

In the case of Japan, its closeness to the Middle East made oil cheaper for Japanese importers than for their competitors in the West. In 1938, Middle Eastern oil had comprised only 6 percent of the world's oil production but by 1955 it jumped to over 20 percent of worldwide production and accounted for more than half of total international trade. This meant that the conditions under which individual countries were able to procure supplies of Middle Eastern oil had already become a major factor in the formulation of basic energy policies and, therefore, Japan was in a unique position to take advantage of the long period of abundant supplies of cheap oil.

Moreover, as suggested in the previous chapter, after its isolation from the international trading community during the war, Japan was now able to select the most advanced technology developed in the war for use in integrated industrial complexes that made the most of geographical conditions and large-scale combinations of technology within an industry and between related industries. One example of this was the Kawasaki Steel complex in the Chiba *konbinato*, but the fruits of the industrial parks concept may be most clearly seen in the large *konbinato* centered on oil refinery complexes during the late 1950s. While such complexes had been prohibited by the Occupation until 1949, the concept of locating steam-powered electric generators near heavy industrial facilities was quickly revived after the Occupation. During the late 1950s, the petroleum industry established refining facilities near port facilities in combination (*konbinato*) with steam-powered electric generating facilities. The concept mushroomed into a much more complex type of *konbinato* in which the large volume of exhaust gas produced during the oil refining process was utilized by the electric power industry, and petrochemicals facilities came to be located in the same *konbinato* near oil refinery plants, which provided their raw materials. Moreover, since the *konbinato* themselves were located near major new ports, all the industries involved benefited from the lower transportation costs, especially of oil. Intense competition developed between domestic and foreign capital as the oil refining industry became the spearhead of Japan's drive toward modernization.

The period of abundant supplies of cheap oil continued until the oil crisis of 1973 and had an enormous impact on Japan's technological revolution and the development of its economic structure. It was also during the 1955–65 period that the issue of peaceful applications of nuclear energy arose. The Basic Law Concerning Nuclear Energy was promulgated in 1955, and the Japan Center for Research on Nuclear Energy was established the following year. However, research and development investment by the government and private industry remained at extremely low levels for some time, largely because of the availability of cheap oil.[2,3]

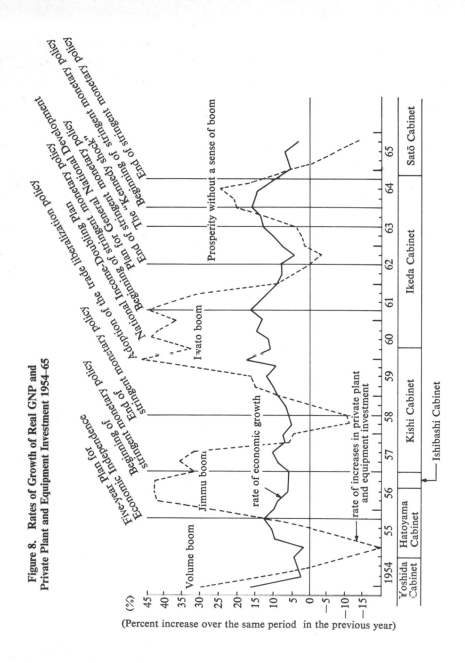

Figure 8. Rates of Growth of Real GNP and
Private Plant and Equipment Investment 1954-65

2. THE JIMMU BOOM

A great deal has been said already about booms in the Japanese economy, but it is probably important to say something about the way booms and recessions are named by Japanese journalists. Such terms as the "consumption boom" or the "plant and equipment investment boom" are easily understandable, but the "Jimmu boom," the "Iwato boom," or the "bottom-of-the-pot recession" (*nabezoko fukyō*) are no doubt mystifying to the Western reader. The Jimmu boom was the name given to the period of economic prosperity beginning in 1956, unprecedented since the reign of the legendary Emperor Jimmu, who, according to Japanese myth ascended the throne in 660 B.C. The following Iwato boom was named for an even more ancient period in Japanese mythology when the Sun Goddess, Amaterasu Ōmikami, was lured from seclusion in a cave (Iwato) by the music of a festival of ancient gods. The Izanagi boom (*see* Chapter Five) was named for Izanagi (the father of the Sun Goddess), who, with his sister, Izanami, created the isles of Japan. While such journalistic devices for announcing major economic changes may seem somewhat farfetched to economists, they have great appeal to the Japanese public, and it is worth retaining them in this study to suggest the extent to which rapid economic development affected Japanese society and culture as a whole. The ten years from 1955 to 1965 remain in the memory of Japanese people as the period during which modernization and rapid economic growth transformed their society, and it was during this period that the Jimmu and Iwato booms clearly demonstrated the amazing potential of the economy.

The so-called volume boom, which had continued since 1955, was rapidly transformed into a boom heavily supported by price rises. While corporate profits did not reach levels of the special procurements boom of 1951, they were certainly the highest in postwar history after the Korean War boom, and the Dow Jones average on the Tokyo Stock Exchange rose 63 percent from January 1955 to February 1957. The atmosphere of the Jimmu boom created unprecedented favorable conditions for labor, and increases in overtime were accompanied by generous overtime allowances. Moreover, summer and winter bonuses, a unique feature of the Japanese wage system, increased from averages of 1.5 months' in 1950 and 1951 to 2.6 months' wages in 1957.

As in previous periods of rapid economic expansion, private enterprises responded by increasing the number of temporary employees at the beginning of the boom, but were soon forced to hire more permanent employees. The Jimmu boom sparked the largest expansion in permanent employees in the history of the postwar economy. In 1957, at the height of the boom, large numbers of new junior and high school graduates were hired and, for the first time since the war, training programs for new recruits were instituted in a number of modernizing industries. The demand for investment capital that accompanied the Jimmu boom far outstripped the ability of city banks to supply financing, and the resulting overborrowing by city banks from the Bank of Japan increased their dependence on the central bank, and its detailed control over their operations grew. The "overloan" phenomenon, in which private firms relied on city bank financing for plant and equipment investment capital, while the city banks relied on the Bank of Japan to guarantee their loans, became more pronounced, eventually producing enormous inflationary pressures.

The Jimmu boom was strengthened by its overlap with the Suez War (called the "second" Middle Eastern war in Japan). The Suez Canal crisis, which erupted on October 27, 1956, resulted in a temporary closing of the canal and the destruction of the Suez oil pipeline. The economies of Western Europe were especially hard hit, but the crisis also resulted in a rapid inflation of foreign trade prices and a sudden increase in shipping costs that extended beyond the Middle East. In fact, the effects of the crisis were felt even in Japan, and there was a sudden sharp rise in domestic wholesale prices. However, these effects did not continue for long, and by February 1957 prices on international markets as well as shipping costs had returned to normal. The canal itself was reopened in April of the same year. In any case, the occurrence of the Suez crisis in the early stages of the Jimmu boom accelerated the domestic price increases that helped to fuel the boom and must be counted as a major factor in getting the boom started.

However, the real driving force behind the boom was private plant and equipment investment, fueled by expectations of a sustained boom and, to some extent, by speculative inventory investment resulting from the Suez Canal crisis. Private plant and equipment investment, adjusted for seasonal fluctuations, increased 80 percent from the first quarter of 1956 to the third quarter of 1957. During the same period, the share of real gross national expenditure (GNE) accounted for by private plant and equipment investment increased from 12.1 percent to 17.4 percent. However, it was also during this period that the postwar pattern of steady, long-term increases in plant and equipment investment, accompanied by relatively sharp cyclical fluctuations, became firmly established. Investment in plant and equipment designed to modernize specific industries rose sharply, but this type of investment comprised no more than 30 to 40 percent of total investment, the remainder being accounted for by induced demand for investment capital due to higher capacity utilization ratios and profitability. Although this latter type of demand for investment capital rose rapidly during the boom, it was to prove unusually susceptible to business cycle fluctuations.

While the end of the Jimmu boom must be traced to the reoccurrence of balance of payments problems, the rapid expansion it occasioned had exposed basic weaknesses in the Japanese economy even before the balance of payments crisis. It is practically an article of faith that any rapidly expanding economy is prone to serious bottlenecks, and the Japanese economy during the Jimmu boom proved to be no exception. Bottlenecks developed in railway transportation, electric power, and steel, resulting in phenomenal increases in wholesale prices. In many cases, particularly in the transportation and electric power industries, these bottlenecks were caused by social capital investment (infrastructure investment by the government) lagging behind investment in new technologies by private industry. The Jimmu boom exposed the inability of the Japan National Railways to keep pace with expansion in private industry, resulting in massive transportation bottlenecks with undelivered industrial products accumulating on station platforms. In cooperation with government planners, private enterprises took emergency steps to deliver these supplies by truck, but these plans were frustrated by the poor quality of the country's highway system. This led to a rapid development of plans to improve highways by constructing a national system of freeways and toll roads but, like many of the other measures adopted during this period, their short-term effectiveness was minimal.

Much the same may be said about the bottlenecks in the electric power and steel industries. Government planners took steps to expand the construction of new facilities and, informally, to hasten the completion of facilities underway. While these policies resulted in increased supplies of electric power and steel in the long term, their short-term benefits were negligible and, in fact, had the opposite effect of putting more pressure on these industries. Any increase in plant and equipment investment by the steel or electric power industries could only result in worsening the supply–demand situation in the steel industry itself.

The failure of policy makers to distinguish between short-term, medium-term, and long-term goals up to this time was highlighted by the development of serious water shortages in key industrial regions, and the accompanying problem of ground level subsidence in these areas. Many of the *konbinato* had been constructed on reclaimed land in coastal areas and, as these industrial complexes expanded, the overutilization of water supplies resulted in serious subsidence problems at such key industrial sites as the Yokkaichi Petrochemicals complex, Kawasaki Steel complex, and Amagasaki Steel complex. On the other hand, it must be pointed out that government planners quickly recognized these problems and took immediate steps to introduce new policies. The problem was not that government economic planners were insensitive to the new issues posed by rapid economic development but that their countermeasures were often aimed at long-term solutions. However effective these policies may eventually have been, they often failed to deal with immediate problems.

There is no question that the gap between aggressive plant and equipment investment on the part of private industry and the relatively slow expansion of government social investment (infrastructure investment) was a major factor in the collapse of the Jimmu boom. However, what really spelled its end was the ubiquitous balance of payments problem. The country was suddenly faced with a balance of payments problem unprecedented since the foreign currency crisis of 1953 and 1954, and foreign currency reserves fell from $910 million at the end of 1956 to $455 million in September 1957. The government was forced to apply for IMF loans of $87 million in July 1957 and $50 million in August of the same year. These loans were not secured without major concessions to the administrative guidance of the IMF, and the government agreed to implement stringent monetary policies in order to rectify the balance of payments deficit.

Another Short-Term Cyclical Adjustment Policy. The immediate cause of the balance of payments crisis was the result not of a decline of exports due to excessive domestic demand but of the increase in demand for imports. The value of imports clearing customs increased 70 percent from the first quarter of 1956 to the third quarter of 1957. A large percentage of this was for increased imports of raw materials, but imports of industrial machinery had also risen rapidly during the boom period. The latter may be explained by the inability of domestic enterprises to meet the demand for new technology that had fueled the boom in the first place.

In the face of this balance of payments crisis, economic planners were in an unusually weak position because of the instability of the political situation. The Hatoyama Cabinet, which had survived negotiations for the unification of the Liberal and Democratic parties, resigned at the end of 1956 (because of Hatoyama's failing health) and the new Tanzan Ishibashi Cabinet suffered the same fate. However, the Ishibashi Cabinet had as finance minister the controversial Hayato Ikeda (*see* Chapter Four), who launched his famous "¥100 billion tax cut, ¥100 billion government expenditure" policy in the budget proposal for 1957. This policy was inherited by the succeeding Kishi Cabinet, in which Ikeda retained his position as finance minister. There were heated debates among politicians and bureaucrats over the pursuit of an expansive fiscal policy when the country was facing a balance of payments crisis.

The debate intensified in the spring of 1957 against a background of explosive domestic expansion and a quickly worsening balance of payments. Its central issues concerned the rapid expansion of domestic inventories that had accompanied the flood of speculative investment in imports during the Suez Canal crisis, and whether the Jimmu boom represented a real expansion or a mere cyclical price inflation boom. The principle contenders in this debate were Osamu Shimomura, Ikeda's closest adviser on economic policy and an advocate of rapid economic growth, and Yonosuke Gotō, a central figure in the economic planning bureaucracy and an advocate of stable economic development. Shimomura's analysis of the situation was superior in the sense that he recognized the root cause of the balance of payments crisis as excessive private investment in import inventories accompanying the Jimmu boom. However, he was overoptimistic in asserting that the balance of payments problem would solve itself without government measures to suppress demand. In fact, the problem was not so easily resolved and, once again, the government found itself making eleventh-hour decisions to avert a foreign currency crisis.

In June 1957, immediately before the first emergency loans from the IMF, the government announced the Emergency Countermeasures Policy for Improving the International Balance of Payments Situation, signaling the beginning of a government-backed deflationary policy. There was a significant attempt to implement deflationary fiscal policies, including a postponement of appropriations for the Fiscal Investment and Loan Plan, public corporations, and the building and repairs budget. However, the monetary policies developed during the post–Korean War recession of 1954 continued to play the most important role in the government's deflationary policy. The most significant difference in 1957 was that increases in the official discount rate replaced "window guidance," or specific credit restrictions on city banks, as the central pillar of stated government policy. However, this supposed policy shift was largely public rhetoric.

General increases in the official discount rate were announced, but "moral persuasion" and "policy signals" from the Bank of Japan continued to remain cornerstones of monetary policy. These policies had been firmly established in the period after 1954, and window guidance, increased deposit requirements for the financing of import transactions, and reduced funding allocations for key industry imports by the Bank of Japan have been much more characteristic of monetary policy than official interest rates policy ever since. As suggested earlier, this emphasis on direct credit restrictions rather than on general increases in the official discount rate is the result of the indirect financing, or overloan system, which makes city banks extremely vulnerable to window guidance from the Bank of Japan. Similar to the administrative guidance exercised by MITI over private enterprises, window guidance has no legal basis but is extremely effective as an anti-inflationary policy. In 1957, once the Bank of Japan began to tighten credit, the government's deflationary policy proved extremely effective.

However effective the policies were, the balance of payments problem had reached critical proportions, and a number of economic planners, led by Gotō, were highly critical of these policies. The Economic White Paper of 1957, whose drafting Gotō had supervised, presented a detailed critique of the government's management of economic policy. While recognizing that the deflationary policy had produced quick results, Gotō pointed out that it would have been equally effective at an earlier stage in the boom and the government's failure to identify the crisis had meant that tight monetary policies had been implemented only after the economy had confronted a full-blown crisis. This "stop-go" approach had not only exacerbated the balance of payments crisis itself but had also worsened the cyclical recession that accompanied the stringent policies. Why, he asked, was it impossible to apply preventative anticyclical policies before the economy had reached the point where heroic, last-ditch measures became necessary? The experience of the Jimmu boom and the subsequent balance of payments crisis suggested all too clearly that government policy makers had taken too light a view of the need to monitor the country's trade balance and foreign currency reserves, and had ignored the importance of countercyclical fiscal and monetary policies. In a period when it could be said that "the immediate postwar period is over," was not the development of policies to stabilize fluctuations in the balance of payments and business cycles as important as policies to promote the technology revolution and modernization?

The Economic White Paper of 1957 concluded with seven basic points concerning needed changes in government economic planning. They may be summarized as follows.

1. The self-regulating function of business cycles should not be over-estimated. In the case of the Jimmu boom, there had been an over-optimistic assumption on the part of planners that, even if the boom developed rapidly, creating inflationary pressures and an unfavorable balance of trade, it would reverse itself without direct countercyclical measures. This assumption persisted despite inflationary pressures created by the Suez Canal crisis, and it was taken for granted that the balance of payments situation would improve by itself. This had not happened and emergency monetary policies had become necessary.

2. If the self-regulating function of business cycles was insufficient to narrow the gap between upswings and downturns in the economy, preventative anticyclical policies should be implemented more quickly, before foreign currency problems reached crisis dimensions.

3. In general, government statistics, the basis for economic planning, were insufficient for effective econometric analysis. This had led to delays in responding to economic fluctuations and, in many cases, to the adoption of wrong policies.

4. Economic policy makers had paid insufficient attention to the clear warning signs in the statistics that were available. In many cases, obvious signs had been ignored out of political considerations, despite the probability that the pursuit of a popular policy would result in even more serious future difficulties.

5. Policies to moderate swings in the business cycle had been extremely ineffective. For example, despite the glut of available capital in the economy, no steps had been taken to absorb the surplus, and excessive interbank competition had resulted in unintended distortions of economic growth during the Jimmu boom.

6. Economic policy discussions within the government had often confused long-term goals with short-term realities. The impending balance of payments crisis had been ignored because of the government's long-term commitment to promoting plant and equipment investment in new technologies. While industrial modernization was

a perfectly valid long-term policy goal, excessive technology imports had been allowed to continue far beyond the point at which the balance of payments could be maintained.

7. The failure to enact stringent monetary policies with a view to long-term structural changes in the economy, as well as to short-term balance of payments problems, could, on the other hand, lead to an unfair imposition of losses on the weaker sectors of private industry and long-term distortions in the distribution of resources.

These policy recommendations were published almost twenty-five years ago, but they continue to have relevance for today's economic planners. Many of us are asking ourselves if economic planning has made much progress since 1957 in developing policies to moderate the impact of business cycles, stabilize fluctuations in the economy and the balance of payments and the inflation rate.

The Bottom-of-the-Pot Recession. Gotō's criticism of the deflationary policies in 1957 as eleventh-hour measures taken only after the balance of payments crisis had become unavoidable is certainly accurate. In fact, however, the stringent monetary policies, centering on window guidance and severe credit restrictions proved extremely effective in reducing demand for imports and moderating domestic inflation, and the shift from an explosive boom to a recession was extremely rapid. By the first quarter of 1958, the total value of imports clearing customs had declined by about 40 percent from the second quarter of 1957, the peak period of the boom, and this reduction was reflected in an immediate improvement in foreign currency reserves. Similarly, wholesale prices and industrial production fell 10 percent during the same period.

The success of the deflationary policy may be explained by the fact that the strict credit restrictions imposed by the Bank of Japan occurred just when the majority of *keiretsu* firms had already taken out loans from city banks up to the highest permissible limits. The window guidance by the Bank of Japan put a brake on further overloans by city banks, and many firms were hard pressed to obtain investment capital or even working capital. The result was that these firms were forced to reduce inventory investments in raw materials and plant and equipment, and to cut back production. The number of industries forced to do this in order to compensate for unplanned inventory increases and poor market conditions was unprecedented. The most extreme cases were production cuts of 55 percent in the titanium industry, 50 percent in rayon, 40 percent in rayon staple and electrolytic copper, and 30 percent in structural steel, polyvinyl chloride, and high-grade paper.

The Jimmu boom, and the subsequent bottom-of-the-pot recession, therefore, reflected the basic pattern of fluctuations in the postwar economy as well as the typical responses of government planners and private industry. The result of a boom in the domestic economy was the development of a deficit in the international balance of payments. In response to the payments deficit, the government adopted short-term stringent monetary policies based primarily on credit restrictions ("window guidance"). Private enterprises, and especially those in the industrial materials industries (such as steel and petrochemicals) responded to the tight monetary situation by forming recession cartels and curtailing operations. These stringent monetary policies led to a reduction of imports and the inauguration of an export drive by private industry. Unlike most industrialized countries in the West, business downturns did not result in more unemployment, at least among permanent employees, reflecting the unique Japanese institutions of "management familialism" and lifetime employment. Indeed, until the period when Japan began to enjoy a permanent surplus in its balance of international payments, this pattern was repeated time and again as government and private industry were forced to respond to cyclical fluctuations resulting principally from their vulnerability to international business conditions.

The bottom-of-the-pot recession actually reached its nadir in June 1958, but it derived its name from earlier expectations that the recession would not follow the pattern of the 1954–55 recession but would continue for some time. That is, rather than developing in a V-shaped curve as in the earlier recession in which the rapid economic downturn was followed by a quick recovery, the current recession would persist over a long period, with recovery tracing a very gradual upward trend as if the curve representing economic indicators were crawling along the flat bottom of a very large pot. This view of private industry was shared by many economic planners, and the Economic White Paper of 1958 was extremely pessimistic concerning prospects for rapid recovery. Private investment in plant and equipment during the Jimmu boom had increased 80 percent in only one year and, despite indications that inventory investment was beginning to recover, there were few signs of a resurgence of domestic demand or an increase in exports to enable private industry to utilize its excess capacity and begin a new round of investment in plant and equipment. Moreover, as the White Paper pointed out, Japan's recession in 1957 was only part of the most orthodox international business downturn since the end of World War II, with rapid declines in plant and equipment investment. leading to recessions in the major economies of Europe and America as well. Given this situation in the West, and the econometric data available at the time, the pessimism of the Economic White Paper of 1958 was not unfounded.

Despite these dire predictions, however, economic recovery began in June 1958 and picked up speed by the end of the year. A number of factors may be cited for this quick turn of events. First, the 80 percent increase estimated in domestic plant and equipment investment in 1957 was based on questionable econometric methods and, in fact, was later revised to less than 60 percent. This meant that economic planners had seriously over-estimated the excess capacity problem. Second, reflecting the economy's dependence on the United States, the brisk recovery of the American economy had an extremely positive effect, both psychologically and because it supported the export drive. Indeed, it was after the recession that financial reporters coined the phrase, "When America sneezes, Japan catches pneumonia." Third, the delayed effects of Finance Minister Ikeda's much-criticized ¥100 billion tax cut in December 1956 sparked a rapid recovery in domestic demand after improvements in Japan's balance of payments situation.

The most important of these factors was the fact that the gap between supply and demand and the problem of excess plant and equipment capacity were not as serious as planners had feared. Many of the moderni-zation plans drafted during the Jimmu boom had just started when the recession hit. While private industries were forced to suspend plant and equipment investment by the stringent monetary policies implemented during the recession, they did not abandon modernization plans, and new plant and equipment investment resumed as soon as credit restrictions ("window guidance") were lifted. More important, during the Jimmu boom and the subsequent recession, the development of a mass consumer revolution was gradually gaining momentum, and personal consumption expenditure continued to rise. Perhaps the most serious error in the predic-tions of the 1958 White Paper was the underestimation of just how strong this mass consumption society had become.

The Advent of the Mass Consumption Society. The wave of modernization during the Jimmu boom had not stopped with heavy plant and equipment investment by industry but, as reflected in the success of Matsushita's home appliances, had spread to the lives of the consumers. It was during the latter 1950s that "the consumer revolution" became a catchphrase. The technology revolution transformed the structure of Japanese industry, but it also brought sweeping changes to the life-styles of Japanese people. Symbolic of this was the popularization of electric household appliances, which had been sparked by the Jimmu boom and which continued to increase through the subsequent recession, playing the leading role in the modernization and Westernization of life-styles. Until 1955, washing machines and televisions could be seen only in the homes of the very wealthy or in restaurants, bars, and coffee shops. Less than 1 percent of Japanese families owned televisions or refrigerators, and less than 5 percent owned washing machines.

However, the situation began to change dramatically in 1956. For example, black-and-white television sets were obtained at an amazing pace, particularly after the announcement of live coverage of Crown Prince Akihito's wedding in April 1959. Domestic production of television sets increased from 310,000 in 1956 to 3.6 million in 1960, representing an increase in their popularization rate from less than 1 percent of Japanese families to nearly 50 percent. Similar phenomena occurred with radios, washing machines, and refrigerators. Domestic production of radios increased from 3 million to 13 million, refrigerators from 80,000 to 900,000, and washing machines from 750,000 to 1.5 million.

The popularization of electric appliances was supported by the development of a highly favorable snowball effect in which rapidly increasing sales enabled firms to maintain high-capacity utilization ratios and to expand capital investment while lowering prices, which in turn spurred consumer demand even further. The most remarkable phenomenon of the boom in electric appliances was the speed with which demand shifted from the relatively inexpensive to the more expensive products. For example, at the beginning of the boom, a black-and-white television set, a washing machine, and a refrigerator were, in popular slang, the "housewife's three sacred treasures." This expression quickly vanished when most families began to acquire these articles, and newer, more expensive products became the objects of consumers' aspirations.

As is normal, the popularization of electric appliances began in urban centers but, in the late 1950s, quickly spread to rural areas. This unusual phenomenon may be explained by rapid structural changes in the agricultural industry that resulted in a greater share of the national wealth for rural families. Bumper crops in 1954 were followed by steady increases in agricultural production that continued at least until the late 1950s. This increase in agricultural productivity was supported by the introduction of modern technology, including such machinery as small tractors and power cultivators adapted for smaller rice plots. The expansion of the chemicals industry promoted increased utilization of chemical fertilizers, insecticides, and herbicides. At the same time that the modernization of agricultural technology was enhancing productivity, the continuation of government subsidies guaranteed that increased production would result in a transfer of wealth from urban to rural areas.

Somewhat after the boom in electric appliances, a boom in the automobile industry gradually transformed modes of personal transportation. The auto boom began with the introduction of motor scooters and motorcycles and, particularly in small and medium industries, quickly spread to automobiles with the announcement of Mazda's Midget 360, a three-wheel minicar. These small, inexpensive vehicles, extremely popular among small businesses, quickly replaced bicycles and carts as delivery vehicles. The development of new passenger cars by Fuji Heavy Industries (Subaru 360 in 1958) and Nissan (Datsun Bluebird in 1959) sparked a boom in the passenger car industry, and competition among firms to produce new models rapidly intensified.

Synthetic textiles had suffered from a very poor image during the first ten years of the postwar period, and rayon had been synonymous with poor quality, and one of the symbols of postwar hardships. With the modernization of the synthetic fibers industry and the introduction of new fabrics, the situation changed completely and synthetics quickly replaced natural fabrics as the leaders in the apparel industry. Similarly, synthetic resins and plastics, which previously had been most evident in kitchen utensils, began to be used in handbags, sandals, and a variety of new products.

Besides clothing, the aspect of daily life most symbolic of hardships of the postwar years had been the chronic shortage of housing, and during his election campaign, Prime Minister Hatoyama had promised that his cabinet would take steps to construct low-cost public housing. The Ten-Year Plan for Residential Construction was launched at the outset of the Hatoyama Cabinet, and the Public Housing Corporation authorized the construction of a series of modern high-rise apartment complexes, the famous *danchi* complexes that have received much comment from foreign visitors. In the late 1950s, however, these *danchi* complexes were the symbol of a new, modern life-style, and the competition to rent apartments in them was intense. Those who were lucky enough to receive a space allotment from the Public Housing Corporation became members of a new urban elite, known at the time as the *"danchi* people" (*danchi-zoku*). The Western-style *danchi* apartments also became showcases for new home appliances, and *danchi* housewives comprised the most conspicuous group of consumers anxious to buy the most up-to-date new products.

The rapid popularization of television made it a new medium for commercializing new products, and the development of the television advertising industry kept pace, helping to transform life-styles with such new slogans as "Consumption Is Virtue" and "The Consumer Is King." Attracted by the potential of television, large newspaper companies competed furiously to enter and expand their positions in the commercial broadcasting industry. During the same period, the field of commercial journalism was transformed by a boom in weekly magazines that began with Shinchōsha's *Weekly Shinchō*. The significance of Shinchōsha's entry into the field was that the publishing company challenged the monopoly on commercial journalism of the big national newspapers, which had been assumed to have a permanent advantage because of their huge reporting staffs and financial resources. Following Shinchōsha's lead, other publishing companies began to publish their own weekly magazines, and news magazines, as well as comics, sports magazines, movie magazines, and women's magazines, appeared in rapid succession. There were soon large racks displaying weekly magazines in front of every drugstore.

The rapid changes taking place in Japanese life could be seen most clearly in the life-styles and attitudes of young people. Shintarō Ishihara, creator of "the sun people" (*taiyōzoku*), won the Akutagawa Prize in 1956 for his novel *Season of the Sun* (*Taiyō no kisetsu*). This novel, which described the rather nihilistic attitudes and life-styles of young high school and college students, was called "juvenile delinquent literature" by established critics, but it remained at the top of the best-seller list throughout the year. The book received even more attention after it was made into a movie, and major studios competed for Ishihara's novels, producing a whole series of "sun people" movies.

While the "sun people" did not represent all of Japan's young, their life-styles and attitudes toward the future certainly reflected a new atmosphere of high expectations and liberation from traditional social conventions that had much appeal, and Ishihara's novels brilliantly captured the spirit of this new generation. The new enthusiasm of young people for sailing, hiking, skiing, mountain climbing, baseball, and other new hobbies that had been far beyond the means of their parents' generation in the immediate postwar period was accompanied by a general atmosphere of affluence, and older people too began to spend more on family outings, dining out, golf, movies, and other luxuries. Indeed, it was this consumer revolution that firmly established the end of the immediate postwar period. Even while many business firms were suffering from the stringent monetary policies of the bottom-of-the-pot recession, the consumer revolution was on the verge of launching the country into a period of high growth and prosperity that was without question the most important period in postwar history in terms of raising the living standards and the quality of life for the average Japanese.

4

THE PERIOD OF
HIGH-SPEED GROWTH
AND FULL EMPLOYMENT

1. THE HAYATO IKEDA CABINET

Economic Policy after the Anti-Anpo Demonstrations. The political situation had been unstable since the formation of the Liberal Democratic Party (LDP) in November 1955, and the forced resignation of the Kishi Cabinet in mid-1960 was only the last of a series of rapid changes that threatened to destroy the dominance of the conservative party. The political turmoil surrounding revision of the U.S.–Japan Security Treaty (*Anzen hoshū joyaku*), or *Anpo*, toppled the government of Nobusuke Kishi and forced the last-minute cancellation of a visit to Japan by President Eisenhower. The anti-*Anpo* movement of 1959 and 1960, a coalition of students, labor, and opposition party politicians, was as important to the Japanese left as the anti–Vietnam War movement was to left-wing political movements throughout the world in the late 1960s.

The Security Treaty had been an important political issue since its conclusion immediately after the signing of the San Francisco Peace Treaty in 1951. Shigeru Yoshida had been successful in resisting U.S. demands for the inclusion of provisions for revisions to Japan's "peace constitution" and for increases in the country's military capability. Nevertheless, it was heavily criticized as unequal, giving America a number of special privileges without obligating it to defend Japan. In the original treaty, the United States had the right to establish bases and station troops in Japan, as well as to deploy troops from Japan to third countries. It also gave America the right to take military action in Japan after consultations with the government not only in the case of an attack by a third country but also in the case of internal subversion or instability. To opposition leaders, this represented a clear case of U.S. interference in domestic politics. An additional problem was that the original treaty had no date of expiration.

The revisions of the treaty were finally signed in January 1960, eliminating most of the points of disagreement between Japan and the United States. However, the anti-*Anpo* movement had arisen not because of these aspects of the treaty—which were as disagreeable to conservative LDP politicians as to left-wing activists—but because of the continuation of the treaty itself, and violent confrontation erupted because of the high-handed tactics of the Kishi government in attempting to quell opposition. From the point of view of anti-*Anpo* leaders, the new treaty resulted in firmly identifying Japan with the antiprogressive policies of the United States, aligning Japan with the United States in its policy of containment regarding China, and serving to intensify the Cold War in a period when international tensions had begun to thaw. Moreover, while the original treaty had been signed when Japan was still an occupied country, the revised treaty would be signed by an independent Japan, thus inviting retaliation from the Soviet Union and China. Even moderates were concerned that the treaty would almost certainly delay normalization of relations between Japan and these two major powers.

The confrontation between the Kishi government and anti-*Anpo* forces was intensified by Kishi's attempt to suppress the movement by hurriedly forcing through the Diet revisions of the Law Concerning the Conduct of Policemen in the Performance of Their Duties (the Police Law). These revisions vastly expanded the powers of the police and were viewed as a direct attempt by the government to squash the demonstrations. In fact, the enactment of the Police Law had the opposite effect of broadening participation in the movement, and the scale and intensity of antigovernment demonstrations exceeded even the expectations of its leaders. The post-treaty political turmoil peaked on June 15, 1960, when a demonstration around the National Diet Building turned into a massive riot resulting in the death of a female university student. The Kishi Cabinet was forced to resign in July 1960, and it was up to the new Ikeda Cabinet to rebuild the fortunes of the LDP and restore public confidence in the country's political system.

Ultimately, it was the strong performance of the domestic economy and the new economic policies of the Ikeda Cabinet that stabilized the political situation and set the stage for a decade of rapid economic growth. Supported by steady increases in personal consumption, the economy recovered quickly from the bottom-of-the-pot recession, and plant and equipment investment following the relaxation of tight money policies signaled the beginning of a new period of expansion. Indeed, the pace of recovery was so swift that the government implemented anticyclical policies in fall 1959, the first time this had happened in the early stages of a post-recession boom. These policies, limited to an increase in the official discount rate and the introduction of a new system of minimum reserve deposits for city banks, had only a moderate effect on domestic demand. Rapid expansion continued, and the wave of expectations that accompanied the boom played a major part in stabilizing the post-Kishi political situation.

The new prime minister, Hayato Ikeda, had had a long career in the planning bureau of the Ministry of Finance before entering politics as a protégé of Yoshida. Subsequently, he had held the posts of minister of finance or minister of MITI in a number of cabinets, and his last post before becoming prime minister had been minister of MITI (June 1959 to July 1960). Ikeda perceived the intimate relationship between economic policy and politics and, indeed, his daring ¥100 billion tax cut in December 1956 as minister of finance had been a major factor in the recovery of the economy and in its ensuing expansion that was taking place as he formed his cabinet. He was thus in an excellent position to make economic policy the cornerstone of his administration, and he proceeded to implement his policies with a vengeance.

The two pillars of his policy were the National Income-Doubling Plan and trade liberalization. The former, as its name suggests, was specifically designed to link commitment to high-speed economic growth to the needs of consumers, while the trade liberalization plan was aimed at meeting growing demand abroad for Japan to open its domestic market to foreign products. There was nothing revolutionary about these policies and, in fact, they were merely extensions of those pursued by Ikeda as minister of MITI in the Kishi Cabinet. The difference was that, as prime minister, Ikeda clearly articulated the two new policies as the foundations of his domestic and foreign policies. By doing so, he was able to overcome the domestic political problems that had beset the Kishi government and win public support for the commitment to rapid economic development and participation in the free trade system envisioned by the General Agreement on Tariffs and Trade (GATT) and the International Monetary Fund (IMF). Even while both plans were criticized as recklessly ambitious, and there was fear that trade liberalization would invite a flood of foreign capital that would overwhelm domestic enterprises, Ikeda was extremely

Table 8.   Comparison of Targets Set by the National Income-Doubling Plan and Actual Economic Performance

	National Income-Doubling Plan		Actual performance	
	Target levels for 1970	Targeted growth rate	Actual levels for 1970	Actual growth rate
Total population (10 thousands)	10,222	0.9%	10,372	1.0%
Persons employed (10 thousands)	4,869	1.2	5,094	1.5
Employers (10 thousands)	3,235	4.1	3,306	4.3
GNP (1958 prices, ¥100 millions)	260,000	8.8	405,812	11.6
Gross national income (1958 prices, ¥100 millions)	213,232	7.8	328,516	11.5
Per capita income (1958 prices, ¥)	208,601	6.9	317,678	10.4
Personal consumption expenditure (1958 prices, ¥100 millions)	151,166	7.6	207,863	10.3
Per capita personal consumption expenditures (1958 prices, ¥)	147,883	6.7	204,079	9.4
Structural components of national income				
(Primary industry)	10.1(%)		7.4(%)	
(Secondary industry)	38.6		38.5	
(Tertiary industry)	51.3		54.1	
Mining and manufacturing production	431.7	11.9	539.4	13.9
Agricultural, marine, and forestry production	144.1	2.8	130.3	2.1
Total demand for energy (unit=1,000 tons of coal)	302,760	7.8	574,095	12.0
Value of exports (customs clearing basis, $100 millions)	93.2	10.0	202.5	16.8
Value of imports (customs clearing basis, $100 millions)	98.9	9.3	195.3	15.5

Notes: 1. Growth rates are in comparison to the average for 1956–58.
2. Figures are based on 1958 prices.
3. For all indexes 1958=100.

successful in coming to grips with the major problems that had to be confronted before the country could proceed toward a new period of long-term economic development.

The National Income-Doubling Plan. In the nearly four decades since the end of World War II to the present, successive governments have adopted a total of eleven comprehensive national economic plans. Of these, several disappeared without evoking any response from the public. There is no question, however, that the one that made the strongest impression was the National Income-Doubling Plan, and that the degree and scope of its influence on Japan's economy exceeds that of any of the others. The Income-Doubling Plan has been judged harshly by some, who argue that it was merely a political ploy to enable Ikeda to take credit for the rising wave of modernization and technological innovation that was already underway when the plan was proposed. Others criticize the plan on the grounds that high-speed economic growth itself was mistaken, citing such adverse effects as environmental damage and urban overcrowding. However, both these views are oversimplifications. While it is true that the Japanese economy was at the threshold of an unprecedented technological revolution, the National Income-Doubling Plan did succeed in arousing public support for the concept of high-speed growth and in creating an atmosphere of high expectation for the future. It was a major factor in mobilizing the country's potential for rapid development.

The stage was set for the National Income-Doubling Plan in the two years before its enactment in November 1960 by widely publicized discussions on the theories of salary-doubling. At the beginning of the 1960s, Japan was still regarded by the United States and Europe as an exporting country that depended on cheap labor and social dumping, and import restrictions placed on Japanese products by European countries were extremely severe. This was a crucial period demanding bold new domestic and foreign policies to change Japan's image abroad and enable the country to join the ranks of the advanced nations. In a visit to Japan in 1958, West Germany's economics minister, Ludwig Erhard, drew the attention of labor unions and business organizations when he attacked Japan's system of low wages and called for positive government policies to increase wages as a step toward creating a healthy export system and expanding the domestic market. At the beginning of 1959, Professor Ichirō Nakayama—then chairman of the Central Labor Commission and soon to become chairman of the planning committee of the Economic Deliberation Council during the drafting of the National Income-Doubling Plan—proposed a bold new strategy for the development of a welfare state, whose basis was an economic policy aimed at doubling wages.

In March 1959, Ikeda supported Nakayama's proposals and became the first politician to advocate the "salary-doubling theory." The essence of Ikeda's theory was that the productive capacity of the economy had increased in recent years at an unprecedented pace, and that the economic growth rate should be increased even further by stimulating domestic demand. He argued that it was by no means impossible to double or even triple salaries in the next five to ten years if government policies were designed to promote the maximum utilization of the labor force and domestic plant and equipment. Ikeda also called for more accurate projections of the economy's performance by economic planning and budget authorities. Previous economic plans, and the projections upon which they were based, had badly underestimated the rate of economic growth, given the potential capacity of the economy. While one result of these low projections had been the phenomenon of large natural increases in yearly tax revenues, they also exacerbated distortions in the growth process by imposing artificially low limits on the growth of government spending. This had meant that increases in social capital expenditure constantly lagged behind the expansion of the private sector, creating infrastructural bottlenecks that impeded further growth. Ikeda did not view large increases in tax revenues as the proper role of economic policy and was highly critical of the practice of underestimating economic growth rates in drafting annual budgets.

In early 1960, Osamu Shimomura, a leading Ikeda adviser, sparked a debate among economists in academia and the government by asserting that far from confronting limits to further expansion, the economy had entered a period of high-speed economic growth during which real GNP could be doubled or even tripled in a ten-year period. While this debate continued, the drafting of the National Income-Doubling Plan was being carried out by the Economic Planning Agency. The original draft projected average annual growth rates of 7.2 percent over the ten years of the plan, but these projections were revised upward at the strong urging of Ikeda and his advisers. The final draft called for average annual increases of 9 percent for the first three years of the plan. This plan differed from previous economic plans in three important respects, which may be summarized as follows.

1. In the public sector, the plan made it clear that the government

would assume responsibility for achieving substantial increases in social overhead capital expenditure and social security. The plan established the National Social Insurance and Pension programs that went into effect in 1961.

2. It emphasized the development of human resources, the first time a government economic plan recognized that maximizing the abilities of the country's population was a basic condition for economic development. Substantial increases were projected for education and research expenditures in science and technology.

3. It established, as a basic economic policy, the elimination of the dual structure of the economy in the course of expansion, outlining specific proposals for reducing wage differentials between large and small enterprises, income gaps between agricultural and manufacturing sectors, and regional income disparities.

Despite favorable public response, the plan was criticized harshly by labor union leaders and opposition politicians. Opposition leaders voiced strong doubts that high-speed economic growth could solve the dual structure of the economy. Moreover, because the plan was overoptimistic about the rise in consumer prices, it was charged with being, in fact, a "price-doubling plan." More important, perhaps, was that while the plan anticipated environmental problems that would accompany rapid economic growth and the necessity of formulating countermeasures, private enterprises attempted to hold down their costs by avoiding increased investments in antipollution facilities, and the government did not commit itself to environmental policies until long after pollution had become a serious national problem.[1,2]

The Concept of Regional Development. The National Income-Doubling Plan was the first comprehensive government economic plan to seriously address the issue of regional economic development, particularly disparities in terms of industrial development and income. As the plan was being drafted, private plant and equipment investment plans for technological modernization were already beginning to seek new industrial locations. At the same time, the various regional and local governments had taken up the problem of reducing interregional income disparities and competed fiercely to offer enticements to private enterprises to locate new facilities in their areas.

With the National Income-Doubling Plan, the Economic Deliberation Council proposed a new industrial location policy called the "Pacific Belt

Region Concept." Recognizing the overconcentration of industry in the four industrialized regions of Tokyo–Yokohama (or the Keihin area), Osaka–Kobe (or the Hanshin area), Nagoya (or the Chūkyō area), and northern Kyushu, the concept called for limiting new locations in these areas of the Pacific belt region while encouraging the construction of new industrial facilities in other areas of this region by channeling government social capital investment there. Needless to say, this proposal met with stiff opposition from the underdeveloped regions outside the Pacific belt region, and the government was quickly forced to formulate a drastically modified policy.

The new policy, established by a cabinet decision in October 1962, was the Comprehensive National Development Plan. It divided the entire country into areas of overconcentration; designated areas for social capital investment; and developing areas. It called for limiting industrial concentration in areas in the first category while promoting industrial development in the latter two by the designation of key centers for large-scale industrial projects. The new plan set off a flood of petition campaigns as regional governments competed to have their respective areas selected for these government-sponsored development projects. Eventually, thirteen new industrial cities and six "special areas for industrial facilities investment" were designated, although there was criticism that the selection was influenced by political considerations and that, in general, decisions were made on the basis of attempting to please everyone. Nevertheless, the National Comprehensive Development Plan had a decisive impact on government infrastructure investment, and new plant construction by private enterprises after 1965 was concentrated largely in the new industrial cities.

The Repercussions of Trade Liberalization. The implementation of radical import liberalization policies from 1960 to 1965 is the second legacy of the Ikeda Cabinet and one of the most epoch-making events of the postwar period. Even after independence, Japan's import trade had been subject to tight government control under the foreign currency allocations system. Calculated according to the Brussels Customs Schedule, the rate of import liberalization when Japan joined GATT in August 1955 had been 16 percent, and this had increased to only 26 percent by 1961. The rationale for the retention of import controls was that Japan's international balance of payments was weak and that, therefore, any further opening of the Japanese market would result in a flood of imports that would produce large deficits in the balance of payments. It was also widely held that the use of foreign products when domestic products were available was an unnecessary luxury. Perhaps the most important aspect of import restrictions was their function as a measure for protecting and nurturing domestic industry, and particularly in such infant industries as automobilies and machinery.

However, the continuance of import restrictions had also created a number of distortions in the domestic economy. For example, under the foreign currency allocations system, the right to import had itself become a vested right in such industries as cotton, wool, and sugar, resulting in the phenomenon of "import premiums." Moreover, since foreign currency allocations were based on the reserve production capacity of each enterprise, they encouraged the practice of competing for guaranteed currency allotments for raw materials imports by resorting to excess investment in production facilities, which led to overcapacity. Overproduction and excessive investment in plant and equipment in these industries became increasingly serious, and clearly revealed that the foreign currency allocation system had reduced the efficiency of the market mechanism, creating distortions in the distribution of resources.

The most direct pressures for trade liberalization came from abroad, particularly from the United States. Rapid increases in the United States' balance of payments deficits had continued long after the end of the worldwide dollar shortage during the post–1945 decade, and the United States had begun to demand that Japan and Europe take measures to remove restrictions on U.S. imports. In 1959, such demands for import liberalization increased in intensity as the volume of Japanese exports to the United States reached record levels and Japan achieved its first balance of payments surplus in its trade with America. Japan already lagged behind Europe, which had moved toward full currency convertibility among its nations in December 1958, and was proceeding to liberalize trade with the United States in the face of what the latter called a "dollar-gold crisis." Pressure from GATT had also intensified.

GATT had been established on the principle of free trade, and its basic premise was the elimination of restrictions on trade volume by individual member nations. Japan and the European nations had joined GATT under Article 14 of the IMF, which recognized temporary, transitional import restrictions by countries that had suffered heavy war damage and were hardest hit by the dollar shortage. However, the advanced nations of GATT had recognized that they were now at the stage of economic development at which they should move to eliminate restrictions on trade by shifting to Article 8 status of the IMF, which required an elimination of government subsidies for exports and trade controls imposed because of balance of payments deficits. The European nations had made the shift to Article 8 status by 1959, leaving Japan as the only advanced industrial country not to have done so. By the early 1960s, trade liberalization and the shift to Article 8 status in the IMF had become unavoidable prerequisites to Japan's entry into the advanced nations club and its future participation in the international economy. Moreover, despite panic and strong opposition in the business community, trade liberalization was perhaps more beneficial for Japan than for any other advanced nation. The free expansion of international trade would greatly contribute to the success of high-speed economic growth policies in Japan, which had pinned its hopes for economic development on increasing industrial exports and was dependent on imports for raw materials. The international division of labor that resulted from worldwide trade liberalization would also contribute to development of a free market system and a more cosmopolitan life-style of the people. However, as the government had been protecting domestic industries through foreign currency restrictions since 1933, the opposition of the business community to trade liberalization was deeply rooted.

Amidst growing anxiety over the repercussions of trade liberalization, the government published its *General Outline of a Plan for Liberalization of Trade Transactions* in June 1960. The plan set the goal of a liberalization rate of 80 percent within three years, to be calculated according to the commodities and products listed on the Brussels Customs Schedule, and it was designed to link trade liberalization with the policies of high-speed growth and full employment. It also established, as general principles, the promotion of modernization and rapid development of the industrial structure with a view to maximizing the advantages of liberalization, as well as the modernization of agriculture and small and medium businesses. More important, perhaps, Ikeda's new plan outlined three basic principles for liberalization, which are summarized below.

1. Liberalization would be implemented first in the raw materials sector, resulting in immediate savings in costs for the manufacturing and processing sectors.
2. Liberalization in specific commodities would be implemented with a view to hastening liberalization in industries in which Japanese products were already competitive internationally, and priority would

be given to imported products that would incur savings for Japanese consumers.

3. Liberalization would be carried out gradually in such industries as automobiles, computers, and heavy machinery, in which Japan was still at the infant stage, requiring nurturing by the government as they achieved international competitiveness.

While Ikeda's plan had been originally designed to achieve 80 percent liberalization three years after its inception, pressure from abroad forced the government to take even more radical measures, and liberalization reached 80 percent by fall 1961.

The swift pace of liberalization brought immediate repercussions. Hardest hit was the coal mining industry, but the electric power, heavy, and chemicals industries benefited a great deal from the rapid liberalization of raw materials imports because of reduced costs for crude oil. Reduced prices for imported oil, however, made the already high price of domestic coal all the more conspicuous and the industry found itself unable to compete. The government attempted to alleviate the situation by enacting the Petroleum Industry Law, which placed heavy restrictions on oil imports, but the energy revolution accompanying the discovery of vast new reserves in the Middle East reduced the price of oil even further. Greater demand for imports of crude oil, and the slackening coal market, threw the mining industry into irreversible decline.

The most important legacy of the period of rapid trade liberalization was the development of the institutions of "public–private cooperation" (*kanmin kyōchō*) that were to characterize the relationship between the economic planning bureaucracy and private business in the postwar period. The public–private cooperation concept had its genesis in the heavy and chemicals industries' move to seek relaxation of the Antimonopoly Law, enabling private enterprises to strengthen existing cartels under the principle of "self-coordination." These enterprises had a marked inferiority complex toward foreign competitors, and viewed the formation of extensive cartels as the only means of resisting capital invasion from big business in the United States and Europe. MITI responded to this by proposing the Special Measures Law for the Promotion of Designated Industries, which embodied the principles of public–private cooperation. The law would have given MITI the power to designate specific industries where there was a need to strengthen international competitiveness, and to approve mergers and other types of "cooperative behavior" (*kyōdō kōi*) for purposes of rationalization under the ministry's administrative guidance.

The conception of this law reflected the panic among young MITI officials in the face of trade liberalization, and the fear that capital liberalization and the influx of foreign capital would break down the barrier maintained by MITI's previous policies of protecting and nurturing industry through trade restrictions.

On March 25, 1963, the cabinet formally voted to sponsor the new law, and it was submitted to the House of Representatives the same day. However, the business community was bitterly opposed to it on the grounds that it represented a revival of strict bureaucratic control over industry, and it died in the Diet as it became too controversial for LDP politicians to support. Nevertheless, the issues raised by the Special Measures Law remained an important by-product of trade and capital liberalization, and the concepts of industrial reorganization and administrative guidance influenced economic policy making throughout the subsequent period. Moreover, MITI–sponsored mergers and rationalization cartels progressed rapidly during the entire process of trade liberalization.

Despite the fears and opposition of the business community, trade liberalization proceeded at a rate unprecedented in other advanced countries, and import liberalization had reached 92 percent by August 1963. With this achievement of liberalization as a passport, Japan shifted to Article 8 status in GATT in spring 1964, and in the same year was admitted to the Organization for Economic Co-operation and Development (OECD), becoming the first Asian country to formally join the ranks of the advanced nations. Ultimately, the domestic frictions created by trade liberalization were not serious except in the case of the coal mining industry, which had been on the decline even before. The heavy and chemicals industries, which had been so pessimistic, reaped enormous profits from the ensuing expansion of world trade and the new international division of labor. Indeed, liberalization significantly increased the efficiency of the Japanese economy as a whole and furthered Ikeda's policies of rapid economic growth and modernization. Both the National Income-Doubling Plan and trade liberalization were inseparable halves of a comprehensive policy. Liberalization was a basic premise of the National Income-Doubling Plan, but without the policy of high-speed growth envisioned in the plan opposition to liberalization would have been much stronger, as would have been the internal frictions resulting from liberalization.[3,4,5,6]

2. THE IWATO BOOM AND THE STRUCTURAL REVOLUTION

The Iwato Boom. The economic expansion that began after recovery from the bottom-of-the-pot recession developed into a boom that surpassed even the Jimmu boom, and by summer 1960 it was being referred to as the Iwato boom. In comparison to the Jimmu boom—which lasted two years and recorded real GNP increases of 6.2 percent in 1956 and 7.8 percent in 1957—the Iwato boom continued for three years, with increases in real GNP reaching 11.2 percent in 1959, 12.5 percent in 1960, and 13.5 percent in 1961. The amazing economic performance during this period can be attributed to the announcement of the National Income-Doubling Plan; rapid increases in plant and equipment investment in response to the promotion of trade liberalization; and expectations for a tremendous growth in the construction industry accompanying the decision to hold the 1964 Olympics in Tokyo. The political commitment to high-speed economic growth, demonstrated by Ikeda's insistence that economic growth targets for the first three years of the National Income-Doubling Plan be raised to annual rates of 9 percent, imbued the business community with expectations of long-term growth. At the same time, the announcement of an extremely rapid schedule for trade liberalization acted as a stimulus to plant and equipment investment as private enterprises rushed to upgrade and modernize in anticipation of stiff competition.

The impact of the Olympics was astounding. The decision to hold the 1964 Olympic Games in Tokyo was announced in 1959, and total expenditures for Olympics-related construction reached ¥1,019 trillion by the time the games were held. This figure represents not only direct expenditure for Olympic facilities but also enormous outlays designed to transform the entire city before the games took place, principally in transportation facilities and luxury hotels. The Tōkaidō Shinkansen was constructed at a cost of ¥38 billion, the Tokyo subway system was expanded, and a new system of freeways completed. The rapid construction of huge, new, luxury hotels sparked the second building boom since the end of the war. In addition to these quantitative indications, the prospect of holding the games in Tokyo provided a psychological boost to business and consumers that combined with Ikeda's National Income-Doubling Plan to encourage optimism concerning Japan's future in the global economy.

The Mass Consumer Revolution. One of the special features of the Iwato boom was the consumer revolution, and it was during this period that the unique traits of Japan's mass consumption society began to take shape. Real personal consumer expenditure as part of GNP showed average yearly increases of 9 percent from fiscal 1959 to 1962, surpassing even the average yearly increases of 6 percent during the previous consumer boom of 1956 and 1957. The most important factor in this rapid increase was the rise in personal income in the face of improvements in labor productivity that resulted from heavy investments in plant and equipment and the transformation of the labor market during the Iwato boom. Due in large part to changes in the supply and demand situation in the labor market, annual wage increases for all industries increased from 5.6 percent in 1955–60 to 10.3 percent in 1960–65. Moreover, the trend toward higher wage increases followed a progressive pattern during this period, from 6.6 percent in 1959, 8 percent in 1960, 9 percent in 1961, and 11 percent in 1962 and 1963. During the same period, annual bonuses also increased from two months' wages to three months' wages by the end of the five-year period ending in 1965. This rapid improvement in real personal income was the basis for the increase in real gross personal consumption expenditure, and these increases were matched by similar increases in the rate of personal savings.

The most conspicuous symbol of the mass consumer society was the boom in household electric appliances, which gained momentum with the increase in retail outlets and improvements in after-sales services as well as the proliferation of the credit purchasing system. The rate of popularization of black-and-white television sets, for example, rose from 7.8 percent in 1957 to 44.7 percent in 1960 and 90.3 percent in 1965. Color television transmissions began in 1960, but their infrequency and high prices impeded the development of this market until the boom that began in 1965. Washing machines and refrigerators followed the trend of black-and-white television sets and, with the popularity of electric appliances priced at ¥50,000 (approximately $139 under the ¥360 exchange rate), this boom came to be called "the ¥50,000 revolution." Products in the same price range, such as living-room sets, stainless steel sinks, stereos, and dining-room sets, displayed similar popularity among the upper and middle classes. Privately owned automobiles began to spread with Nissan's Bluebird in 1959, and the ownership of passenger cars increased from 2.8 percent in 1961 to 9.2 percent in 1965.

The textile and apparel industries also reflected the new mass consumer society as demand for synthetic fibers grew at an extraordinary rate. The development of the textile industry was the result not only of the rise in consumer demand accompanying the new prosperity but also of the technological revolution taking place in the industry itself. The introduction of new synthetics, as well as new blends of synthetics and wool, cotton, and silk, appealed to the increasingly sophisticated tastes of Japanese consumers, and similar technological advances in the dyeing industry produced a new range of choices that resulted in a fad for colorful clothes at considerably lower prices. The consumer revolution in clothes was not limited to the new synthetic fabrics and blends, for technological advances in the production of natural fabrics also signaled the start of mass consumption of ready-made cotton, wool, and silk apparel. Children's wear, women's fashions, and underwear were plentiful as well as inexpensive, and the buying of new, fashionable clothes became the norm. In women's fashions, this new market also reflected the change from kimono to Western-style clothing.

A similar shift in tastes may be observed in foods. Daily consumption of rice reached a peak of 130 grams in 1962, only about 70 percent of the highest prewar levels, rising very little or even declining thereafter. On the other hand, vinyl packaging and processed foods enabled consumers to buy a wide variety of foods regardless of the season, and new food products such as ham and sausage became popular alternatives to the traditional Japanese diet. The rapid rise in income and the new urban life-style brought about changes not only in the daily diet but also in attitudes to cooking, ushering in a new era of instant foods. Instant coffee, instant *rāmen* (noodles), and packaged sauces and seasonings became symbolic of the new consumer society.

The popularity of washing machines, detergents, synthetic fabrics, ready-made clothing, and instant food products, as well as the shift from firewood and charcoal to gas, electricity, or kerosene as the principle source of energy for most households, revolutionized Japanese attitudes, especially in nuclear families and the growing middle class. New labor-saving appliances and instant foods reduced the hours housewives devoted to housework, and there was a general reduction in working hours as large enterprises introduced the five-day week and annual summer vacations. Even in the traditional service industries, restaurants and shops began the system of closing one day per week. Such phrases as "free time" became popular as expressions of a new consciousness that at once symbolized the rise of a new middle class and created a huge new market for consumer goods and the leisure industry.

By 1961 the percentage of household budgets devoted to leisure spending had already reached 22 percent, surpassing the West German average. With the popularity of sightseeing trips, excursions to beaches, mountain climbing, hiking, skiing, and golf, came a boom in hotels, traditional Japanese inns, hostels, restaurants, and large enterprises in the leisure industry, as well as large private railway companies, increased their investments in new facilities. However, the new leisure industry, still in its infancy, was hard pressed to meet the explosion of demand. Beaches were overcrowded, trains on the Japan National Railways routes between urban centers and popular resort and ski areas were so packed on weekends that people were forced to stand in line for hours, and the highways were packed bumper to bumper.

In the case of Japan, the rise in personal income was matched by increases in expenditure for education as new middle class parents who grew up during the war and just after were determined to give their children a better education than they had received themselves. The number of high school, junior college, and university students nearly doubled between 1955 and 1965, with the number of high school students increasing from 2.6 million to 5.07 million, and college and university students rising from 600,000 to 1.09 million. The hopes of the postwar generation for a better future for their children were not frustrated, and the expenditure for education during the late 1950s and early 1960s paved the way for the transformation of Japanese society in which educational background became the fundamental prerequisite for social status.

The Explosion of Private Plant and Equipment Investment. The consumer revolution was a major force supporting the post-recession recovery and the subsequent economic expansion that launched the Iwato boom. However, the driving force of the boom itself was the unprecedented explosion of private investment in plant and equipment that followed trade liberalization and the National Income-Doubling Plan. Real private investment in plant and equipment increased 2.5 times from the first quarter of 1959 to the first quarter of 1961, and rose as a component of real gross national expenditure from 14.8 percent to 21.2 percent in the same period. On a yearly basis, private plant and equipment investment recorded the largest increases in postwar history: 27 percent in 1959; 38.8 percent in 1960; and 29.4 percent in 1961; and comprised nearly one-third of gross national expenditure in each year. These figures represent increases four percentage points higher than increases at the peak of the Jimmu boom and suggest the enormous role of new plant and equipment investment in the boom.

Moreover, an examination of the components of private capital investment during this period reveals that the boom in private plant and equipment investment differed in a number of important respects from the expansion that occurred during the Jimmu boom. The immediate cause of the boom in plant and equipment investment was intense competition among domestic enterprises to modernize and rationalize operations in the face of trade liberalization, and this quality of the boom had far-reaching effects not only on the structure of investment itself but also on the institutions of high-speed growth. These unique characteristics of the boom may be summarized as follows.

First, a major factor in the expansion of plant and equipment investment was a spectacular increase in investment for construction of huge new facilities and for land for new industrial locations. The movement toward large, integrated facilities in new, systematically organized industrial parks had already begun during the Jimmu boom but had been concentrated during that period in the oil-refining, petrochemicals, and steel industries. During the Iwato boom, this spread to all industries as enterprises responded to the rapidly expanding domestic market and began to make investment decisions based on expectations of a prolonged period of high-speed growth. Firms in a wide range of industries now found it impossible to achieve desired increases and improvements in productivity by introducing new technologies into existing facilities; in many cases existing sites were simply too small to achieve the economies of scale promised by the construction of large, integrated assemblies of advanced technology capable of high-speed, continuous operation.

The boom in the construction of new facilities generated enormous demand for new locations, particularly in the industrial parks in the Pacific belt region, which offered modern port and harbor facilities and were close to major population centers. This demand, in turn, was the driving force behind a surge in public and private investment in civil engineering construction, including land reclamation projects, dredging operations to improve existing harbors and create new ones, infrastructure investment for new industrial parks, road construction, and construction of new facilities to supply water for industrial use. One adverse consequence of the competition for new sites was the inflation of land prices. Price increases, and the expectation of even higher prices, drove national land price averages up to levels five times higher in 1963 than in 1955.

Second, the rapid implementation of Ikeda's trade liberalization policies acted as a major new stimulus for domestic plant and equipment investment, and in a way that revealed the characteristic structural features of the economy. Investment was particularly brisk in the automobile, industrial machinery, and chemicals industries, in which a self-image of weak international competitive ability combined with fears of an imminent influx of foreign capital to accelerate plans for "modernization investment." Faced with import liberalization, automobile manufacturers abandoned previous modes of production, in which passenger cars and trucks were assembled in the same facilities, and rushed to construct new factories equipped with automated assemblies, specializing in passenger cars. Large makers such as Toyota and Nissan also took the lead in drafting and financing modernization plans for their subcontractors.

The industrial machinery and chemicals industries attempted to deal with the threat of import liberalization by expanding imports of foreign technology, entering into cooperative agreements with foreign firms, and by a series of large-scale mergers. It is certainly true that these industries, which had been protected and nurtured by MITI since their development, now found themselves in a life-or-death struggle with foreign capital, and the infant oil-refining industry faced a very real threat as domestic and foreign enterprises competed in the general rush to secure market shares by expanding plant and equipment capacity. In retrospect, however, the threat of import liberalization was largely psychological, and in the greatest number of cases served only to promote fierce competition among domestic firms in the same industry. Important as trade liberalization was as a stimulus for domestic competition, most of the rapid increase in plant and equipment investment during this period may be explained by the determination of domestic enterprises to get ahead of the competition or, at the very least, not to fall behind.

Third, competition among domestic firms was paralleled by keen competition among financial *keiretsu* and a strengthening of the "one group, one set" management ideology, in which each group acquires an outstanding firm or creates a new one in each new industry. The strengthening of *keiretsu* financial lineages was an inevitable result of the competition for investment capital and strong structural links among *keiretsu* industrial firms. These new structural links took a variety of forms: the most interesting of the new industrial groupings were the famous *konbinato*, in which firms in the same *keiretsu* combined to form vast complexes that integrated production of refined petroleum products, petrochemicals, and electric power. More traditional arrangements, such as the relationship between large auto makers and their subcontractor parts manufacturers, were strengthened by the parent company helping the smaller firms to design and finance their modernization plans. The demand for investment capital was enormous and, under the system of "indirect financing" (*kansetsu kinyū*), competition for capital made *keiretsu* firms even more dependent on their respective banks. The equity capital ratios of Japanese firms are very low, and almost all of the increase in plant and equipment investment during the boom was financed by overloans from large city banks.

The banks responded aggressively to the demand for capital and competed fiercely to expand their shares, particularly in industries designated as "growth industries" by MITI under the National Income-Doubling Plan. Moreover, both the established city banks of the *zaibatsu*-related *keiretsu* and newer competitors attempted to secure market shares in newly developing and growth industries for their respective *keiretsu* by extending preferential financing to new entries into industries in which the *keiretsu* did not have a company. The famous "one group, one set" ideology of modern *keiretsu* groupings achieved full development during the high-speed growth period that began with the Iwato boom.

Fourth, while previous plant and equipment investment had been concentrated in the industrial materials industries, such as steel, petrochemicals, synthetic fibers, and oil refining, the Iwato boom was characterized by equally spectacular increases in investment by small and medium-size companies in the processing industries. Increases were especially rapid in industries in which technological innovations in the materials industries resulted in new products that stimulated similar advances in related processing industries. For example, the introduction of new specialized steel products led to new plant and equipment investment in the machinery industry. A similar pattern can be seen in the plastics, garment, and processed foods industries. Moreover, the rapid development of the mass consumer society encouraged large increases in capital investment for expanding wholesale and retail facilities.

Fifth, it was during the Iwato boom that a new type of business enterprise began to play a major role in economic expansion and modernization. These firms, which began to attract attention during the early 1960s, took an aggressive posture toward plant and equipment investment and technological innovation unparalleled even in the rapidly modernizing firms of giant *zaibatsu*-related *keiretsu*. Matsushita (Panasonic), which started out as a small company before the war, Sony and Honda, both of which were established after the war, grew so quickly during this period that they received much more attention from abroad than the larger *keiretsu* firms. These and other corporate innovators maintained their independence of financial *keiretsu*, each developing new technologies and innovative management techniques that enabled it to achieve relative superiority over much larger firms in specific foreign and domestic markets. During the Iwato boom, these companies took advantage of the interbank competition for new credit customers to expand their plant and equipment investment, increasing the size of their operations to the level of large firms. Besides the companies cited above, examples of this new type of enterprise may be cited in almost every industry in which the commercialization of state-of-the-art technology offered unprecedented opportunities for new entries: Omron-Tateishi, Alps Electric, Murata Manufacturing, and Kyoto Ceramics in electronic parts; Pioneer, Clarion, and Akai in audio equipment; Copal in cameras; Sankyō Seiki in music boxes; Yoshida Manufacturing in zip fasteners; and Hitachi Seiki and Makino Milling Machines in industrial machinery.

In addition to major structural changes in the economy, the massive plant and equipment investment during the Iwato boom fueled a transformation of operations and management that amounted to a virtual facelift for Japanese industry. The rapid introduction of computer technology provided the foundation for modernizing production, business, and sales operations, and was accompanied by surging demand for automated control equipment and other automated technology in small, medium, and large enterprises. The trend toward automation was particularly striking in in-plant transportation and packaging systems. The development of gigantic coastal industrial *konbinato* was symbolic of the general trend toward rationalizing transportation, and it was paralleled by a large increase in the use of trucks for transporting materials from factories and final assembly plants to wholesalers, retailers, and consumers.

The Advent of the Full Employment Economy. Perhaps the most significant structural change wrought by the Iwato boom was the transformation of the labor market. The boom brought the country to the threshold of a full employment society for the first time in modern history, irrevocably destroying the basis for an economy with an excess supply of labor. The transition to full employment had far-reaching effects for every sector of the economy and guaranteed the success of the National Income-Doubling Plan.

As we shall see in this and the following sections, the shift from a surplus to a shortage in the labor market also hastened the realization of Ikeda's goal of reducing wage differentials created by the dual structure of the economy. However, precisely because this transformation of the labor market occurred so quickly, and the scope of its effects on the economy was of such magnitude, the amount of friction generated by fear and uncertainties concerning its impact on prices and economic growth during the transition period was also substantial. Confronted by the prospect of a long-term labor shortage, a mood as much psychological as based on an immediate crisis developed among enterprise managers, threatening to touch off a wage–price spiral that could have created serious distortions. The advent of full employment presented real problems, both for enterprises and for society as a whole, which demanded realistic and creative solutions rather than panicky responses.

The shift in labor supply and demand occurred during 1960 and 1961, much more quickly than had been envisioned by the National Income-Doubling Plan. The swiftness of the transition may be explained in part by a temporary phenomenon in the population structure. The new school graduates (especially junior high school but also high school graduates) entering the job market in 1960 and 1961 represented the generation born at the end of the war or in the immediate postwar period, when the birth rate had been abnormally low. The postwar baby boom generation had just begun secondary education, and would not enter the job market for a few more years. At the same time, the number of students continuing their education beyond junior high school was increasing, reducing even further the number of junior high school graduates entering the labor force. This reduction in the number of new school graduates, combined with increases in labor demand spurred on by the Iwato boom, created a sudden, abnormal labor shortage. However, once the shortage had developed, the strength of the Iwato boom and expectations of long-term labor shortages combined to make what appeared to be a temporary aberration into a permanent feature of the labor market.

The demand for labor generated by the Iwato boom was staggering. During the three-year period from 1959 to 1961, total employment in all enterprises increased by 3.39 million workers, and the number of permanent employees in the manufacturing industries increased by 44 percent. In the same period, the number of totally unemployed workers declined by 340,000, and overall unemployment dropped from 2 percent to 1.4 percent. The labor shortages created by this excess demand were most serious in the

Table 9. Changes in Demand for Labor and Wage Increases in the Period of High-Speed Growth

	Units	1953	1957	1961	1967	1973
Effective ratio of job offers to applicants	ratio	0.35	0.48	0.73	1.05	1.74
Ratio of job offers to applicants for new school graduates						
Middle-school graduates	//	1.06	1.18	2.73	3.45	5.79
High-school graduates	//	0.69	1.07	2.04	3.05	3.13
Starting salaries of new school graduates						
Middle-school graduates	¥1,000	9.7	11.2	15.7	26.2	57.0
High-school graduates	//	3.5	4.7	7.3	15.5	37.6
Wage differentials based on scale of enterprises	(see note)	60.4	56.1	61.7	67.7	70.9
Special allowances (e.g., bonuses)	no. of months	1.83	2.61	3.16	3.43	4.39
Wages increases after spring wage offensives	%		4.4	13.8	12.5	24.1

Note: Wage differentials are expressed as the wage index in firms with 30–99 employees when wages in firms with more than 500 employees=100.

market for new junior high school graduates, in which shortages had begun much earlier (*see* Table 9). In June 1961, the effective ratio of openings to applicants reached 2.7 to 1 and the number of openings filled amounted to only 30 percent of those offered. The market situation for new high school graduates was only marginally better, with the ratio of openings to applicants reaching 2 to 1.

With the transformed labor market as a background, there was a gradual increase in worker mobility between enterprises, and it was this increase that hastened the erosion of the dual structure. The salient feature of the dual structure is the system of lifetime employment offered by large firms, which, before the development of labor shortages, was virtually closed to applicants other than new school graduates. Until about 1960, it was almost impossible for a worker already employed in a small firm to enter a large enterprise as a lifetime employee. Within the large firms themselves, the permanent work force of lifetime employees was supplemented by temporary and seasonal employees, whose wages were about half those of the former and whose numbers could be reduced at will. It was the existence of wide productivity and wage differentials between the lifetime employees in large enterprises and the workers in small enterprises, and between lifetime employees and temporary workers in large enterprises, that had spawned the dual structure.

The labor market institutions that characterize the dual structure were in large measure reflections of the system of "familial management" that had developed before the war and had relied heavily on a surplus labor supply in the agricultural sector. (Indeed, the differentials in productivity and incomes between the agricultural sector and the modern industrial sector may be said to constitute the traditional dual structure of the economy.) Labor shortages, especially the severe shortages of new school graduates, forced large enterprises to hire their lifetime employees from those already employed in small enterprises and to upgrade temporary workers to the status of lifetime employees. Firms also began to compete in recruiting trained technicians from other large firms, and this competition intensified as private firms attempted to lure skilled technicians away from government bureaucracies.

This competition for labor during the Iwato boom sparked a sharp increase in wages that affected every sector of the economy. Because demand for labor was concentrated on new school graduates, the most dramatic increases were recorded in the starting wages of new lifetime employees in large firms. New school graduates were sought by large firms offering lifetime employment not only because they were considered the most ideal candidates for training in new technologies but also because their starting wages were relatively low in the seniority wage structure. This situation changed drastically as wages for new graduates, which up to then had increased only a few percentage points each year, rose in 1960 by 14 percent for junior high school graduates, 10 percent for high school graduates, and 5 percent for university graduates. The full impact was felt in 1961, and wage increases for these three categories reached 24 percent, 21 percent, and 20 percent, respectively, as the higher wages offered junior high school graduates in 1960 were reflected in greater wage increases for high school and college graduates. These rapid rises for new entrants narrowed wage differentials within large firms, serving to flatten the seniority wage curve, which had revealed a steep gradient during the 1950s.

Excess demand and increased worker mobility in smaller enterprises also served to narrow wage differentials between large enterprises and small and medium firms. Indeed, the magnitude and scope of wage increases tended to be larger in inverse proportion to the size of the firm.

Figure 9. Changes in the Industrial Structure during the Period of High-Speed Growth

1. Changes in the Employment Structure

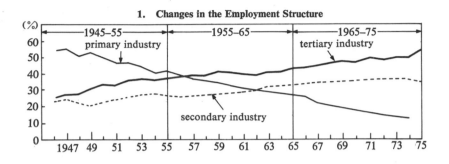

2. Changes in the Industrial Structure (Share of GNP)

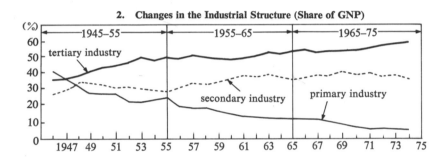

This was due to the fact that smaller firms not only had to compete with larger firms offering more prestigious employment and better training opportunities but these firms also had to increase the wages of present employees in order to stabilize their work forces. Given the new willingness of large enterprises to hire previously employed workers, and the higher wages being offered new workers by smaller firms, it was inevitable that the scale of wage increases would be even greater in such firms. This narrowing of wage differentials proceeded at a much faster pace than government planners had predicted, and in fact the goals set by the National Income-Doubling Plan for eliminating the dual structure by 1970 were surpassed in 1962.

The transformation of the labor market also brought far-reaching changes in labor relations, resulting in a dramatic strengthening of labor's bargaining position vis-à-vis management. The national labor movement, which until then had tended to overemphasize political and social issues due to its relationship with opposition political parties, gradually shifted its focus to the issues of wages, working hours, and working conditions. It was during the Iwato boom that the "spring wage offensive" (*shuntō*), which had started shakily in 1955, began to play a leading role in yearly negotiations between individual unions and enterprises. The number of union members participating in the spring wage offensive increased dramatically from 700,000 in 1955 to 4.4 million in 1960. Under the leadership of pragmatic labor leaders like Kaoru Ōta of the General Council of Trade Unions (Sōhyō), the spring wage offensive rapidly became the primary means for labor to present its demands for better wages and working conditions. Wage increases resulting from this, which averaged only 4 or 5 percent until 1959, reached 6.9 percent in 1959, 8.7 percent in 1960, and 13.8 percent in 1962. Unlike the prewar and war years, during which the song "If I Could Only Get a Raise" had become an instant hit, large annual increments were now taken for granted. Of course, the large increases in wages after the spring wage offensive were not entirely due to labor's enhanced bargaining position.

It is possible to argue that, especially during the Iwato boom, the so-called spring offensive wage hikes themselves were pushed up by increases initiated by large firms competing to employ new school graduates and the related increases in small and medium enterprises, many of which had no unions. However, it is impossible to deny the importance of the national labor movement and the spring wage offensive in creating a public consensus supporting wage increases, and in influencing the decisions of small enterprises in negotiating wage settlements with non-union workers. Moreover, they were similarly influential in the negotiations between farmers and government authorities on setting official prices for the yearly rice harvest.

Rapid Changes in Agriculture and Small Enterprises. The sector of the economy most affected by the shift to full employment was agriculture (including the forestry and fishing industries). Dramatic increases in the wages of urban workers in the secondary and tertiary industries started an enormous flow of population from agricultural to urban centers. This was true especially among new school graduates, for whom the attractions of city life and nonagricultural employment would have exerted a strong pull even without the huge wage increases of the Iwato boom. However, there was also an acceleration of the trend among household heads and eldest sons to seek nonagricultural employment in nearby urban areas while farming part-time. Moreover, income differentials between farmers and those employed in other industries widened in inverse proportion to the size of agricultural operations, and among small-farm families, the problem of eldest sons refusing to succeed their fathers as household heads became increasingly serious. The total population employed in agriculture declined by 1.5 million persons in the five-year period from 1955 to 1960, and continued to decline by an annual average of 0.7 million persons thereafter. The share of agriculture in the total employed population showed a similar rapid decline, from 37.9 percent in 1955 to 30 percent in 1960, and to only 21 percent in 1965. It was during this period that journalists began to coin such phrases as "Sunday farmers" for farmers who worked only nominally in agriculture in order to keep their land while relying primarily on income from nonagricultural employment, and "*sanchan* agricultural" for the situation in which *kāchan* (momma), *jiichan* (grandpa), and *bāchan* (grandma) ran the farm while *tōchan* (poppa) went off to work in the city. The number of farmers who earned 50 percent or more of their incomes from nonagricultural employment increased from 20 percent in 1950 to 30 percent in 1960 and 50 percent in 1970.

Agricultural policy as envisioned by the National Income-Doubling Plan, which was implemented in 1961, was consistent with the goal of eliminating the dual structure. Specific provisions for agriculture called for eliminating the traditional dual structure between agriculture (primary industry) and nonagricultural industries (secondary and tertiary industries) by absorbing the underemployed and potentially unemployed work force existing in agriculture into secondary and tertiary industries as the labor market in these industries expanded during the process of high-speed growth. In turn, this process was expected to lead to rapid increases in per capita productivity of the remaining agricultural population, resulting in a balance in income levels between agriculture and other industries. In fact, however, rapid economic growth had already brought agriculture to a crucial point, presenting problems that could not be solved merely by relying on automatic productivity increases due to a shift of the agricultural population to nonagricultural industries. Rapid wage increases in the nonagricultural sectors had further exacerbated income differentials, changing life-styles had put a limit on increases in rice consumption, and import liberalization had adversely affected wheat production. By the time the National Income-Doubling Plan went into effect in 1961, it was already clear that basic structural changes would have to be made, and there were loud demands that the government develop new policies for agriculture.

Against this background the Basic Agricultural Law was enacted in June 1966. It was essentially a resolution recognizing that agricultural policy had been out of step with changes in the economy, and it established three basic goals for subsequent policy.

1. The reduction of productivity differentials between agriculture and other industries and the promotion of a balance between the incomes and living conditions of agricultural families and other classes of the population.

2. The selective expansion of agricultural production with the aim of increasing production of commodities for which demand was rising. For example, production of livestock was to be tripled and production of fruit doubled during the subsequent ten-year period.

3. The nurturing of independent farm families, including the maintenance of secure agricultural incomes at levels that would enable them to live as well as workers in other industries while engaging in agriculture.

The first step toward realizing these goals was the Agricultural Modernization Financial Assistance Law, designed to mobilize excess capital accumulated in various financial institutions established by agricultural cooperatives. The law provided for government subsidies that would enable these institutions to extend low-interest, long-term loans to individual farmers, enabling them to invest in new technology and new areas of production. The goal was a general increase in agricultural productivity through mechanization and modernization that would compensate for the decrease in the agricultural population.

In fact, this law produced some remarkable results in promoting the mechanization of rice cultivation and the development of other designated areas of agriculture. Livestock breeding advanced quickly, with economies of scale achieved by increasing the size of herds and introducing new feeds. The poultry industry gradually became a large-scale manufacturing industry. Similarly, fruit growers achieved outstanding increases by expanding the size of orchards, introducing new technologies, fertilizers, and insecticides, and modern techniques and mechanization in harvesting and delivery.

However, while large-scale farmers took advantage of the new law to increase productivity and, in some cases, to transform their farming operations into large business enterprises, the basic structure of land ownership, which had been imposed by Occupation reforms, remained virtually intact. While the policy makers responsible for the Agricultural Modernization Financial Assistance Law had envisioned sweeping changes as small landowners gave up their land to seek employment in secondary and tertiary industries, these expectations were not fulfilled. Increased reliance on nonagricultural income and the expectation of further large increases in land prices resulted in a steady decline in the number of farmers engaged exclusively in agriculture but an increase in the number of farmers who kept their land but relied primarily on nonagricultural income. Moreover, the new price-fixing policy for rice implemented in 1961 introduced the production-cost income-compensation formula, resulting in large increases in the government's buying price for rice each year thereafter.

Generally, the entire food supply administrative system shifted to a protectionist position as regards agriculture, which was highly colored by political considerations. In the face of rapidly changing conditions in the labor market, the government's agricultural policy attempted to pursue the contradictory goals of extending the concept of economic rationality and modernization to agriculture while maintaining a protective stance through a system of price supports. The political realities underlying these policies were abundantly clear to politicians both in the ruling LDP and in the opposition parties. Elections simply could not be won by calling for the modernization of agriculture and the rectification of income differentials between agriculture and nonagricultural industries through large-scale outmigrations of the agricultural population. Strong political pressure was exerted on policy makers to devise compromises to enable agriculture to adapt to high-speed economic growth but at the same time maintain the status quo of agriculture and rural society. In fact, this meant that severe limitations were placed on policies designed to modernize agriculture and, while significant progress was made in reducing differentials in income between agriculture and nonagricultural industries, productivity differentials remained high. The losers in this compromise were the consumers, who continue to pay high prices for rice and other agricultural products.

As suggested in the previous section, the changes in the labor market also presented serious problems for small and medium enterprises. Especially in the case of small businesses in traditional commercial enterprises, these problems paralleled those of small farmers, and it is not surprising that initial opposition to the high-growth policies of the

National Income-Doubling Plan was strongest among these two groups. Small and medium enterprises in general had relied on low wages and labor-intensive operations, and the labor shortages created by the Iwato boom forced them to confront the reality that their labor force could not be maintained without large wage increases.

Against this background, the government shifted the emphasis of its policies from nurturing and protecting small businesses to promoting modernization by enacting the Basic Law for Small and Medium Enterprises in July 1963. Based on this, a series of ten related laws were enacted at the same time, including the Small and Medium Enterprises Modernization Promotion Law and the Small and Medium Enterprises Modernization Financial Assistance Law. These laws designated industries in which the modernization of small and medium enterprises could contribute to the rapid growth and international competitiveness of the industry as a whole, and established basic modernization plans for small and medium enterprises in each industry. These plans set standards for product design and quality control, and outlined goals for cost reductions and production increases. Other measures provided special subsidies, tax exemptions, and preferential financing from the Small and Medium Enterprises Finance Corporation. Twenty industries were designated in the first year of the plan, and this number grew to sixty-eight in 1966 and to one hundred and eighteen in 1974, covering about 70 percent of the total sales volume of small and medium enterprises. These policies deserve high praise for their contribution to progressive changes in the industrial system. They encouraged small and medium enterprises to increase profits through rationalization, modernization of plant and equipment, product specialization, and increased production. Furthermore, they supported rapid increases in the introduction of automation and labor-saving operations by small enterprises acting on their own initiative in the face of labor shortages and import liberalization.

However, small and medium enterprises existed in both the secondary and tertiary industrial sectors of the economy, and there were wide disparities in their ability to adapt to the historic changes taking place. One extreme is represented by smaller firms in high-growth industries such as automobiles, household electric appliances, industrial machinery, and plastics. Anticipating rapidly expanding markets in the near future, these first acted aggressively to confront the new period of high wages by emphasizing capital accumulation and rapid increases in productivity. At the other extreme were firms in traditional commercial, service, and manufacturing industries, in which progress in rationalization and modernization tended to be negligible. These firms either passively accepted the necessity of passing on increased labor costs to consumers in the form of higher prices, or were forced to do so by the nature of their operations.

This period proved to be a turning point for small and medium enterprises, and there were many failures and some outstanding successes in adapting to the new economic situation. Indeed, while many traditional industries declined, others made rational decisions to limit their markets to higher-income groups. Similarly, as we saw previously, such firms as Honda, Sony, and Matsushita were able to take advantage of innovative management and maneuverability to expand their operations. These patterns reflect those in agriculture, in which traditional rice cultivation declined while large-scale operations were able to improve productivity, and selective development of new products enabled fruit growers and livestock breeders to expand into new markets. The course taken by government toward small and medium enterprises also parallels its policies toward agriculture. Laws related to the Basic Law for Small and Medium Enterprises attempted to promote modernization and rationalization, but provisions of the Small and Medium Enterprises Organizations Law, the Environmental Protection Law, and the Department Store Law were clearly protectionist, and promoted cartels that were contradictory to the goal of stabilizing consumer prices.

A New Type of Consumer Price Inflation. The transition to full employment occurred during a period of high-speed economic growth and it, therefore, played a major role in eliminating the income disparities that characterized the dual structure of the economy. As we have seen, however, the advent of full employment presented new problems for every sector of the economy and for the consumer. The Iwato boom was accompanied by rapid increases in consumer prices, representing a new type of price inflation that differed in character from previous ones. In this sense, too, the Iwato boom period was a turning point.

In retrospect, the most stable period in postwar history in terms of inflation was the years between 1955 to 1959. Even in 1957, at the peak of the Jimmu boom, the consumer price index rose by only 2.8 percent, and annual inflation rates during the rest of the period hovered around 1 percent, almost unbelievable from today's perspective. However, after 1959, consumer prices began to rise from 3.6 percent in 1960 to 5.3 percent in 1961, 6.7 percent in 1962, and 7.9 percent in 1963. This was not caused

Table 10. Increases in the Consumer Price Index and Composite Factors

	1960–65		1965–74	
	Increase	Contribution to CPI	Increase	Contribution to CPI
	%		%	
Total	6.2	100	4.9	100
Agricultural, marine, and livestock products		(35)		(28)
Rice and other grains	6.1	11	7.4	12
Fresh fish	4.4	4	5.9	6
Seasonal commodities	12.3	20	5.8	10
Manufactured goods		(32)		(35)
Processed food products (large enterprises)	2.0	2	2.2	3
Processed food products (small and medium enterprises)	7.2	17	4.6	11
Other products (large enterprises)	1.1	2	2.6	7
Other products (small and medium enterprises)	4.6	11	4.4	14
Services		(33)		(37)
Private	11.8	27	7.4	28
Public	3.5	6	3.5	9

Source: Economic White Paper, 1970.

by any of the factors that had pushed prices up during the two previous inflationary periods, both of which had resulted from unusual circumstances. (The period of rampant inflation in the immediate postwar period had been caused by widespread shortages and excessive money supply, while inflation during the Korean War period had been the result of excess demand created by special procurements. Moreover, the increase in consumer prices during these two periods was not accompanied by significant increases in wholesale prices, which recorded annual increases of only 1 or 2 percent.)

Price inflation during the Iwato boom was deeply rooted in the new structure of the economy and affected an extremely wide range of products and services. Only the products of large enterprises, in which productivity gains had been substantial, rose at relatively moderate rates. Predictably, increases were especially steep for the products of traditional small and medium enterprises where improvements in productivity were difficult to achieve. Thus, bread, noodles, bean paste, soy sauce, tofu, rubber shoes, and textiles recorded the most striking increases. Similarly there were large increases for agricultural products such as vegetables, fruits, and fresh fish. Perhaps the most remarkable component of these increases, and one that has been neglected so far, was the rapid rise in service costs: restaurants and bars, beauty shops, tailor shops, laundries, and public baths posted large increases, and the cost of deliveries of newspapers and milk rose. The public sector also contributed to inflation with higher train and subway fares, higher postage charges, increases in school and tuition fees, and higher official prices for rice. Finally, rapid increases in rents and lease rates reflected not only general inflationary pressures but also the staggering increases in land prices.

As indicated by the data presented in Table 10, the only commodities that recorded moderate price gains were such consumer durables as electric home appliances produced by large enterprises. Inflation was by no means the result of wage increases outstripping productivity improvements in the economy as a whole. On the contrary, as demonstrated by the relative stability of wholesale prices compared with those of the United States and Europe, brisk gains in productivity were more than sufficient to offset a large-scale general increase in wages, even though these gains were concentrated in large enterprises in the heavy and chemicals industries.

What caused the rapid inflation during this period was a transitional adjustment of the price structure for labor-intensive goods and services accompanying the full employment economy. These prices had lagged far behind levels in the United States and Europe, and increases of wages in these industries were pushing prices up to levels comparable to those in other advanced nations. This new type of inflation resulted in heated debates concerning its causes and the countermeasures to deal with it. The most extreme position held that high-speed economic growth policies, and especially the promotion of private plant and equipment investment, had generated excessive demand and spiralling land prices and that, therefore, the only effective way to deal with it was to suppress private investment.

However, Osamu Shimomura, one of the planners most directly responsible for the National Income-Doubling Plan, took the opposite view that since wholesale prices, which were the principle yardstick of international competitive ability, were stable in comparison to other advanced countries, the increases in consumer prices should not be regarded as inflation. Moreover, he argued that there was no need to worry about this kind of inflation because the price increases for such things as personal services reflected a healthy upgrading of the value attached to human labor, which up to then had been too low.

Countering these views, Ryūtarō Komiya and Ryūichirō Tate of the University of Tokyo argued that the basis of the inflation was administered pricing by oligopolistic enterprises and administrative intervention by government policies that nurtured and protected industry. In fact, the basic cause of rapid increases in consumer prices during this period was what might be called "productivity differentials inflation," which may be explained in the following manner. Despite the wide gaps in productivity levels between the high-productivity sector—comprised principally of large enterprises in heavy industries—and the low-productivity sector—comprised of agriculture, small enterprises, and services—annual wage increases did not show a marked difference. In fact, wage increases in the low-productivity sector tended to outstrip those in the high-productivity sector as enterprises in the former attempted to hold on to their work force. Therefore, due to the highly apparent wage increases in the high-productivity sector, wage increases in the low-productivity sector were pushed up even more, resulting in severe pressures on consumer prices.

Despite a conspicuous rise in consumer prices, the government optimistically viewed these increases as temporary inflation. Countermeasures were limited to attempts to calm the inflationary mood by placing selective controls on designated commodities and taking steps to check opportunistic price increases. It gradually became clear, however, that inflation of consumer prices was not temporary but was caused by fundamental structural changes in the economy during the transition to full employment. It was at this point that long and mid-term policies to eliminate productivity differentials by promoting the modernization of agriculture and small and medium enterprises became focal points of discussions. It was also during this period that the University of Tokyo's Professor Shūji Hayashi proposed the theory of the "distribution revolution," pointing out the need to modernize the distribution system. However, when the government finally bowed to political pressure to adopt concerted anti-inflation policies, it once again resorted to suppressing demand through a freeze on public spending and the imposition of a tight monetary policy.

The Iwato boom marked the end of abundant, cheap labor, and this fact was symbolized by a number of changes in life-styles. Rising wages and increased costs forced junk dealers and secondhand stores out of business and, beginning with old newspapers and magazines, junk quickly lost its value. The hiring of maids and servants declined drastically as middle-class housewives turned to labor-saving household appliances, instant foods, and ready-made apparel to cut down time spent on housework. As the wages of Japanese workers rapidly approached American and European levels, it was no longer possible to take advantage of the dual structure, and the realities of the full employment society were reflected in new social values and new life-styles, as well as in the management of business enterprises.

3. THE AFTERMATH OF THE IWATO BOOM

From the Tokyo Olympics Boom to the Recession of 1965. The Iwato boom came to an end in December 1961, exactly one year after the National Income-Doubling Plan. The boom had continued for forty-two months, almost one year longer than the thirty-one months of the Jimmu boom. During this period, shortages of port and harbor facilities, rail transportation, public highways, and industrial water supply developed into serious obstacles impeding further economic expansion. The duration and pace of the boom, as well as the rapid growth of private plant and equipment investment, had highlighted the inadequacy of government social capital investment in the economic infrastructure.

As with the Jimmu boom, however, the basic cause of the economic downturn was not the infrastructural bottlenecks but the worsening of the international balance of payments situation and subsequent tight monetary policies. The fact that 1961 was the first year of the National Income-Doubling Plan had created unique political exigencies for economic planners, who were pressured to devise policies to bolster expansion. Ambitious programs had been implemented to expand public investment, including the social security and pension systems, and similar measures were taken to promote an expansive monetary policy. At the beginning of 1961, the Ministry of Finance adopted a policy encouraging reductions in the official discount rate. At the same time, the Bank of Japan began to shift from the indirect financing system to the direct investment system, and authorized the issuance of public bonds and debentures in the first three months of 1961. The impending balance of payments problem during this period was obscured by a short-term inflow of foreign capital and by a temporary delay in the payment of foreign capital usances.

By summer, however, the balance of payments deficit began to grow at an alarming rate, and foreign capital reserves declined from $2 billion at the end of April to $1.6 billion by the end of September. The principle cause of this was the rapid increase in industrial raw materials and technology imports resulting from the prolonged high demand created by plant and equipment investment during the three-year Iwato boom. The problem was further intensified by the fact that high domestic demand had blunted the desire of private firms to promote exports. Finally, in September 1961, the government had no choice but to institute emergency measures and, as in the past, stringent monetary policies were assigned the leading role.

While these policies were implemented under the banner of the New Financial Adjustment System, which promised an end to such practices as window guidance, the most important policy tools still continued to be window guidance, increases in the official discount rate, and higher minimum deposit reserve ratios. The New Financial Adjustment System empowered the Bank of Japan to conduct open market operations and to implement prohibitive interest rate penalties on city banks that exceeded a specified ceiling on total borrowing from the central bank. The latter differed from window guidance in the sense that it imposed general limits on borrowing rather than selective restraints on borrowing by each city bank. It had been implemented with the aim of normalizing financing by curtailing the practice of overloans by city banks and replacing it with a system of stable financing for private enterprises attempting to cope with the new problems posed by import liberalization. In theory, the new system constituted a lower level of interference in city banks than window guidance, but in practice it differed little.

The business downturn resulting from these monetary policies continued until fall 1962, but was extremely mild compared to the recessions of 1954 and 1958, causing only marginal increases in unemployment and very few bankruptcies. The moderate impact of anticyclical policies, and the brief duration of the downturn, were due principally to the rapid expansion of exports supported by vigorous business upturns in the United States and Europe. The government had also taken steps to soften the impact of these stringent policies on small and medium business by instituting special financial assistance measures at an early stage in the business downturn. Moreover, the amelioration of wage differentials under the dual structure, and the institution of the income-parity formula in setting official rice prices, not only reduced disproportionately adverse effects on low-income groups but also accelerated recovery from the

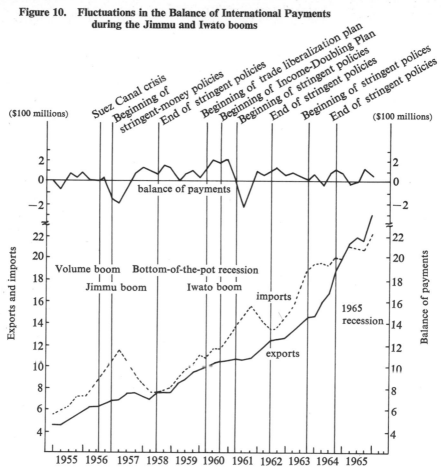

Figure 10. Fluctuations in the Balance of International Payments during the Jimmu and Iwato booms

Suez Canal crisis
Beginning of stringent-money policies
End of stringent policies
Beginning of trade liberalization plan
Beginning of Income-Doubling Plan
Beginning of stringent policies
End of stringent policies
Beginning of stringent polices
End of stringent policies

($100 millions)

($100 millions)

balance of payments

Exports and imports

Balance of payments

Volume boom   Bottom-of-the-pot recession

Jimmu boom   Iwato boom

imports

1965 recession

exports

1955 1956 1957 1958 1959 1960 1961 1962 1963 1964 1965

Note: Figures on imports and exports are seasonally adjusted and based on customs statistics.

business downturn. A rapid growth in exports improved the balance of payments situation, and the subsequent relaxation of tight monetary policies was followed by another period of brisk economic activity that continued until the fall of 1964.

This rapid economic growth period was unique in that it was supported by an expansion of construction investment and a general increase in business activity in anticipation of the Tokyo Olympics. Fiscal spending under the National Income-Doubling Plan expanded rapidly as the government moved to implement spending programs for social overhead capital investments and public investment programs designed to deal with the bottlenecks in the economic infrastructure. As the opening date for the Tokyo Olympics drew near, there was a rush to complete public and private projects such as the Tōkaidō Shinkansen. Large neon signs at department stores and banks announced the number of remaining days before the Tokyo Olympics, and department store sales of "dream super-express" models symbolized the atmosphere that fueled the boom. Announcements of meetings of the IMF and the World Bank in Tokyo in September and the Tokyo Olympics in October had stimulated a boom in hotel construction, and large new hotels sprang up one after the other. Revisions of the Building Standards Law in January 1964 had eliminated restrictions limiting the height of buildings to thirty-one meters, and the Hotel New Otani and the Kasumigaseki Building marked the beginning of the age of skyscrapers. It was also during the year of the Tokyo Olympics that *manshon,* or apartment complexes or condominiums constructed by private enterprises, replaced *danchi* as the object of public aspiration and the symbol of affluence. While only sixty-two of these complexes had been constructed during the three-year period from 1961 to 1963, fifty-six new construction projects were launched in 1964 alone, with prices for individual units increasing more than three times.

Thus, public and private construction investment played the leading role in the pre-Olympic boom of 1964, and the one-year period from fall 1963 to fall 1964 witnessed the most sweeping changes in the postwar construction industry. The strength of the boom itself, however, resulted in renewed balance of payments problems as demand for imports of industrial raw materials threatened once again to create large deficits. Moreover, the Cuban missile crisis in October 1963 had driven up the price of sugar on international markets, and a disastrous wheat crop had necessitated unexpected imports of food, producing more pressure on the balance of payments. The second "defense of the dollar" policy of July 1963, implemented by the Kennedy administration, again resulted in an unforeseen decline in foreign currency income from foreign trade and in influxes of foreign securities investment capital. The deterioration of the balance of payments situation, and the surge of consumer prices accompanying the boom, suggested that the economy was overheating and, in the interest of stabilizing it before the IMF conference and the Tokyo Olympics, anticyclical policies were implemented at the end of 1963. These took the form of a one-year deferment of public investment financing as well as the usual stringent monetary policies.

In October 1964, more than five thousand young atheletes from forty-four countries gathered in Tokyo for the Olympics, marking the first time this major international event had been held in an Asian country. As suggested earlier, the Tokyo Olympics symbolized a new stage of development for Japan. Immediately before the games, the Tōkaidō Shinkansen, the Tokyo Monorail, the Shuto Expressway, and the Meishin Expressway had been completed, representing a total public investment of over ¥1 trillion. During the same year, the government achieved its goals for liberalizing imports (although the liberalization of completed passenger cars was delayed until 1965) and had taken important steps toward a fully opened economy by shifting to Article 8 status in the IMF and joining OECD. For the Japanese people the Tokyo Olympics created the atmosphere of an international festival—and we are famous for our love for festivals—celebrating Japan's entry into the community of advanced nations. In the *Pillow Book* of Sei Shōnagon, a famous court lady of the Heian period, the author laments that "one is especially sad and lonely after a festival," and the aftermath of the Tokyo Olympics was certainly such a period for Japan. The unexpected death of Prime Minister Ikeda soon after the games seems, in retrospect, almost to have been an omen of the end of the period of high-speed growth, which had been sustained in no small measure by the power of his vision. In the following year the economy entered its worst recession in postwar history, the so-called recession of 1965.

In the first half of 1965, corporate profits fell to their lowest levels since the post–Korean War recession of 1951. This decline was intensified by the sluggish stock market, which had been in a slump since the "Kennedy shock" of 1963, when an interest equalization tax on exports of capital, part of the second "defense of the dollar" policy, was imposed. The "Kennedy shock" had a disastrous effect on Japan's securities market, which was heavily dependent on foreign investment capital, and in June 1965, two major firms, Yamaichi Securities and Ōi Securities, announced they were in serious trouble and were saved only by a drastic government-secured loan program unprecedented since the financial panic during the Dodge Line. There were also a great number of bankruptcies among industrial firms, including large firms. Japan Special Steel, Sun Wave, and Sanyō Special Steel represented the biggest bankruptcies that had yet occurred in postwar Japan. During the period of high speed economic growth that began with the Iwato boom, intense competition to expand capital investment and increase market shares had resulted in a corresponding expansion of corporate indebtedness on the one hand, and holdings of accounts receivable on the other. Once uncertainty developed in the credit market, the same firms that had been expanding plant and equipment investment and sales based on indirect financing did an about-face, instituting financial retrenchment schemes and drastically reducing stock issues. To the extent that these were large, influential firms, they also had the effect of creating a recessionary psychology in related industries, and it became clear that, if unchecked, this snowball effect could result in a prolonged, self-sustaining recession.

The Theory of Structural Recession and the Emergence of Fiscal Policy. There was considerable debate during this critical period over the nature of the recession and the proper steps to deal with it. A number of analysts referred to it as a stock market recession or as a credit recession, revealing a clear view of the symptoms of the recession but little grasp of underlying causes. Also, it is true that the leveling-off of demand for electric home appliances, which had continued to grow steadily during previous recessions, and the end of the construction boom following the completion of projects related to the Tokyo Olympics, contributed to the intensity of the recession. However, the most important factor in the 1965 recession was the plant and equipment (or capital stock) adjustment function, and the recession may be viewed as the result of medium-term adjustments in the plant and equipment investment cycle. To this extent, it differed significantly from the recessions experienced in 1954 and 1958.

It is untrue that the recession developed suddenly and without warning from economic analysts. Professor Miyohei Shinohara of Hitotsubashi University, who was later to join the Economic Planning Agency, was one of the first to argue that there was the possibility that business fluctuation could develop in the economy due to the plant and equipment investment cycle, or Juglar cycle. The Economic White Paper of 1962 also suggested that there would be an economic downturn due to adjustments in plant and equipment investment, referring to this phenomenon as a "structural recession." The theory of structural recession, which was widely debated at the time, argued that business activity would change as a result of fluctuations in private plant and equipment investment, and that this transformation would, in turn, result in changes in future economic growth. Plant and equipment investment during the Iwato boom had grown rapidly as firms competed to introduce modern technologies and expand operations in the face of impending import liberalization. (This was the period when economic planners confidently began to use the phrase "investment begets investment.") However, this unusual expansion of private plant and equipment investment to levels of more than 20 percent of gross national expenditure (GNE) had resulted in the unbalanced growth of the economy as a whole.

Against this background, the fact that plant and equipment investment has a two-tiered effect, in which there is first an increase in demand followed by an increase in productive capacity, would lead to a large supply and demand gap in plant and equipment investment itself as the economy adjusted to balanced growth. This adjustment process would result in a stagnation of private plant and equipment investment that might be prolonged for some time. At the same time, according to the structural recession theory, the pattern of economic growth after balanced growth had been achieved would have to be transformed into one in which a much greater share of GNE would be accounted for by fiscal spending and personal consumption. Of course, the implication of this analysis for economic policy was that positive measures should be taken to make this transition as smooth as possible by expanding fiscal spending and encouraging personal consumption. Unfortunately, Economic Planning Agency economists responsible for drafting the White Paper were well aware that any clear statement of this prescription for the economy would meet with strong opposition from budget authorities, and even stronger opposition from private industry, and they contented themselves with presenting a basic outline of their theory of imminent structural changes.

In fact, the ideas proposed by Shinohara and the White Paper proved to be an accurate assessment of the changes that were taking place during this period. Private plant and equipment investment in the manufacturing industry (firms capitalized at over ¥100 billion) reached a peak in the fourth quarter of 1961 and declined for four years thereafter, and the term "structural recession" became a catchphrase among economic analysts. As is often the case with catchphrases, however, the term was used indiscriminately and with little understanding of the theories of Shinohara and the White Paper. Often structural recession implied a justification for pessimism and an attitude of helplessness in the face of "chronic recession."

In any case, the implications of the theory of structural recession became crucial during the recession of 1965. If the theory was correct in arguing that the effects of the plant and investment cycle were playing a central role in the recession, then the potential of the economy for self-sustained recovery would remain weak regardless of the balance of payments situation or the application of monetary policies. Indeed, with the amelioration of the balance of payments problem and the relaxation of monetary restraints in 1965, it became clear that the domestic economy was responding only weakly and that monetary policy alone was no longer sufficient to deal with the gap between supply and demand. There was a clear need for positive fiscal policies to stimulate domestic demand. Government economic policy had reached a turning point.

It was against this background that the new cabinet of Eisaku Satō confronted its first economic policy decisions after taking over from Ikeda. Frankly, the new cabinet got off to a very poor start. After succeeding Ikeda in November 1964, Satō was faced with the task of halting what seemed a self-sustaining recession and developing new policies to lead the economy toward recovery. At least until the summer of 1965, new policies simply did not materialize, and the policy makers persisted in a stubborn adherence to past policies. Based on the experience of three previous postwar recessions, they were convinced that economic recovery could be achieved merely by relaxing restrictive monetary policies. Moreover, it must be remembered that policy makers were restricted during this period by the principle of balanced fiscal budgets, which had prevailed since the enactment of the Finance Act of 1947, and the view that long-term national bond issues were strictly taboo.

This left absolutely no room for a positive fiscal policy. For example, the Medium-Term Economic Plan, which was enacted in January 1965 to replace Ikeda's National Income-Doubling Plan, clearly stated that the government would not issue national bonds in the future. Moreover, the budget proposal for 1965 was drafted on the principle of fiscal neutrality, or no stimulation of the economy. Indeed, when revenues from corporation and indirect taxes fell below government projections, the budget was revised to reduce expenditure further by the implementation of a ¥100 billion reserve in the public works budget. These policies were completely inappropriate given the stagnation of the economy, and fiscal policy during the first half of 1965 had less the character of achieving balanced growth in the economy as a whole than of protecting the principle of yearly balances in the national budget itself.

Confronted with the reality of deepening recession, fiscal authorities finally recognized the necessity of a major reappraisal of the principles that had dominated fiscal policy in the past. In July 1965, the government rescinded the 10 percent reserve requirement on public works expenditure and carried out a drastic revision of the budget. The fiscal loan and investment program was expanded by ¥210 billion, and the issue of ¥250 billion worth of bonds was authorized under the Special Finance Law to cover the increase in fiscal spending. Moreover, the budget proposal for 1966 called for bond issues of ¥730 billion and a tax cut of ¥310 billion.

These changes represent an important shift of emphasis toward greater reliance on fiscal policy as a major anticyclical policy tool. The stimulation of domestic demand following the application of these policies demonstrated their effectiveness as a "pump-priming" policy as the economy began to recover at a steady pace. Moreover, the issue of national bonds provided the opportunity for private firms to increase their liquidity by participating in the bonds market, thus reducing their reliance on overloans from city banks. Nevertheless, beneficial as the new policies were, the issue of national bonds continued to be viewed as an irregular and dangerous policy. This view was shared by policy makers and private enterprises alike, and was based on poignant recollections of the vicious cycle between excessive issues of national bonds and inflation during the immediate postwar period.

However, it is simply not true that increases in the national debt automatically produce inflation. Rather, what is important is the extent to which fiscal authorities are able to guard against the attitude that once fiscal debt financing is accepted it can be increased at will whenever new funds are needed for public investment or to stimulate the economy. The attitude that national bonds were a panacea led to the extraordinary increase in national debt and the rampant inflation of the immediate postwar period. In contrast, fiscal authorities maintained firm control over the increase of national debt, at least from 1965 to 1975, and, while national bonds issues increased steadily during the period, deficit fiscal policy did not become a major source of inflationary pressures. Indeed, the principle of resorting to national bonds as a temporary measure remained a pillar of fiscal policy during this period and impeded the nurturing and development of a domestic capital market. For some time, a large majority of national bonds continued to be held by authorized financial institutions under a quota system and were redeemable only by the Bank of Japan. While this negative attitude toward fiscal policy, and especially toward fiscal deficits, persisted throughout the postwar period, fiscal policy began to play an increasing role in government policy after the recession of 1965, and the recession provided a precedent for its much greater role in the early 1970s.

5

AN ECONOMIC
SUPERPOWER

1. THE IZANAGI BOOM AND THE ADVENT
OF LONG-TERM PROSPERITY

The impetus for recovery from the recession of 1965 was provided by
the adoption of new fiscal policies to stimulate the economy as well as a
strong export drive by private industry. The increase of public investment
financed by national bonds and the implementation of a large tax cut
stimulated industrial production and plant and equipment capacity
utilization ratios, resulting finally in recovery from the prolonged stagnation of plant and equipment investment. The tax cut stimulated personal
consumption, and the sustained export drive led to spectacular export
increases (over 27 percent in 1965 and over 16 percent in 1966). Moreover,
the fact that industrial products with higher degrees of processing accounted for an increasingly larger share of total exports magnified the
effect through the demand-induced rise in production in related domestic
industries.

As suggested in Chapter Four, the development of such strategic
industries as steel and petrochemicals during the high-growth period of
the late 1950s and early 1960s stimulated related processing industries
such as automobiles, machinery, and synthetic fibers. During the recovery
from the 1965 recession, the expansion of exports by firms in the processing
industry stimulated parallel increases in the key industrial materials
industries, markedly strengthening the competitive abilities of both
sectors. The aftereffects of the recession continued to be evident until
summer 1966, and the number of corporate bankruptcies remained high
even in the following year. However, with the reduction of involuntary

inventory surpluses accompanying the resurgence of demand, private plant and equipment investment recovered from its four-year-long slump, and the economy was on the road toward the longest period of sustained high-speed growth in Japan's postwar history, the Izanagi boom.

New International Challenges. The greatest challenge facing policy makers as the economy emerged from the recession of 1965 was the problem of capital liberalization. With Japan's admission to the OECD on April 29, 1965, the country was committed not only to trade liberalization but also to the removal of controls on capital transactions, and by 1967 the government was under strong foreign pressure to take concrete steps to comply with the OECD agreement. Capital liberalization implied the relaxation, and eventual elimination, of domestic restrictions on the acquisition of controlling stock interests in Japanese companies by foreign firms, as well as on the establishment of foreign-owned subsidiaries in Japan. It would also liberalize direct foreign investment by domestic enterprises. With the exception of a small group of progressive economists, the prospect of opening up the economy to this extent brought a general panic similar to that in the early stages of import liberalization. The press, which had run headlines of THE SECOND COMING OF THE BLACK SHIPS when trade liberalization measures were announced in 1961, now had THE SECOND SECOND COMING OF THE BLACK SHIPS. These references to Admiral Perry's black ships in 1868 reflected the widely held view that the opening of the Japanese economy would result in the same kind of economic takeover by American multinationals that had taken place in Europe during the early 1960s. Whether it was based on a realistic interpretation of what had happened in Western Europe following capital liberalization or not, this view also dominated the thinking of MITI officials and industry leaders, and MITI assumed an extremely passive stance in formulating policies to promote liberalization.

This attitude was further supported by the principle of protecting domestic industry from foreign competition by restricting capital investment by foreign firms, which had been well established since the beginning of the Meiji period (1868–1912). Moreover, the low capitalization of Japanese firms, a consequence of the indirect financing system, made them easy targets for foreign acquisition, and MITI officials feared that once American multinationals invaded the Japanese market, they would be able to take over domestic firms and dominate major domestic markets. Mainstream MITI officials, who were firmly committed to the system of administrative guidance, cited existing conditions in the oil-refining industry and warned that even if their worst fears of takeovers did not materialize, it would be extremely difficult to maintain the system in an economy dominated by all-out war between domestic and foreign capital. This attitude of those officials most directly responsible for its implementation resulted in the creation of a characteristic Japanese-style of capital liberalization.

Complete liberalization was carried out only in those industries in which foreign competition was unlikely: saké brewing and the making of Japanese wooden clogs (*geta*), for example. The so-called 50 percent liberalization formula, the most characteristic Japanese-style liberalization system, limited direct foreign investment to joint ventures with at least 50 percent Japanese participation. In major strategic industries, such as automobiles and computers, MITI made every effort to postpone liberalization as long as possible. All these strategies to soften the effects of liberalization were accompanied by steps encouraging large-scale mergers among domestic firms, and horizontal mergers between firms capitalized at over ¥1 billion were a frequent occurrence after 1965.

The most controversial of these mergers, and the one that most clearly symbolized MITI's plan for industrial reorganization in the face of capital liberalization, was that between Yawata Steel and Fuji Steel to form New Japan Steel, the largest steel company in the world. The news that the merger was being planned was broken by the press on April 17, 1968, generating a highly publicized debate between MITI officials and those opposed to the merger. A group of progressive economists at the University of Tokyo, led by Professor Tadao Uchida, issued a formal statement opposing the merger, and the Tokyo High Court held public hearings on it during June 1969. The merger finally received the formal assent of the Fair Trade Commission in October 1969, but the period between April 1968 and March 31, 1969, when New Japan Steel formally came into existence, was one of intense debate concerning the propriety of these large-scale mergers and whether MITI's plans for industrial reorganization were economically sound.

During the same period, Japan was forced to confront a second challenge from abroad resulting from the devaluation of sterling by 14.3 percent in November 1967. This was quickly followed by devaluations in the sterling zone and in Northern Europe, and the resulting "gold rush" of 1968 led to a strengthening of "defense of the dollar" policies by the United States. Japan's balance of payments suffered a deficit in 1967 and, after stringent

Table 11. International Comparison of Japan's Production Levels

1. Total Domestic Production

	1950	1960	1965	1970	1975
U.S.	100.0	100.0	100.0	100.0	100.0
Japan	3.9	8.4	12.8	19.8	32.3
West Germany	8.1	14.2	16.6	18.9	28.1
France	10.0	12.0	14.3	15.0	21.6
U.K.	12.9	14.1	14.4	12.2	15.0
Italy	6.0	6.9	8.5	9.4	11.4

Source: Economic Planning Agency.

2. Industrial Production

	1958	1960	1963	1968	1972
U.S.	100.0	100.0	100.0	100.0	100.0
Japan	15.6	20.5	25.5	36.7	49.0
West Germany	23.0	24.0	24.0	23.1	25.9
France	21.2	20.2	20.6	19.7	23.6
U.K.	19.5	19.3	17.7	16.0	14.8
Italy	13.6	15.1	17.3	17.5	17.7
U.S.S.R.	59.4	63.6	71.9	81.6	95.7

Source: Estimates by Professor Miyohei Shinohara.

Table 12. Japan's Share of World Production of Major Industrial Products

	1960	1970
Steel (raw steel)	6.4%	③ 15.7%
Zinc	5.5	② 13.7
Aluminum	3.0	④ 7.5
Ships	20.7	① 48.3
Passenger cars	1.3	③ 14.2
Industrial vehicles	1.6	① 30.5
Radios	30.1	① 40.3
Televisions	21.5	① 30.4
Synthetic fibers	16.9	② 21.0
Nitrogenous fertilizer	9.4	③ 6.5

Note: Figures in circles represent Japan's rank in world production.
Source: Bank of Japan, *Kokusai hikaku tōkei* (Comparative international statistics).

monetary policies, had just begun to take a turn for the better when the pound devaluation was announced. The international currency crisis was viewed as a serious threat, and there was a good deal of discussion on the possibility of a devaluation of the yen. There was little recognition of the strength of the yen either in Japan or in international financial circles during this period, and rumors of a yen devaluation were widely accepted as an obvious outcome of the international situation. Ultimately, this did not happen, but the international currency crisis only encouraged Japanese economic planners to underestimate the yen's strength in international markets.[1]

Japan as Number Two. Despite the challenges posed by capital liberalization and the international currency crisis after devaluation of the pound, the most salient feature of the economy during the second half of the 1960s was the Izanagi boom. This journalistic nickname likened the boom to the creation of the islands of Japan by Izanagi, progenitor of the Sun Goddess Amaterasu Ōmikami. The boom lasted for fifty-seven months, from November 1965 to July 1970, outstripping the forty-two months of the Iwato boom. The average annual increase in nominal GNP was 11.8 percent for the period 1966–70, and the growth in real GNP was higher than 10 percent each year. These phenomenal rates of growth, sustained over a period of five years, symbolized the advent of long-term prosperity and a new period of high-speed economic growth.

A number of factors combined to make the Izanagi boom possible, and one of the most important was the impact of the United States on the international environment. The aggressive economic policies of the Kennedy and Johnson administrations, as well as increased military spending with the escalation of the Vietnam War, generated a boom in the American economy that lasted for one hundred and six months, or almost nine years. The Japanese economy was highly dependent on developments in the U.S. economy, and the pattern of domestic business upswings supported by export increases when the U.S. economy was flourishing was already well established. The booming U.S. economy and Vietnam War expenditures also had the indirect effect of rapidly increasing the total volume of world trade, with more rapid increases in the total value of world trade due to inflation. Thus the economic policies of Kennedy and Johnson contributed both directly and indirectly to the rapid expansion of Japanese exports.

The second major factor in the boom was the fact that the high-speed growth policies of Ikeda in the early 1960s were now bearing fruit, and the accumulated effects of these policies provided the groundwork for a new stage of high-speed growth. Sustained efforts to promote modernization through plant and equipment investment had produced remarkable improvements in the international competitiveness of Japanese industry, especially in the heavy and chemicals industries, which could now boast of relative superiority in international markets. Moreover, the share of total exports accounted for by these industries rose from 44 percent in 1960 to approximately 65 percent by the end of the boom in 1971. During the same period, 1966–71, exports increased at the phenomenal average annual rate of 20 percent, about twice the growth of total world trade, and after 1968 large surpluses in the international payments balance were taken for granted.

Indeed, the achievement of a strong competitive position in international trade and liberation from the limits on growth imposed by the balance of payments ceiling must be counted as the most direct factor in the strength and duration of the boom. One final factor that is often overlooked is the favorable domestic political environment for economic expansion. Eisaku Satō had inherited the policies of Ikeda, and the success of these policies in promoting economic growth not only enabled him to hold office longer than any other postwar prime minister (almost eight years) but also insured that he would continue to support these policies.

During this period of high-speed economic expansion, the growth of private plant and equipment investment once again assumed boom proportions, registering average annual increases of more than 20 percent. This figure does not match the annual 31.5 percent gains recorded during the Iwato boom, reflecting the fact that a better balance was struck between plant and equipment investment and personal consumption, housing investment, and exports. Nevertheless, yearly increases of 20 percent in plant and equipment investment were by no means inconsiderable in an economy that had assumed the international stature of Japan's in the late 1960s. While plant and equipment investment increases during this period resembled the expansion of the Iwato boom, a number of special features should be noted.

1. Capital liberalization replaced trade liberalization as the stimulus to investment of private enterprises.
2. A worldwide movement toward capital investment in "mammoth industrial plants," inspired in part by the Japanese example, prompted

private enterprises to seek even greater economies of scale in new modernization plans.

3. As labor shortages became increasingly severe, plant and equipment investment in labor-saving devices and automation assumed a greater proportion of the overall capital investment of small and medium enterprises.

4. The range of plant and equipment investment expanded to include tertiary industries such as transportation, wholesale and retail sales, and leisure industries, which moved quickly to modernize.

5. There was a second boom in the construction industry, supported by a general movement of large firms in every industry to build skyscrapers in major metropolitan areas for their corporate headquarters.

Economic theory holds that annual growth rates of 11 percent will increase the national economy by 1.7 times in five years and will triple it in ten years. In actual fact, the Japanese economy expanded at a phenomenal rate. Between 1966 and 1968, Japan's economy overtook those of France, England, and West Germany in rapid succession in terms of GNP and, by 1968, Japan was second only to the United States among advanced nations of the noncommunist world. Exactly one hundred years after the Meiji Restoration of 1868, which marked the beginning of contact with the West and the long struggle for modernization, Japan had recovered from World War II to become an economic superpower. However, the speed of Japan's expansion itself and the fact that many of the people most directly responsible for the "economic miracle" still had an inferiority complex toward the West meant that perceptions of Japan as an economic superpower developed much more quickly abroad than among the Japanese themselves.

This gap in perception resulted in a good deal of misunderstanding as Japanese delegates at international conferences continued to respond to demands for increased foreign aid efforts and speedier compliance with capital liberalization agreements by insisting that Japan was a poor country with an economy dominated by agriculture and small traditional enterprises. Foreign countries, and particularly the developing countries of South and Southeast Asia, understandably viewed such assertions as excuses, but many Japanese were genuinely convinced that Japan was still a backward country compared to America and Western Europe. Ironically, it was not until the high praise of Japan's economic performance by foreign observers began to turn to impatience at Japan's reluctance to open its markets and participate more actively in international economic assistance programs that serious discussion began in Japan of the country's responsibilities as a major economic power and its future role in the international community.

With the rapid growth of the economy as a whole and the expansion of the domestic market, productive capacity and the scale of large enterprises also increased at a remarkable pace. In 1970 Japan was the world's largest producer of ships, televisions, transistor radios, and trucks; it ranked second in synthetic fibers, synthetic resins (plastics), synthetic rubber, and newsprint; and third in steel, automobiles, chemical fertilizers, sulphuric acid, cement, and wool yarn. Moreover, in many of the latter industries Japan was already challenging the second-ranked producer, or even the leader. In the steel industry, for example, Japanese firms had introduced the world's most advanced technology and, by combining such technology in huge production complexes, had developed the most competitive steel industry in the world. Similarly, Japanese firms in the automobile industry had combined the development of competitive production facilities with aggressive behavior in international markets to expand their share of world trade.

Indeed, by 1971, Japan was the largest exporter of automobiles in the world and, in the same year, more Toyota Corollas were produced than any other make. During the same period, Japanese big business expanded at a fantastic rate and, in terms of scale of operations, labor productivity, and capitalization, reached levels at which they could compete favorably with American and European multinationals. In fact, as the largest firms began to approach the size of American multinationals they also began to outstrip their largest European competitors by wider and wider margins. These huge firms were developing not only in the steel and automobile industries, but also in home appliances, heavy electrical machinery, industrial machinery, textiles, chemicals, plate glass, and cement. Viewed in this way, the period from 1965 to 1970 was the most brilliant of the Japanese "economic miracle." However, it was also during this period that the country experienced most painfully the distortions resulting from high-speed economic growth.[2]

Shōwa Genroku: "The Age of Peace and Prosperity." As the Izanagi boom progressed and Western perceptions that Japan was in the midst of an "economic miracle" began to gain currency among the Japanese, a new mood of peace and prosperity transformed Japanese society. The term "Shōwa Genroku," which enjoyed a great vogue in the mass media, was coined by Takeo Fukuda, later to become prime minister, both to describe the ebullience of the period and to satirize the showiness of new urban life-styles. The Genroku era (1688–1704) was one of brilliant activity in literature and the arts, of unprecedented prosperity, and of prolonged peace, and Fukuda's Shōwa Genroku refers to the reoccurrence of such an atmosphere in the Shōwa period (1926 to the present). Moreover, the brilliance of the Genroku era is symbolized by the rise of the "townsmen's culture," the culture of the non-samurai populations of Japan's major urban centers. Art and literature took as their themes the Kabuki and the pleasure quarters, and urban life was characterized by a concern for the new, the spectacular, and the not quite respectable.

It was in this sense that Fukuda's phrase concealed a rather bitter lampooning of the new life-styles that developed with the rapid rise in personal consumption. Unused to their prosperity, people had a tendency to spend foolishly, run wildly from one fad to another, and adopt life-styles more to shock their peers than from any sense of personal identity. Nevertheless, prophetic as it may have been of the enormous problems that would emerge in the early 1970s, Fukuda's implicit criticism of urban life-styles during this period was soon lost as Shōwa Genroku was adopted by the media as a celebration of the new prosperity.

Huge increases in personal consumption expenditure during this period reflected the rapid rise in income resulting from high-speed growth in a full employment economy. Indeed, prolonged high-speed growth during the Izanagi boom completed the transformation of the labor market, and labor shortages became more severe each year. An indication of just how serious the problem became is provided by the critical index of job offers to job seekers, which reached 1.4 in both 1969 and 1970. This ratio also suggests how strong the bargaining position of labor was. Wage increases won during the spring wage offensive escalated from 10.6 percent in 1966 (¥3,273) to 18.5 percent (¥8,983) in 1970. During the same period, annual bonuses increased from three months' to four months' basic wages. By the end of the boom, one of the slogans of the spring wage offensive had become "¥10,000 increase in basic monthly wages for everyone," and this was no longer considered unrealistic.

Large increases won by workers in the private sector were followed by salary increases for public employees, based on recommendations by the National Personnel Authority. Moreover, these increases, which in the past had often lagged behind those in the private sector due to "fiscal considerations," achieved parity in 1970, and the practice of attempting to hold down increases or delay them was discontinued. The improvement of salary levels for public employees, in fact, was one of the most conspicuous results of the shift to full employment. The basic monthly wages of workers in the manufacturing industries more than doubled during the five years of the Izanagi boom from ¥40,000 to ¥81,000 and, even after adjusting these figures for inflation, real wages increased by more than half.

Nevertheless, while Japan had the second largest GNP in the noncommunist world in 1970, it only ranked nineteenth in real per capita GNP. This reflects the fact that productivity and incomes were still low in agriculture and the distribution industries compared to the United States and Europe, and that the high levels of productivity in the manufacturing industries were still not sufficient to make up the difference. Nevertheless, hourly wages in the manufacturing industries finally reached levels comparable to those in the United States and Western Europe, thus realizing the long-term goal established by the Japanese labor movement in the early 1960s. In 1973, average hourly wages reached $1.91, and, while this was still below West Germany's $2.94, they were higher than England's $1.82 and France's $1.85.

As suggested above, the general rise in incomes during this period did not completely eliminate the dual structure, and there were rapid changes in the social class structure. The agricultural population suffered further declines, and by 1970 workers in primary industry accounted for less than 20 percent of the total employed population. During the same period, the share of blue-collar workers increased to 34 percent and that of white-collar workers to 22 percent. Together they accounted for more than half the employed population, and the number of families that considered themselves "middle class" also exceeded 50 percent. This consciousness of being "middle class" may mean little more than a vague sense of being situated on the social scale somewhere between the lower and upper classes, but it was very important in the transformation of Japanese society. The new life-styles and personal consumption habits developed by this new middle class were major factors in making Japan an economic superpower not only in terms of GNP but also as a major mass consumption market for domestic and foreign products.

The new society was characterized by an abundance of "things," and for the new middle class the phrase "Shōwa Genroku" symbolized the

**Table 13.   Rates of Popularization of
Consumer Durables in Urban Households**

	Over 20%	Over 50%
Before 1955	Cameras	Radios, sewing machines, bicycles
1956–60	Black-and-white TV's, washing machines, electric fans, rice cookers	Western-style chests of drawers
1961–65	Refrigerators, vacuum cleaners, kerosene or gas heaters	Cameras, washing machines, electric *kotatsu* (under-table heaters)
1966–70	Color TV's, automobiles, Western-style living-room sets, stainless steel sinks	Vacuum cleaners, kerosene or gas heaters
1971–75	Western-style beds, electric organs	Color TV's, stereos, stainless steel sinks, gas water heaters

Source: Economic Planning Agency.

advent of a period in which they were at long last able to enjoy the fruits of high-speed economic growth. The boom in personal consumption was again led by electric household appliances. Black-and-white television sets began to disappear in 1971, by which time half the families in urban areas and one family in three in rural areas owned color sets. By 1973, the popularization of color television had reached almost 100 percent. Similarly, a number of other popular new consumer durables replaced older appliances: refrigerators with freezer units, fully automatic washing machines, microwave ovens, tape recorders, stereo equipment, stainless steel sinks, gas water heaters, and electric blankets. Interior furnishings, Western-style living-room and dining-room sets, beds, and carpets also enjoyed a great vogue. The popularization of kerosene and gas heaters doomed the traditional firewood and charcoal business, and dealers in lamp oil were forced to switch to distributing propane gas. Charcoal dealers disappeared one after another, with only a few large makers remaining to supply the dwindling demand from *yakitori* (broiled chicken) restaurants.

Clothing reflected the mood of the period, and both Western-style clothing and kimono were rapidly changing in style. With the rising prestige of the new white-collar class, blue-collar workers and workers in traditional industries began to imitate its clothing styles and, after working hours, it became impossible to guess a person's occupation by a casual glance at his clothing. A vogue for kimono accompanied the new popularity of tea ceremony and ikebana lessons, and dress at weddings, whether

Western or Japanese-style, became the subject of intense competition among women. Indeed, it was during this period that the Japanese custom of throwing large, expensive parties at famous hotels to celebrate almost any occassion became well established.

The biggest winners in the large-scale increase in wages were the new school graduates, and the increased affluence of young workers gave rise to a new journalistic catchphrase to describe their life-style, the "singles aristocracy." Even though young, unmarried workers still received relatively low wages under the lifetime employment system, disproportionate increases in starting wages and revisions of the income tax system that reduced their share of the tax burden enabled young, male workers to spend money on hair driers, clothes, televisions, stereos, sports equipment, and entertainment. Office girls were inclined to spend money on expensive clothes or weekend trips with friends, and the custom of groups of young women saving up for a trip abroad together before marriage became increasingly popular.

Perhaps the most striking symbol of the new affluence was the popularization of the automobile. In 1970, 22 percent of all families owned one and, by 1975, the rate had risen to 41 percent. Moreover, the automobile during this period gained popularity as rapidly in rural areas as in the cities. On the one hand, weekend drives or dinner at suburban drive-ins became a popular mode of recreation. On the other hand, the exodus of office workers to suburbs further away from the city began to make the automobile indispensable both for commuting and for getting around in suburban areas where mass transportation was not available. Farm families were forced to adopt urban consumption patterns, including the purchase of automobiles, in order to keep their children from leaving for the city and to make it possible for the heir to find a wife.

Another symbol of the new middle class was a tremendous leisure boom, supported by the reduction of working hours and the institution of the five-day week in many large companies. A fad for golf spread among young and old, male and female, and in 1974 the total acreage of golf courses and practice ranges in Japan reached 700 square kilometers, or roughly 1.2 times the area of Tokyo.

For the majority of Japanese people, Shōwa Genroku was a new period of affluence and rising expectations, but the vogue for miniskirts was accompanied by the appearance of long hair and hippies, and violence erupted on campuses throughout the country from 1967 to 1970. The suicide of Yukio Mishima in 1970 was the climax of a period of intense unrest among students and intellectuals, who were questioning the values of the society that had made the "economic miracle" possible and, indeed, the "economic miracle" itself. In part a rebellion against the establishment, this movement nevertheless raised specific issues concerning the consequences of the single-minded pursuit of economic growth and Japan's role in international affairs. Moreover, there were other indications that the brilliance of Shōwa Genroku masked basic problems in the country's economy. The most important of these was the result of a serious imbalance between the expansion of the private economy and public social overhead investment in the economic infrastructure and in welfare.

The increased affluence and the steady expansion of the economy served only to highlight the inadequacy of economic policies in the public sector. The National Income-Doubling Plan was revised a number of times during Satō's eight years as prime minister. However, the economic plans that replaced it consistently underestimated the performance of the economy, and the old pattern of public investment lagging behind actual increases in tax revenues once again became characteristic of fiscal budget policy. This resulted in the relative paucity of public spending for social overhead capital and welfare, which, in turn, exacerbated social and economic problems, inviting more social instability. For example, the failure of new road construction to keep pace with the rapid automobile expansion resulted in serious traffic congestion and large increases in road deaths. Traffic-related deaths increased from 600,000 to 1 million between 1966 and 1970, a 50 percent increase in five years.

Similarly, the increased availability of affordable consumer durables served to intensify the feeling among middle-class families that they were doomed to a "rabbit-hutch" existence. One of the motivations for the Japanese worker's famous devotion to work is his desire to own a larger home, and it is the dream of every man to move his family out of a cramped apartment into a house of his own. However, since land prices rise much more quickly than monthly salaries, this dream is seldom realized. Even if he manages to save enough to make the down payment on a long-term mortgage, the best that the typical employee can hope for is a small tract of land in a far-flung suburb with, due to the slow pace of public investment in new mass transportation facilities, long commutes on packed trains to and from his job in the city.

In the early 1970s the ideal of the new middle class was a condominium in new architect-designed *manshon* complexes near a park in the city, but it was far beyond the reach of the vast majority. Moreover, attempts by the government to rectify this situation only produced contradictory results. The land tax system was revised in 1969 to provide a temporary reduction of selective taxes on profits from land transfers. The aim was to encourage landowners to sell their land to residential housing developers, thus stabilizing the price of land and moderating the demand for housing. In fact, the result of this measure was the creation of a new class of nouveau riche. Ninety-five of the one hundred "wealthiest men" in 1971 were members of this new class who had made their fortune by taking advantage of the new land tax. Needless to say, the sensational press coverage of this phenomenon intensified feelings that the government merely supported the unfair acquisition of wealth by people in a position to exploit the predicament of average city dwellers.

The proliferation of disposable products and overpackaging created a serious problem in dealing with the mounting quantities of waste. Moreover, the vicious cycle of high repair costs and vanishing repair shops produced the attitude that it was, for example, easier and cheaper to buy new umbrellas or shoes than to have old ones repaired. A similar attitude developed in private industry. Rising costs for collection of recyclable materials and low prices for imported raw materials convinced most managers that it was more efficient to import new supplies of raw materials than to recycle scrap material. In short, the problem of waste disposal grew in direct proportion to increases in GNP. At the same time, the growing consumers' movement resisted government projects to locate new garbage disposal facilities in crowded urban areas. The same groups began to protest against the dual price system, the increase of defective merchandise, and the steadily worsening pollution problem. Prime Minister Satō's principle accomplishments during his eight years in office were not in economic planning but in foreign policy (the Japan–Republic of Korea Basic Relations Treaty, the reversion of Okinawa, agreement with the U.S. on automatic extension of the Security Treaty, and Expo '70). In part because Satō himself was not well versed in economic planning, however, his economic policy was borrowed almost intact from Ikeda's National Income-Doubling Plan.

The facile assumption that the policies pursued so successfully by Ikeda in the early 1960s could meet the new challenges of the "economic miracle" persisted long after it had become clear that the free market system and the unique institution of administrative guidance were insufficient by themselves. The consumers' movement was a symptom of this lack of creative policy making, and was symbolic of the emergence of new interest groups no longer satisfied with the single-minded pursuit of large annual increases in GNP. The most striking example of the consequences of this failure was pollution.[3]

Expo '70 and the Pollution Problem. The year 1970 was not only the peak of the Izanagi boom but also of high-speed economic growth. It was the year of Expo '70, the first world fair held in Asia, and the year in which the problem of pollution burst upon the national consciousness. The pollution problem symbolized more than anything else a growing dissatisfaction with high-speed economic growth, and it was during this period that citizens' movements began to use such slogans as "To hell with GNP." Moreover, soon after the end of Expo '70, the economy slipped into a prolonged recession, triggering large increases in Japan's balance of payments surplus. These increases account in part for the radical change in American economic policy in 1971 that Japanese call the "Nixon shock." In this sense, too, 1970 may be considered a crucial year in the postwar history of the economy.

Expo '70 opened in Osaka on March 14, 1970, with exhibitions from seventy-seven countries. During the six months of the fair, it was visited by more than 64 million people. Its theme, "Progress and Harmony for Mankind," served to demonstrate to the world the level of modernization and economic development that Japan had achieved in the one hundred years since the Meiji Restoration. In fact, Expo contributed much more in encouraging the Japanese to look outward, and thus to the development of an international consciousness within the country. Of the 64 million visitors to Expo '70, only 1.7 million were foreigners. The 62 million Japanese visitors represented 60 percent of the Japanese population in 1970. With 340,000 visitors a day, there were long lines at the popular American and Soviet pavilions, and large numbers collapsed from exhaustion or heat stroke.

The economic impact of Expo was enormous. Direct investment for construction projects related to Expo, including freeways, the Osaka subway system, and the Osaka International Airport, reached ¥350 billion, and related personal consumption expenditure amounted to about ¥330 billion during the six months of the fair. During the same period, passengers on the Tōkaidō Shinkansen increased by 34 percent, hotel guests in the Osaka area by 58 percent, and purchases of color film by 60 percent. Expo is also considered to have been a major factor in the rapid increase in foreign travel after 1970.

Table 14.   The Increase in Pollutant Emissions, 1960–70

1.   Sulfur Dioxide (SO_2, 1,000 tons)

	1960	1970	Increase (%)
Due to consumption of fuel oil	1,069	4,976	
Heavy fuel oil	1,052	4,880	16.6
Light fuel oil	17	96	18.9
Due to consumption of coal	452	263	−5.3
Other factors	132	400	11.7
Total emissions	1,653	5,799	13.4

2.   Nitrogen Dioxide (NO_2, 1,000 tons)

	1960	1970	Increase (%)
Fixed sources of emissions	536	1,390	10.0
Liquid fuels	148	945	20.3
Gaseous fuels	33	150	16.3
Solid fuels	336	196	−5.3
Others	18	98	18.4
Mobile sources of emissions (vehicles)	153	571	14.1
Total emissions	689	1,961	11.0

The unexpected success of Expo '70 was clouded by a series of incidents that brought into focus the enormity of Japan's pollution problem. Industrial pollution and environmental damage had already become serious issues after the outbreak of Minamata disease in 1953 caused by mercury poisoning of the water around Minamata village in Kyushu's Kumamoto Prefecture by the Chisso Fertilizer Company. In 1958, there had been rioting by fishermen against wood pulp factories along the Edo River and in 1959, the outbreak of Yokkaichi asthma, caused by sulfuric oxide emissions from big petrochemical complexes, had resulted in the first citizens' movement against the location of *konbinato* in their respective areas. The cadmium poisoning of rivers by mining companies became an issue with the outbreak in 1959 of Itai-itai disease in the Jinzū River area of Toyama Prefecture, and a second Minamata disease epidemic began in the Agano River area of Niigata Prefecture. It was also during the late

1950s and early 1960s that the first cases of Thalidomide babies and of SMON disease were reported, raising the issue of the government's responsibility for establishing standards and testing procedures for pharmaceuticals.

Against this background, the government finally promulgated the Pollution Countermeasures Basic Law in 1967, which set standards for several kinds of pollution: air, water, noise, vibration, subsidence, and soil (added in 1970). In 1969, the Special Measures for Pollution-Related Damage to Health Law was established to provide financial relief for the treatment of victims of the epidemics at Minamata, Yokkaichi, the Agano River area, and the Jinzū River area. However, the government's attitude toward the pollution problem before 1970 is illustrated by the fact that the original Pollution Countermeasures Basic Law contained the stipulation that antipollution measures must be "in harmony with the healthy growth of the economy."

Confronted with the problems posed by impending capital liberalization, private enterprises attempted to avoid or delay investing in antipollution facilities, and the absence of strong governmental measures enabled them to ignore the rising public outcry. Moreover, in many cases, the new pollution problems were being encountered for the first time in the world, and the government simply lacked the scientific expertise to define the nature and scope of pollution-related incidents. Even when the cause of a new pollution disease had been determined, the sectionalism inherent in Japanese bureaucracy often served to delay the formulation of effective countermeasures. While a certain progress had been made in considering antipollution measures in new industrial cities and areas designated for industrial development, little attention was paid to scientific evidence concerning the scale of the problem, and higher priority was placed on narrowly defined questions of industrial efficiency than on antipollution facilities. Despite the growing awareness of the pollution problem, it was virtually impossible to make needed changes in development plans, and the regional development program only intensified the problem.

In addition to industrial pollution, environmental damage in Japan's dense urban areas had become a serious issue. The rising living standards and changing life-styles of the new urban middle class also resulted in new environmental problems. By 1970, air pollution by exhaust gases, river pollution due to synthetic detergents, and waste disposal problems due to disposable containers and the tendency to replace consumer durables had reached serious proportions. Thus, just as Japan was celebrating its new international status as an economic superpower, the country was rocked by a series of major pollution-related incidents, whose gravity left a deep impression both on the Japanese and on foreign observers.

In May 1970, a public sensation was created when the National Medical Students Union published the results of a study in which toxic levels of lead had been detected in blood samples taken from citizens living near a busy intersection in Tokyo's Ushigome district. The National Police Agency took widely publicized steps to restrict the flow of traffic at busy intersections, and MITI announced plans to promote a switch to unleaded gasoline. In the same month, cadmium-poisoned rice was discovered in the same area of Toyama Prefecture in which Itai-itai disease had broken out earlier, raising the issue of soil pollution for the first time. In July the first cases of photochemical smog poisoning were reported among high school students in the Suginami area of Tokyo, and in August a citizens' group from the village of Taganoura Bay filed suit against the area's pulp manufacturing company, which had created a disastrous sludge problem by dumping waste in the bay. Also in late 1970, the Maritime Safety Agency disclosed that it had substantiated charges that Ishihara Industries in Yokkaichi was disposing of liquid sulfuric acid waste by pumping it into the ocean.

The mass media gave wide coverage to these incidents and launched an aggressive campaign to arouse public opinion. This campaign was highly successful in driving home the point that pollution was no longer limited to a few isolated areas or a few rivers but was threatening extensive environmental damage throughout the Japanese archipelago. Large-scale demonstrations led by citizen's movements, focusing their attack on pollution by private industry, demanded stronger government actions against offending firms. In late July 1970, the cabinet established the Central Pollution Countermeasures Headquarters. The result was the famous "Pollution Diet" from November 24 to December 18, 1970, which removed the phrase "in harmony with the healthy growth of the economy" from the Pollution Countermeasures Basic Law and revised or passed fourteen antipollution laws.

In July 1971, the government created the Environment Agency, which combined all the sections and bureaus dealing with pollution in the various ministries into a single agency responsible for pollution prevention and environmental protection. During the same period, antipollution measures were adopted by regional and local governments throughout the country. Also in 1971 and 1972, high court decisions were handed down in the four big pollution cases (Minamata, Yokkaichi, the Agano River area, and the Jinzū River area) awarding victories to the citizens' groups and severely criticizing the conduct of the companies involved and the government authorities responsible for pollution prevention.

In this way, the implementation of strong antipollution measures and administrative reforms proceeded in fits and starts as the government began to respond to public demands for positive action. Nevertheless, 1970 marks the turning point in antipollution policy and the beginning of one of the most effective industrial clean-up campaigns in history. Recently, environmental standards have been strengthened even more, and good progress has been made in reversing the effects of air and water pollution. However, the progress since 1970 should not obscure the fact that prolonged neglect of the problem resulted in great damage to the environment and huge numbers of innocent victims. The wasted lives of the people of Minamata are only the most extreme example of human loss, and the mistrust and resentment of the late 1960s and early 1970s toward private industry and the government remain deeply rooted today. Moreover, private industry's tardiness in introducing antipollution facilities meant that they had to bear higher installation expenses after the period of high-speed growth.

While the pollution problem affected the advanced nations in various ways, Japan's case must be considered unique. The cumulative effects of high-speed growth and intense urban concentration are suggested by the facts that in 1970, 73 percent of industrial production was concentrated in a narrow belt along the east coast, and 32 percent of the nation's population was living on 1 percent of the land. Thirty-three million people were living within thirty miles of one of the three largest cities (Tokyo, Osaka, and Nagoya). As a great number of these people had experienced the hardships of the postwar period, their single-minded commitment to high-speed economic growth and better living standards is, perhaps, understandable. Nevertheless, their indifference to environmental protection during the period of high-speed growth and the long delay in the shift of values regarding antipollution measures resulted in the most terrible pollution disasters in the world, and Minamata is still a painful memory for the Japanese.

2. THE "NIXON SHOCK" AND THE INTERNATIONAL CURRENCY CRISIS

The Yen's Achilles Heel. One aspect of the policies of Satō was to try to maintain the ¥360 exchange rate even after the balance of payments surplus had become a permanent feature of the economy and foreign exchange reserves began to increase. In this and the following sections, I would like to consider the consequences of this policy for the domestic economy and for international relations immediately before the "Nixon shock."

The journalistic phrase "internal weakness, external strength" refers to the contradictory phenomenon of rapidly rising consumer prices in the domestic sector at a time when wholesale prices remained the most stable among the advanced nations. The productivity differentials inflation that had made its appearance in the early 1960s continued through the Izanagi boom, and the "internal weakness, external strength" problem was a direct outgrowth of this. While wholesale prices did begin to rise more quickly in the late 1960s, the disparity between wholesale and consumer prices actually widened. Consumer prices, which posted average annual increases of 4.6 percent from 1965 to 1968, rose 6.4 percent in 1969 and 7.3 percent in 1970.

There were a number of special factors in these increases, such as large price rises following a drought in 1970, but the basic cause of the acceleration of inflation was the exacerbation of the wage-price spiral as high-speed growth continued under conditions of full employment. The tight labor market produced wage increases of 16 to 17 percent each year, and it was impossible for small and medium-size enterprises, farmers, and firms in the distribution and service industries to keep up with increased labor costs through productivity improvements alone. Enterprises in the low-productivity sectors had no choice but to pass on higher labor costs to the consumer. This pattern is the same as that which emerged in the early 1960s. In 1969 and 1970, however, increased labor costs and higher prices on the international market for raw materials began to affect the prices of consumer goods produced by large firms as well. Labor's strong bargaining position enabled workers to win large raises in real wages despite inflation, but for those on fixed incomes this spiral of wages and prices was a source of considerable anxiety.

On the other hand, among advanced nations, Japan's wholesale prices remained the most stable during this period of worldwide inflation. At 3.4 percent in 1969 and 2.3 percent in 1970, increases were higher than the annual average of 1.6 percent from 1965 to 1968. These higher levels of increase may be explained in part by higher costs and oligopolistic pricing, but the most important factors were increases in prices for imports of raw materials and for exports. As indicated by the data in Figure 11, however, the disparity between wholesale and consumer prices widened dramatically during the late 1960s and early 1970s.

This contradictory phenomenon reflects the fact that the purchasing power of the yen was being steadily eroded by inflation at home and abroad at the same time that the ¥360 exchange rate—combined with steady increases in productivity and inflation abroad—was serving to increase the international competitiveness of Japanese products. Despite the new competitiveness achieved by what amounted to a face-lift for the economy during the Izanagi boom, the yen remained undervalued at the ¥360 exchange rate, leading to foreign charges that Japan had an unfair advantage, thus complicating Japan's international relations. Both domestic inflation and international trade frictions could have been solved by moderate adjustments in the exchange rate. However, as we shall see, the political situation at home made such a move impossible, and the policies aimed at curbing inflation only served to worsen trade frictions.[4]

An Unprecedented Tight Money Policy despite Trade Surpluses. The period of mounting international balance of payments surpluses began in 1968 and 1969. From the beginning of the National Income-Doubling Plan in 1961 to mid-1968, Japan's foreign currency reserves had fluctuated around $2 billion, a figure considered by economy planners to be the "scrimmage line" for domestic policy. When deficits in the balance of payments threatened to lower reserves to below $2 billion, stringent monetary policies were implemented to suppress domestic demand. Conversely, when the balance of payments situation improved sufficiently to maintain foreign currency reserves at $2 billion, fiscal and monetary authorities could switch to expansionary policies. Unlike economic planners in Western Europe, Japanese planners never attempted to expand foreign currency reserves or convert the increases into gold reserves. Rather, as we have seen, the most important goals up to 1969 were the realization of annual economic growth rates of 10 percent, the promotion of Japan's competitiveness through plant and equipment investment in ultramodern technologies, and a steady balance of payments situation. Of course, in the long run, these policies proved more far-sighted than those pursued by Western Europe in terms of maintaining and strengthening Japan's competitiveness in international markets.

Given these policy objectives, occasional deficits in the balance of payments did not mean that the yen was inherently undervalued. Indeed,

Table 15. Fluctuations in Japan's International Balance of Payments

($1 million; annual averages)

	Period of reconstruction	Period when economic independence was achieved	Period of high-speed growth	Period of large trade surplus	Period of adjustments to "oil shock"
Trade balance	−233	−360	686	6,105	3,411
(Exports)	(661)	(2,041)	(5,573)	(21,562)	(48,522)
(Imports)	(894)	(2,401)	(4,887)	(15,457)	(45,111)
Invisible transfers	100	211	−492	−1,701	−4,927
Transfer payments	316	12	−77	−261	−320
Current balance	183	−137	117	4,143	−1,836
Long-term capital balance	−8	23	−115	−2,807	−4,616
Basic balance	175	−114	2	1,339	−6,452
Short-term capital balance (corrected for errors)	17	33	68	2,680	−78
Overall balance	192	−81	70	4,019	−6,530
Changes in foreign reserves	143	−58	182	3,869	−1,850
Others					
Changes in debt to official overseas organs	49	23	112	150	−4,680

Note: − indicates deficit.
Sources: 1. Before 1962, MITI, *Sengo no Nihon bōeki nijūnen shi* (A twenty-year history of Japan's postwar foreign trade).
2. From 1962, Bank of Japan, *Kokusai shūshi tōkei* (International balance of payments statistics).

until 1970, the application of moderately stringent monetary policies when excess domestic demand led to a worsening balance of payments situation had always effectively suppressed demand and restored a healthy payments balance. In short, economic planners worked on the principle that as long as economic growth could be sustained at 10 percent a year over the medium and long terms, the balance of payments situation would take care of itself. However, with the advent of the full employment economy and increased labor costs, these policies also resulted in inflationary trends in consumer prices.

From mid-1968, Japan's international trade pattern changed radically and, once foreign currency reserves began to exceed the $2 billion level

Figure 11. Internal Weakness, External Strength: Price Differences between Japan and Major OECD Countries

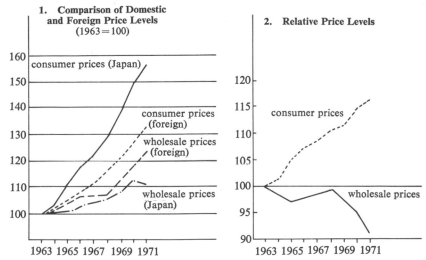

1. Comparison of Domestic and Foreign Price Levels (1963=100)

2. Relative Price Levels

Notes: 1. Foreign prices are the simple arithmetical average of prices in the six major OECD countries excluding Japan (U.S., U.K., W. Germany, France, Italy, Canada).

2. Relative price levels were obtained by dividing Japan's price indexes by the price index averages of the six OECD countries listed above.

by a wide margin, it became impossible to halt the trend toward large surpluses. Foreign currency reserves increased to $3.5 billion at the end of 1969, $4.4 billion at the end of 1970, and $7.6 billion in June 1971. Moreover, these increases occurred despite the implementation of the so-called yen shift policy by foreign exchange authorities. Rather than converting all the surplus into foreign currency reserves, it encouraged foreign exchange banks and private firms to repay outstanding loans held by foreign financial institutions. Besides moderating nominal increases in foreign currency reserves, this policy also made good economic sense in terms of improving the financial position of domestic enterprises and banks. However, given the magnitude of the surpluses that still occurred, it did little to stem the rising tide of criticism from abroad. During this period, the only two countries among the advanced nations that were recording substantial trade surpluses were Japan and West Germany, and both were subjected to a good deal of criticism concerning their undervalued currencies. The pace at which Japan advanced its share of the overall trade surplus held by the advanced nations is revealed by

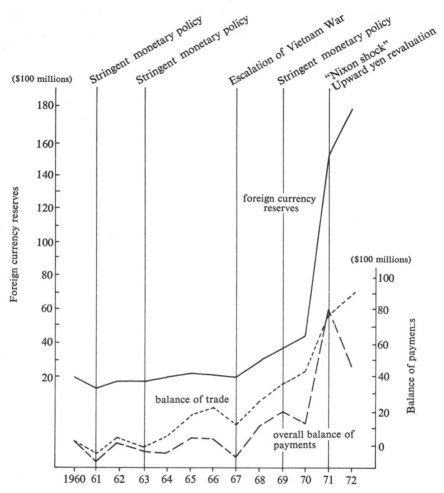

Figure 12. Large-Scale Balance of Payments Surplus and the Rapid Increase in Foreign Currency Reserves

trade surplus figures for the OECD countries as a whole. In 1969 and 1970, Japan's share of the $3.9 billion annual trade surplus recorded by the OECD countries was $2 billion. In 1971, OECD countries had an overall trade surplus of $7.4 billion, of which $5.8 billion was accounted for by Japan.

Despite this steady increase in annual balance of payments surpluses, stringent monetary policies were implemented in September 1969 that continued until fall 1970. This was an unprecedented decision, but a

174 AN ECONOMIC SUPERPOWER

number of factors may be cited to explain why policy makers viewed it as being essential.

1. The pace of consumer price increases had accelerated, giving rise to fears that the economy was overheating. Moreover, a surge of inflation in international markets was affecting domestic wholesale prices, threatening to force consumer prices up.
2. There was strong pressure from Prime Minister Satō to stabilize prices before Expo '70. This was combined with a general feeling that as the host, Japan had to take appropriate measures to provide a good atmosphere for this important event, including policies to bring inflation under control.
3. Policy makers hoped that the early implementation of anti-inflationary measures would effectively check inflation and bring only a moderate downturn in the business cycle, and that long-term expansion of the economy could be maintained at a high growth plateau.

This had been the strategy for the stringent monetary policies of 1967, and it had been extremely successful in moderating price increases without producing a major cyclical downturn. Unfortunately, it was not successful in 1969 and 1970, and the economic situation after the end of Expo '70 was similar to the aftermath of the Tokyo Olympics. Domestic businesses slumped and it proved extremely difficult to increase private plant and equipment investment. Moreover, monetary stringency did have the usual effect of causing a stagnation in demand for imports and an increase in exports, and this combined with a stabilization of import prices to produce even larger balance of payments surpluses. Thus, while the implementation of stringent monetary policies was appropriate for checking inflation, it was not effective in avoiding a large-scale recession, and seriously exacerbated international frictions resulting from Japan's trade surpluses.

More important, in retrospect, is the fact that Japan missed an important opportunity to implement an upward revaluation of the yen independently. In fact, secret investigations into the possibility of an upward revaluation and its effects were carried out within the Ministry of Finance during November and December of 1969, but a number of domestic political factors combined to frustrate any hope that these investigations would result in concrete policies. First, Japan had experienced an international payments deficit as recently as 1967 and, despite criticism from abroad, there was no consensus among economic planners that balance of payments surpluses had become a permanent feature of the economy. Even when policy makers agreed that an upward revaluation of the yen would eventually become necessary, they viewed it as something to be considered in the distant future. Moreover, this view was shared by the business community, and there simply was no public support for upward revaluation either as an alternative to stringent monetary policies or as an appropriate policy to follow them.

Second, Prime Minister Satō, who had staked his political reputation on a smooth settlement of the return of Okinawa to Japanese sovereignty without nuclear weapons, was strongly opposed to the idea of a yen revaluation, which he believed would complicate negotiations with the United States. Third, the fact that the ¥360 rate had been maintained so long had the contradictory function of making revaluation, which was actually an economic and administrative problem, into a difficult political problem. A book entitled *The Upward Revaluation of the Yen: What Will Happen When It Comes?* (published by the prestigious Nihon Keizai Shimbun-sha) topped the best-sellers list, and LDP politicians had reason to worry about the political ramifications of revaluation. Finally, perhaps the most important political factor was the delicate situation within the LDP itself. The question of when Satō would step down as prime minister and who would be his successor had divided the party, and there was little likelihood that LDP politicians on either side of the factional struggle would champion an unpopular policy.

All these domestic factors combined to make revaluation a political impossibility in the period before Expo '70, and when Expo had started any change in the exchange rate was unthinkable. Thus, an important opportunity was missed, and the issue of the ¥360 exchange rate did not arise again until after the end of Expo, when surging balance of payments surpluses intensified international frictions and contributed to the deterioration of trade relations with the United States.[5]

Deteriorating U.S.–Japan Trade Relations: The Quagmire Negotiations. Noncommunist nations are characterized by both trade surplus countries and trade deficit countries, thus giving rise to the problems of balance of payments adjustments and exchange rate adjustments. Ironically, the country most directly threatened by Japan's strong competitive position was the United States. The strengthening of the yen on international markets coincided with the lowered prestige of the dollar, and Japan's trade surplus affected the international currency system, in which the dollar was the key currency.

Frictions between the strong yen and the declining dollar were most directly reflected in the trade imbalance between the two countries. U.S. trade deficits with Japan grew from $400 million in 1967 to $1.2 billion in 1968, $1.6 billion in 1969, and $1.5 billion in 1970. Against this background, trade relations between the two became increasingly strained, even while substantial progress was being made in such diplomatic negotiations as the reversion of Okinawa and cooperation in regional security. While the focus of economic clashes would shift in 1971 to the revaluation of the yen, the central issues from 1969 to early 1970 were the trade imbalance and the remaining Japanese import restrictions after the first round of trade liberalization in 1961. On June 9, 1970, Zenith filed a suit charging that Japan was dumping television sets in the United States, and, during the same period, negotiations were bogged down by disputes concerning tariffs and Japanese restrictions on American imports.

The most unproductive of the several economic conflicts between the two countries was the dispute over limiting Japanese exports of synthetic textiles and wool to the United States. The negotiations, later dubbed the "quagmire negotiations," dragged on from 1969 to 1971 with little progress. The textile dispute originated from the 1968 election campaign, during which Richard Nixon attempted to secure his lead in the Southern states by promising to negotiate reductions of textile imports. Soon after the Nixon administration took office in January 1969, Secretary of Commerce Maurice Stans was dispatched to Japan and other textile exporting nations to press for an international agreement limiting exports of synthetic textiles and wool. Japan took the position that the United States' proposal violated the principle of free trade and that, if U.S. textile producers were affected by Japanese imports, the United States should take up the issue through procedures established by GATT.

The Diet passed a resolution unanimously rejecting U.S. proposals for a bilateral "orderly marketing agreement." The latter, however, continued to press its demands, and the stage shifted to the Satō–Nixon summit conference in Washington (November 19–20, 1969), at which Nixon attempted to arrange a situation whereby the United States would agree to Japan's terms for the return of Okinawa in exchange for a textiles agreement. Satō actually agreed to this but was unable to keep his word in the face of strong domestic opposition. During 1970, U.S. demands became more strident and its terms more severe, but the year ended with no progress toward a solution. After arduous negotiations with the domestic textile industry, the Japanese government attempted to break the deadlock in March 1971 by announcing that the Japan Textile Federation would voluntarily restrict exports to the United States. Nixon refused to accept this, insisting on a government-level agreement, and the negotiations were right back to where they had started. The textile dispute was not settled until October 15, 1971, two months after the "Nixon shock." Kakuei Tanaka, who had taken over as minister of MITI in July, accomplished this by accepting all of the Nixon administration's demands without the consent of the Japan Textile Federation. The conclusion of the textile dispute provides an excellent illustration of the Nixon administration's high-handed approach to trade issues on the eve of the "Nixon shock," and of Japan's vulnerability to accede to U.S. demands against the interests of domestic industry.

Even while the United States was pursuing this blatant protectionist policy as regards textiles, it was also attempting to shore up its deteriorating balance of international payments by putting pressure on the European Community (EC) to eliminate import tariffs and on Japan to abolish residual import restrictions. (Residual import restrictions are any restrictions on imports maintained without specific waivers from GATT by countries holding Article 8 status in the IMF.) In effect, America was demanding a second round of Japanese trade liberalization measures. Ministerial-level discussions of the trade liberalization issue had taken place in Geneva in November 1968 and in Tokyo in December 1968. At that time, Japan maintained residual import restrictions on some one hundred and twenty-two products, an undeniably high figure compared to forty-three for West Germany, twenty-two for England, and seventy-four for France.

Although there·were a number of products for which there was no reason to maintain restrictions, such as rope, straw matting, and charcoal, many of the products targeted by the Americans for liberalization were those that posed problems for the Japanese government in terms of domestic reactions. For example, the United States was most impatient for the elimination of restrictions on computers and integrated circuits, which U.S. companies enjoyed a substantial competitive advantage, but these were exactly the industries that MITI hoped to protect. The case of leather and leather products is a good example of an industry with a unique Japanese problem that, understandably, was difficult for U.S. negotiators to understand. The small population of *eta*, or outcasts, who had been excluded from most occupations since the premodern period of Japanese history, had carved out a traditional monopoly in the leather industry, which was considered "unclean." Long after the taboo against leather had disappeared, the rising social consciousness of the 1960s had strongly supported government protection of this monopoly, including protection against foreign competition.

Similarly, strong U.S. demands for liberalization of restrictions on agricultural products coincided with the government's new policy of promoting selective development of agriculture. In particular, the liberalization of trade in mandarin oranges and grapefruit would have hurt those farmers who were just beginning to realize profits on new operations designated for preferential treatment. Much the same thing may be said for the beef industry, in which large operations were still a recent phenomenon. Moreover, many of the U.S. demands involved difficult international problems. Both before and after reversion, Okinawans opposed the liberalization of canned pineapples, and the elimination of restrictions on fish imports would have met with strong opposition from Japan's Asian neighbors.

Confronted with these problems, the Japanese government attempted to avert further friction with the United States by offering to eliminate restrictions on thirty-six products within two or three years and to increase import quotas on a number of others. Needless to say, these proposals fell short of U.S. expectations, and U.S.–Japan trade relations still continue to be a source of considerable friction. It should be noted, however, that the government has continued to support trade liberalization despite strong domestic opposition and that, by 1975, the number of products subject to residual import restrictions had fallen to thirty, of which twenty-three are agricultural.

While it is true that trade liberalization was slow by international standards and that it was accomplished in part to avoid an upward revaluation of the yen, Japan's record by 1975 was equal to or better than that of Western European countries. Moreover, while trade friction between the United States and Japan intensified, with U.S. demands extending to more and more industries and Japanese resistance stiffening, the elimination of import restrictions had very little effect on the balance of trade between the two countries. As this fact became more evident, the stage of conflict between the two countries shifted once again from trade negotiations to an upward revaluation of the yen.

The Dollar, the Mark, and the Yen just before the "Nixon Shock." The year 1971 was one of turmoil for the international economy and for Japan.

The international currency system established at Bretton Woods and maintained for a quarter of a century was thrown into complete disarray, and the IMF system was severely challenged. Ultimately, with the devaluation of the dollar and the large upward revaluation of the yen, the ¥360 exchange rate maintained for twenty-two years became irrevocably a thing of the past. The root of this upheaval was the international dollar crisis, and its magnitude and significance makes it worth examining in some detail.

Under the IMF system, established at the Bretton Woods Conference in 1944, the U.S. dollar was the central currency in the international currency system, the key currency with convertibility into gold. By 1971, however, the deteriorating prestige of the dollar had exposed the contradictions of the IMF system. The overwhelming economic superiority enjoyed by the United States at the end of World War II had declined sharply, and the United States was rapidly losing its ability to provide leadership in the international monetary system. Despite this, it continued to pursue its role as the self-proclaimed policeman of the free world, and the outflow of dollars resulting from escalation of the Vietnam War during the late 1960s was a major cause of both rising U.S. balance of payments deficits and worldwide inflation. Moreover, this dollar drain was compounded by the neglect by successive administrations of the problem of enormous capital outflows resulting from foreign investment by U.S. multinationals.

As we have seen, the United States failed to deal with the domestic causes of its deteriorating balance of payments but chose instead to pursue an ineffective policy of forcing its allies to make trade concessions, exacerbating frictions in its relations with Japan and Western Europe, and accomplishing little in the way of improving its balance of payments. The worldwide inflation resulting from the outflow of dollars only made the situation worse. The sudden large increases in Japan's trade surplus were not only reflections of competitive gains achieved by modernization, technological innovations, and improved productivity. They were also the result of a competitive advantage due to stable Japanese export prices in the context of worldwide inflation. The large surpluses achieved in the late 1960s far exceeded the expectations of Japanese economic planners themselves, who were by no means pursuing a policy of increasing the trade surplus.

The Nixon administration added to these problems in 1971 by pushing forward with an expansionary fiscal policy designed to win votes in the coming election year despite opposition from Japan and the EC. The results of this policy were even higher domestic inflation rates and the worst balance of payments deficit since 1935, a staggering $29.8 billion. Despite economic problems at home and a declining international position, the United States continued to insist that the dollar standard under the IMF system be maintained. The Nixon administration held that if other countries were unwilling to absorb the flood of dollars, they should revaluate their currencies. On the other hand, if other countries were unwilling to revise their exchange rates, they should welcome the influx of dollars and actively cooperate with the United States in its international policies. This amounted to a declaration that solution of the problem of the U.S. international payments deficit was not the responsibility of the United States but of the countries that enjoyed surpluses. Needless to say, this high-handed demand that other countries take responsibility for U.S. policies over which they had no control met with strong protest from abroad.

Developments in Europe during early 1971 served to intensify the crisis mood. Following statements on the international monetary situation by the governor of West Germany's Federal Bank and Economic Minister Schiller in late April, four leading German research institutions published recommendations for a shift to the floating exchange rate system. These reports sparked a rush of speculation on the mark and the Swiss franc in early May, forcing West Germany and many neighboring countries to close their exchange markets. At the same time, the mark and the Dutch guilder were allowed to float, and Switzerland and Austria announced large upward revaluations of their currencies.

The United States welcomed these moves, taking the naive view that the upward revaluation of these strong currencies was just what was needed to stabilize the dollar. However, this optimistic view was quickly frustrated by subsequent developments that forced the United States to recognize the seriousness of the crisis. The dollar capital that had been shut out of German, Swiss, and other European exchange markets flowed into France and Belgium, where it was promptly converted into gold. The ensuing gold rush represented a serious threat to U.S. prestige as U.S. gold reserves came dangerously close to falling below the crucial $10 billion mark. In fact, developments in Europe, far from working to improve the situation, had the reverse effect of worsening U.S. balance of payments problems, throwing the international monetary system into a full-fledged crisis.

Against this background, Japan was under continuous pressure to do something about its balance of payments surplus and the undervalued yen. Having observed the rush of exchange rate speculation in West Germany, the government took immediate steps to strengthen controls on foreign exchange transactions in order to avoid a massive accumulation of foreign currency reserves and, on June 4, the cabinet adopted an Eight-Point Yen Policy designed to ease mounting friction with the United States. This policy envisioned the following measures.

1. Promotion of the elimination of residual import restrictions;
2. Preferential tariffs for imports from developing countries (effective August 1, 1971);
3. Reduction of customs duties and tariffs;
4. Promotion of capital liberalization;
5. Elimination of nontariff import barriers;
6. Promotion of economic cooperation, including the expansion of direct government development aid;
7. Establishment of an "orderly" export structure through the elimination of subsidies and tax incentives encouraging exports;
8. Effective management of fiscal and monetary policy.

The announcement of this policy was accompanied by repeated statements by the finance minister that the government had no intention of revising the ¥360 exchange rate. However, the Eight-Point Yen Policy offered little that was new in the way of response to the currency crisis, and most of the points merely represented offers to accelerate the implementation of measures demanded by foreign countries for some time. It could hardly be hoped that it could effectively answer foreign demands for large-scale reductions in Japan's balance of payments surplus and for a revaluation of the yen. Rather, many policy makers felt that the most effective way to avoid a yen revaluation was to eliminate the cyclical factors underlying the sharp increases in the balance of payments surplus by promoting recovery of the economy and by increasing imports. With this in view, the government effected a whole series of measures designed to stimulate the economy.

Despite measures by the Ministry of Finance to tighten controls on the foreign exchange market, foreign currency reserves mounted at an unprecedented rate due to the "leads and lags" phenomenon. Large private firms, unconvinced by the government's insistence that it had no intention of revaluating the yen, attempted to avoid exchange rate losses by obtaining prepayment for exports, moving up export schedules, and converting dollar income from exports to yen as quickly as possible. On the other hand, they delayed imports and payments for imports as long as possible in the hope of reaping exchange rate gains after the anticipated revaluation. Rapid increases in foreign currency reserves resulting from this "leads and lags" phenomenon effectively destroyed the basis for maintaining the ¥360 exchange rate. On July 10, 1971, the Exchange Rate Study Group, organized by Professor Tadao Uchida's Modern Economists Group at the University of Tokyo, published a proposal calling for a series of small revaluations of about 1 percent every three months until the exchange rate had been raised to a level at which foreign reserves decreased to a more suitable amount, the "crawling peck adjustment" approach to revaluation. Professor Miyohei Shinohara, on the other hand, argued that the yen should be floated.

In fact, the crisis had become much too serious for such painless solutions as the "crawling peck" approach and, given the international situation, the only realistic options were a sizable revaluation or a shift to a floating exchange rate. However, determined not to repeat West Germany's experience, the Japanese government continued to issue statements to the effect that the ¥360 exchange rate would be maintained, and assumed a posture of awaiting further developments on the international scene. In short, the government followed the usual wait-and-see and follow-the-crowd approach that has characterized Japanese foreign policy since the war.

The "Nixon Shock." The first "Nixon shock" occurred in July 1971, when the Nixon administration announced its new China policy and Nixon visited Beijing without coordinating this major foreign policy shift with the Japanese government. It is unclear to what extent this decision was affected by the economic clashes between the two countries, but certainly it reflected the Nixon administration's increasing insensitivity to the domestic political problems and international positions of its major foreign allies. The second "Nixon shock" occurred on August 15, 1971, with the announcement of Nixon's New Economic Program, and was directly related to the United States–Japan friction and, more generally, to the deepening international currency crisis. The massive U.S. balance of payments deficit, the flight of U.S. capital in the form of foreign investment, and the attack on the dollar in French and Belgian exchange markets had marked a serious decline in the dollar's prestige, and the fact that the dollar was the only key currency in the international monetary system meant that the dollar crisis threatened the survival of the whole system.

The crisis was finally resolved by a multinational currency adjustment, in which the dollar was devalued against gold, and most of the major currencies were revalued upward against it. It was within this framework that an upward revaluation of the yen was finally carried out, and the announcement of Nixon's New Economic Program set the stage for rapid movements toward a new international monetary system.

The New Economic Program was a comprehensive one designed to end domestic inflation and restore equilibrium in the U.S. balance of payments. Its essential points may be summarized as follows.

1. Suspension of convertibility of the U.S. dollar into gold and other currencies;
2. A 10 percent surtax on imports;
3. A 10 percent reduction in foreign aid expenditure;
4. A ninety-day freeze on domestic wages and prices;
5. A tax cut designed to stimulate the domestic economy.

The first three of these "new international economic policies," sent shock waves throughout the world. Essentially, they amounted to economic war, and the surtax on imports, in particular, was viewed as a blatant attempt to force other countries to revalue their currencies. The United States, which had stood at the forefront of the free trade movement after World War II, was now implementing measures that ran directly against this principle and, regardless of justifications based on the seriousness of the nation's problems, the surtax on imports resulted in chaos in the world economy. The feeling that the United States had created a crisis in the free trade system was now added to the prevailing fears that the international currency system was collapsing. As suggested by the Japanese term "Nixon shock," it was Japan that felt the effects of the new U.S. policy most acutely.

The Tokyo stock market suffered the most disastrous slump in its history, and the economy, which had just begun a slow process of recovery, slipped once again into recession. Panic over the import surtax and the growing realization that a large-scale revaluation of the yen would soon be unavoidable cast an atmosphere of gloom over the future. Unlike Western Europe, which had closed its exchange markets immediately after the announcement of the New Economic Program, reopening them after shifting to the float system, Japan maintained the ¥360 exchange rate until August 27, 1971, keeping its exchange market open. To other advanced nations, Japan seemed to be determined to resist the Nixon policies to the bitter end, even if it meant standing alone. Between August 16 and August 27, the Bank of Japan's dollar purchases reached $5 billion, which means that ¥1.8 trillion flowed into Japan in the eleven days before the yen was finally allowed to float on August 28.

However, foreign perception of the Japanese government's policies during this period by no means reflected the actual situation. Policy makers did not see themselves as being locked in a samurai-like duel with the United States and neither were they so naive as to think that the ¥360 exchange rate could be maintained. Rather, they were legitimately concerned that a sudden change in the exchange rate would compound the prevailing panic and confusion, and gave top priority to avoiding the loss of confidence that would follow a hasty reversal of the ¥360 exchange rate policy that had been publicly reiterated even after the "Nixon shock." It is true, however, that the government overestimated the ability of the new foreign exchange controls to check the inflow of dollars, and purchases of dollars by the Bank of Japan wildly exceeded all expectations. The huge dollar inflow, and the subsequent flood of yen into the domestic economy, even though transitory, became a major cause of excess liquidity, which, in turn, became the most important factor in the inflation that shortly followed revaluation.

Japanese domestic enterprises were severely shaken by the "Nixon shock," and the only businesses that managed to maintain some semblance of their former prosperity were bowling alleys, golf courses, and supermarkets. Hardest hit were companies that were heavily dependent on exports, particularly small and medium-size enterprises. These were attacked on both flanks, by the 10 percent import surcharge and by the floating yen. Moreover, compared to large enterprises, they were far down the list of companies designated for preferential export financing. Exporting industries such as ceramics, silverware, pots and pans, and shoes manufactured from synthetic materials, in which small and medium-size firms abounded, suffered enormous losses and found it increasingly difficult to sign new contracts as well as to collect payments on previous sales and arrange financing. Many of these firms were threatened with bankruptcy unless positive steps could be taken to stabilize the situation.

The case of Okinawa is a good example of the unique problems that confronted the Japanese government. The U.S.–Japan agreement on the reversion of Okinawa to Japan in May 1972 had been signed in June 1971, and it was ratified by the Diet at the end of the year. In the period before reversion, however, Okinawans suffered most directly from the floating yen. While the dollar was still the standard currency in Okinawa, more than 80 percent of daily necessities were imported from Japan. Therefore, the yen float resulted in an enormous inflation of consumer prices and a huge devaluation of the yen value of privately held assets. This problem was taken up in the Diet session convened to ratify the U.S.–Japan agreement on Okinawa, and it was decided that the Japanese government would compensate Okinawa losses due to exchange rate revisions with subsidies based on the ¥360 exchange rate.

Finally, the growing mood of pessimism that the so-called yen revaluation recession would deepen into a prolonged economic downturn evoked strong demands from both opposition and LDP Diet members that the government implement a large tax cut to stimulate the economy. In October 1971, the cabinet announced a series of measures designed to soften the blow of the impending yen revaluation, including the issue of ¥90 billion in new government bonds and an unprecedented mid-year ¥165 billion tax cut.

The Smithsonian Agreement. After several months of negotiations the escalating monetary crisis was finally brought to an end by an agreement signed by the Group of Ten (the United States, the United Kingdom, Japan, West Germany, France, Italy, the Netherlands, Belgium, Sweden, and Canada) at the Smithsonian Institution in Washington on December 19, 1971. The decision to entrust negotiations for a new international currency system to ministers of these ten nations was based on the fact that it would be difficult to reach agreement in a meeting of all IMF countries and on the desire to agree, at least, on basic principles before the end of the year. Nevertheless, as late as September 1971, negotiations were still bogged down because the United States refused to yield to demands by the other nine participants that the dollar should be devalued and that the 10 percent surcharge represented a violation of the principle of free trade. It was not until November that the United States began to seek exchange rate adjustments by the other advanced nations in exchange for a devaluation of the dollar and the elimination of the surcharge on imports. This decision was based on the realization that a prolongation of negotiations could only lead to worsening of the worldwide recession and a contraction of international trade, both of which would further exacerbate the U.S. balance of payments deficit.

Agreement on the basic outlines of a plan for reconstructing the international financial system through multilateral currency adjustment was finally reached on December 16 and 17 at the Smithsonian Institution. The Smithsonian Agreement (or the Smithsonian system) was based on two principles. First, the U.S. dollar, which was the key currency of the international monetary system, was devalued by 7.89 percent against gold; the official price of gold rose from $35 per ounce to $38 per ounce. This was the first time the dollar had been devalued against gold since 1934. Second, the currencies of other advanced nations were revalued upward against the dollar. Since the IMF formula for international exchange rates was based on gold, the other countries had the option of revaluing their currencies against gold or maintaining their existing exchange rates, which would amount to a de facto upward revaluation against the dollar. For example, England and France chose to maintain the par value of their currencies against gold, effectively raising the value of the pound and the franc by 8.6 percent against the dollar. The par value of the mark against gold was increased by 4.6 percent, which amounted to an upward revaluation of 13.5 percent against the dollar. The upward revaluation of the yen was by far the largest, an increase of 7.66 percent in the par value of the yen against gold and an upward revaluation of 16.88 percent against the dollar.

The large upward revaluation of the yen, which, unlike the mark had not been revalued since World War II, was the most important purpose behind these talks, and it quickly became clear to Japanese negotiators that a settlement of the multilateral currency adjustment issue could not be reached without an upward revaluation of the yen of at least 17 percent against the dollar. The Japanese government concluded that there was nothing to be gained by prolonging discussion over the scale of the yen revaluation, and a final agreement was reached on December 19, 1971. The Smithsonian Agreement provided for fluctuations of 2.5 percent either way in the new exchange rates, a substantial increase over the range allowed under the old IMF system. Canada maintained the float system.

With the signing of the Smithsonian Agreement, the 10 percent surcharge on imports was abolished on December 20, 1971. One hundred and fourteen noncommunist countries carried out currency adjustments, the majority revaluating their currencies upward against the dollar. Compared to the twenty-four countries that revalued their currencies after the devaluation of the pound in 1949, the number of countries affected by the "Nixon shock" had increased enormously. The 16.88 percent revaluation of the yen had established a new exchange rate of ¥308 to the dollar, even higher than the ¥310 to ¥320 rate predicted by analysts in Japan.

The government attempted to moderate the resulting panic by immediately announcing a series of policies to stimulate the economy. In a press conference on December 19, 1971, Prime Minister Satō said that the government would draft an expansionary budget for 1972 and would issue nearly ¥2 trillion worth of new bonds. In fact, the budget for 1972 authorized an increase of 22 percent in expenditures from the general account and an increase of 32 percent in the Fiscal Investment and Loan Program. In this sense, yen revaluation and, by extension, the "Nixon shock," resulted in enormous losses for Japan, not only in terms of their direct impact on private industry but also in terms of their influence in distorting the efficient management of fiscal and monetary policy.

6

NEW CHALLENGES
AT HOME AND ABROAD

1. YEN REVALUATION AND EXCESS LIQUIDITY
INFLATION

A Plan for Rebuilding the Japanese Archipelago. The phrase "yen revaluation recession" was coined for the severe economic downturn of 1971, with the prediction that the large upward revaluation of the yen would have a deflationary effect on the economy for some time. However, the recession bottomed out at the end of 1971 and, by the first half of 1972, the economy began gradually to recover. While the growth of exports remained sluggish after revaluation, the national budget for 1972 included substantial increases for public works, social security, and social insurance, which supported the recovery of domestic demand. In July 1972, Satō finally ended his long career as prime minister and was succeeded by Kakuei Tanaka. Tanaka had campaigned on his image as a decisive, activist administrator who got results, on the issue of normalizing relations with China, and on his "plan for rebuilding the Japanese archipelago." In fact, after taking office, he proceeded rapidly to deal with China, adopting the unprecedented strategy (for an LDP politician) of seeking help from private individuals and opposition party leaders who had strong ties with Beijing to carry out negotiations on normalization. By September 1972, Tanaka was in Beijing to sign the Joint Communiqué on Sino-Japanese Friendship (the Sino-Japanese Trade Agreement was signed in January 1974).

Having started off well in international diplomacy, Tanaka turned his attention to domestic policies. In June 1972, just one month before the LDP convention at which he defeated Takeo Fukuda for the party presidency, Tanaka published his best-selling book *A Plan for Rebuilding the Japanese Archipelago* (*Nihon rettō kaizō ron*), which called for a visionary policy of industrial relocation and regional development. With his victory in the contest for prime minister, his vast, government-sponsored development plan contributed immensely to the revival of business activity. Based on the New Comprehensive National Development Plan, which had been adopted by a cabinet resolution in 1969, and the Industrial Relocation Promotion Law, established in June 1972, while Tanaka was still minister of MITI, it called for massive regional development with priority given to industrial relocation through strong tax incentives and government investment to encourage industries to move out of the Pacific belt.

More important, while the New Comprehensive National Development Plan had set goals for development based on average annual growth rates of 7.5 percent and a GNP of ¥200 trillion by 1985, the Tanaka plan was based on average annual growth rates of 10 percent and a ¥300 trillion GNP by 1985 (based on prices in 1970). These projections grossly overestimated the economy's potential for continued high-speed growth and further increases in productivity, and produced unrealistic expectations for increased government investment in social overhead capital, especially in such vital infrastructural areas as transportation. Nevertheless, in the gloomy period after the yen revaluation, the promise of new possibilities in the Tanaka plan was received enthusiastically.

Against this background, academics, bureaucrats, and business leaders clamored to be part of the advisory group for the plan, which was set up in August as a brains trust for the new prime minister. By the end of the year, the government had acted on the recommendations of the study group, proposing revisions to the National Lands Comprehensive Development Law, the establishment of a National Lands Comprehensive Development Agency to coordinate development administration at the national level, and a National Lands Comprehensive Development Corporation to act as its operational arm. These proposals encountered stiff opposition in the Diet and were not adopted until June 1974, after being substantially revised and submitted under new titles (National Land Use Planning Law, National Land Use Agency, and Japan Regional Development Corporation). In February 1973, the government put out its Basic Economic and Social Plan, designed to make the Tanaka plan official government policy.

The Basic Economic and Social Plan envisioned annual growth rates of

9.4 percent from 1973 to 1977, and outlined an enormous program for expanding the Shinkansen and freeway systems. The fiscal budget for 1973 reflected the ambitious nature of this plan. Total government outlays were to increase by 25 percent over the original budget for 1972, and the Fiscal Investment and Loan Program was to be increased by 28 percent. Moreover, while the expansive 1972 budget had concentrated on increases in social security and the national pension program, the most substantial increases in the 1973 budget were in the area of public works. The implementation of this budget revealed a great lack of concern for the effect such increases in fiscal spending would have on consumer prices and on the price of land.

Even before the 1973 budget was adopted by the Diet, the Tanaka plan had sparked off enthusiasm nationwide, and private enterprises, flush with excess capital, rushed to buy up land in anticipation of its implementation over a long period. This land rush was not limited to real estate companies but extended to trading companies, construction companies, banks, investment companies, and, in the manufacturing industry, textiles and nonferrous metals companies. Given the steadily increasing value of land as collateral for loans, domestic financial institutions were all too eager to support the growing land speculation with generous financing arrangements, and this insertion of finance capital into an already tight market sparked an explosion in land prices. Increases were especially steep in areas that had been designated for development under the Tanaka plan, such as Mutsu-ogawara in northern Honshu, Tomakomai in southern Hokkaido, and Shibushi in Kyushu. The explosion in land prices resulted in more land speculation, which, in turn, led to even higher land prices, a vicious cycle that lasted from fall 1972 until early 1973. It seemed that private enterprises throughout the nation were under the spell of a collective hallucination called "inflation hedges." Kiichi Arita, then director general of the Economic Planning Agency, described the situation as follows: "In our haste to deal with the recession and ameliorate the balance of trade situation with the United States, I wonder if the government as a whole did not view the problem of prices too lightly. It is especially unfortunate that the 'plan for rebuilding the Japanese archipelago' became the cause of an explosion in land prices." (*Keizai kikakuchō sanjūnen-shi* [A thirty-year history of the Economic Planning Agency]).

During the same period, there was an unprecedented rise in stock prices. The Dow Jones average, which had finally recovered to the ¥3,000 level in March 1972, skyrocketed to ¥5,000 by the end of the year. The publication of the government's version of the Tanaka plan was partly responsible for this huge increase, but the most important contributing factor was speculation by private firms. Private firms devoted more of their efforts during this period to the accumulation of capital gains than to the expansion of business. Capital gains from land price increases reported by private corporations in 1972 amounted to ¥15 trillion and those from securities appreciation amounted to ¥5 trillion. The effect of this kind of speculation on prices in general was so great that journalists described the subsequent inflation as a "capital gains inflation." In any case, the reckless mood created by the Tanaka plan and the excess liquidity resulting from Japan's enormous balance of payments surplus produced an inflationary psychology that pushed up wholesale prices, then consumer prices.[1]

The Collapse of the Smithsonian Agreement. Even while policy makers attempted to cope with the effects of the yen revaluation at home, a new crisis was developing in the international currency system. It had been recognized from the very beginning that about two years would be required for the multinational currency adjustment outlined by the Smithsonian Agreement to begin to show results and that, in any case, success in stabilizing the international currency situation depended entirely on improvement of the U.S. balance of payments. In fact, for a very short time immediately after the signing of the Smithsonian Agreement, the dollar market did show signs of stabilizing as part of the dollar capital that had flowed to foreign countries, before and after the "Nixon shock," began to return.

However, the strengthened dollar position proved a transitory phenomenon and, in February and March 1972, Japan, West Germany, and the Netherlands were forced to buy large amounts of dollars to support their exchange rates. This weakening of the dollar on foreign exchange markets was influenced by a loss of confidence in the dollar due largely to the United States' delay in implementing the Smithsonian Agreement until congressional debate on its ratification. The purpose of this delay was to enhance its bargaining position with other advanced nations. However, the basic cause of the new dollar crisis was the Nixon administration's failure to enforce stringent monetary and fiscal policies at home in order to raise confidence in the dollar abroad, even at the risk of a decline in Nixon's popularity. The administration implemented even more expansionary policies, including a large-scale tax cut, encompassing income tax, sales tax, and large increases in depreciation allowances, an increase in the money supply, and lower market interest rates. It is hardly surprising, therefore, that the U.S. balance of payments problem worsened. Imports increased $10 billion in a single year, and the U.S. balance of payments deficit increased in 1972 to $6.8 billion, compared to $2.7 billion in 1971. The Nixon administration's decision to give priority to policies aimed at stimulating domestic demand and reducing unemployment meant that the new international currency system was skating on thin ice from the very beginning.

With the exception of the United Kingdom, the other nine countries attempted to maintain the Smithsonian Agreement's central rates by reducing their balance of payments surpluses and stimulating their domestic economies. The United Kingdom shifted to the floating exchange rate system in June 1972 and devalued the pound, but this had been necessitated by the pound being overvalued at the time of the agreement. Despite efforts to reduce their trade surpluses, both Japan and West Germany recorded substantial increases. Japan's balance of payments surplus increased from $7.8 billion in 1971 to $9.0 billion in 1972, while Germany's increased from $4.3 billion to $6.2 billion. Japan, which continued to record the largest surplus in the world even after the Smithsonian Agreement, came under increasing pressure from abroad to take positive steps to amend the situation.

The OECD proposed that Japan should stimulate domestic demand by implementing an even more expansionist budget, increasing outlays for such social insurance programs as the national pension program, and enacting a large tax cut. The most difficult problem was friction with the United States over the large increase in Japanese exports, which grew from $3.4 billion in 1971 to $4.0 billion in 1972. As the United States became more adamant in demanding that other countries cooperate in reducing its balance of payments deficit, and as its commercial diplomacy began to be colored by international politics, Japan made greater efforts to reduce its trade surplus with the United States. At a U.S.–Japan discussion held in Hakone in July and during the Nixon–Tanaka summit in September, the new prime minister found himself hard pressed on the issue of trade imbalance. Indeed, it is perhaps one of the great ironies of history that the Nixon–Tanaka summit later became an issue in the famous Lockheed scandal.

Given this background, it is unclear whether it was wise to defend the fixed exchange rate set by the Smithsonian Agreement. The government, however, continued to give priority to avoiding another yen revaluation in the formulation of economic policy. In part, this reflected fears that a second yen revaluation would spark a resurgence of the panic created by the first one. More important, however, was the political judgment that there was a good deal to be gained if the balance of payment surplus could be reduced by getting the Japanese economy back on the track of high-speed growth, and the "plan for rebuilding the Japanese archipelago" was designed to provide the psychological atmosphere in which such a policy could be pursued. It was also during this period that high government officials and leaders of the financial community began to advocate publicly the "readjustment inflation theory," which argued that a period of domestic inflation was an acceptable trade-off for avoiding a second yen revaluation. Having given top priority to avoiding a second revaluation, the government became desperate to reduce the balance of payments surplus, which continued to grow despite the first revaluation to a fixed exchange rate of ¥308.

On October 10, 1972, a meeting of the cabinet adopted the "third yen policy," which lowered customs duties by 10 percent across the board, increased existing import quotas by 30 percent, and established restraints on exports of commodities that had shown rapid export increases under the Trade Control Law. At the same meeting, the cabinet adopted a supplementary budget proposal calling for large increases in public works expenditure, an issue of ¥360 billion in new government bonds, and orders to launch the Industrial Location Plan. This plan, one of the pillars of the Tanaka plan, contained a number of controversial provisions, not least of which was the designation of specific regions for future industrial development. As Professor Hiromi Arisawa suggests in his *Shōwa keizai shi* (Shōwa economic history, Nihon Keizai Shimbun-sha), "The suggestions, countersuggestions, negotiations, haggling, impatience, uproar, and heated emotions of the period immediately before this cabinet meeting were no trivial matter and, while there were a lot of people working day and night on the problem, one somehow had the feeling that it was all much ado about nothing." Moreover, all of this was followed by the drafting of an expansionary budget for 1973.

Despite the government's struggle to support the Smithsonian Agreement with expansionary domestic policies and highly publicized trade concessions, the agreement was extremely short-lived. At the end of 1972, foreign pressure for a second yen revaluation had subsided, but by the beginning of 1973, the international currency system was clearly headed for another crisis. At the end of January, Italy shifted to the double exchange rate system and the Swiss franc was allowed to float. This was followed at the beginning of February by a large sale of dollars by the West German central bank. On February 8, Volcker, assistant treasury secretary, interrupted a European tour to fly to Japan for secret talks with Kiichi Aichi, the finance minister. Japan closed its exchange market on February 10, and the major European nations followed suit on February 12. On February 13, the dollar was devalued 10 percent against Special Drawing Rights (SDR's) and, on the following day, Japan reopened its exchange market after announcing that the yen would be allowed to float. This resulted in an immediate 5 percent upward revaluation of the yen against the dollar. Finally, on March 12, West Germany announced a 3 percent upward revaluation of the mark, and the EC countries (with the exceptions of England, Ireland, and Italy) announced a "joint floating exchange rate system," under which they would maintain fixed exchange rates between community members but would allow their currencies to float against the dollar.

These moves signaled the end of the Smithsonian Agreement, only fourteen months after the meeting of the Group of Ten in Washington. After Japan floated the yen in February 1973, its value increased rapidly against the dollar, and the dollar dropped below the ¥280 level in the second half of July. Underlying this decline was a deeply rooted lack of confidence in the dollar, which sustained heavy setbacks on all the major international exchange markets, increasing concern about the instability of the international currency system. The reasons for this lack of confidence have been suggested by Professor Shōichi Kase in his *Kokusai tsūka kiki* (International currency crisis, Iwanami Shoten.)

> First, one may cite the growing political scandal connected with Watergate. The Nixon administration's loss of authority and prestige is one more example of the way a loss of political confidence gives rise to a loss of confidence in a nation's currency. Second, the uncertainty about the future of Japan's economy that accompanied the acceleration of domestic inflation was combined with increasing doubts about the prospects for an improvement in the U.S. balance of payments. Finally, there was a good deal of concern over the threat of renewed conflict in the Middle East.

In short, the international political scene in general and the international currency situation in particular were badly disrupted by the Nixon administration's irresponsible policy of "making America strong again" by exporting domestic inflation and U.S. balance of payments deficits to its major trading partners. The Japanese government stuck to the policy of avoiding a second yen revaluation much too long and rushed headlong into Tanaka's overambitious "plan for rebuilding the Japanese archipelago," hoping to ease frictions over Japan's trade surpluses by resuming high-speed economic growth. The price for these policies was the development of severe inflationary pressures that erupted with full force after the collapse of the Smithsonian Agreement.

Excess Liquidity Inflation. The most serious problem confronting non-communist countries after the prolonged international monetary crisis was worldwide inflation. Inflationary pressures created during the turbulent changes in the international economic order after the "Nixon shock" were compounded by the development of worldwide shortages, followed by the food supply crisis and then by the oil crisis. Inflation escalated into a full-scale international problem and continued to attack Japan, forcing it to go through a period of "crazy prices" after the first "oil shock" in 1973. The underlying causes of this worldwide inflation were the huge dispersal of dollars, the "dollar drain," from the United States, and the inability of individual governments to control the resulting excess international liquidity in the form of dollar capital. According to IMF statistics, worldwide international liquidity nearly doubled in a period of only two years and three months: from $92.6 billion at the end of 1970 to $179.2 billion in early 1973. Indeed, it would have been surprising if this huge outflow of dollars had not caused inflation on an international scale. Ultimately, the collapse of the Bretton Woods system may be traced to the sharp decline of U.S. industry's competitiveness due to the Vietnam War, the Nixon administration's irresponsible stimulation of demand through expansionary economic policies, and the failure of the attempt to check domestic inflation by unilaterally suspending the convertibility of the dollar into gold.

On the other hand, the other advanced nations must share responsibility for the inflationary pressures that developed. Even after the United States had suspended the convertibility of the dollar into gold and into other currencies at fixed exchanged rates under the Bretton Woods system, the advanced countries attempted to maintain fixed exchange rates by making large dollar purchases. The total volume of dollars purchased in support of the dollar had a direct bearing on the seriousness of inflationary pressures due to excess international liquidity in their economies. Moreover, relying on steadily expanding foreign exchange reserves, the governments of these countries attempted to take the easy approach to reducing balance of payments surpluses by adopting expansionary domestic economic policies. The resulting inflation in all advanced countries had a cumulative effect that inevitably resulted in worldwide inflation. Indeed, to the extent that domestic booms occurred simultaneously in all advanced nations, 1973 was an extremely unusual year. It is hardly surprising that the world economy was unable to supply the resultant explosion of demand, and severe shortages in both primary raw materials and basic industrial materials drove prices even higher on all markets.

Japan was by no means an exception to this worldwide phenomenon. In fact, however much it feared that other advanced countries were about to gang up on Japan unless it did something about its balance of payments surplus and foreign reserves, the government's recklessly expansionary policies gave the Japanese economy the most inflationary bias of all. Overly concerned with avoiding a second yen revaluation and reducing Japan's trade surplus, the government was pushing the economic accelerator with all its might at precisely the period when it should have been applying the brakes to check inflation. The result was that Japan suffered the worst inflation in the world during this period.

As suggested above, the character of this inflation was quite different from the productivity differentials inflation of the past, and can best be understood as an excess liquidity inflation. Unlike the former, in which wholesale prices remained stable, the symptoms of excess liquidity inflation appeared throughout the price structure of the economy, with large increases in wholesale prices leading directly to even higher rates of inflation in consumer prices. The danger of this type of inflation was not completely overlooked by economic planners. The Economic White Paper of 1971, published at about the same time as the "Nixon shock," had taken up the problem long before the fact.

> If the tempo of foreign currency reserves increases seems likely to accelerate further, it will become necessary to develop policies to absorb excess liquidity even if business conditions are stagnant. Moreover, in the event of an economic upturn and increased demand for capital, excess liquidity will present new problems for monetary adjustment policies. There is a need to develop effective monetary adjustment policies now to avoid disruptions in the domestic flow of capital in the future if a large inflow of foreign capital occurs under the conditions of a balance of payments surplus.

Unfortunately, this timely warning went unheeded. Finally, after the yen was allowed to float, the Bank of Japan raised deposit reserve requirements for city banks and imposed various stringent monetary policies, but they were too late and their effects too weak. Moreover, interest rates remained relatively low even after inflation had become a major problem, and there was a rush among private enterprises to obtain financing for new buildings and inventory investment before interest rates were raised. The phenomenon of excess liquidity extended to small and medium-size firms, and banks and private enterprises alike had large quantities of cash on hand. Given this background, speculation was no longer limited to land and securities, and the craze for gambling spread to golf club memberships, art and antiques, jewelry, and rare coins. The scope of the problem may be illustrated by the fact that the expansion of the money supply (M_2) during this period amounted to 23 percent in 1971, 27 percent in 1972, and 20 percent in 1973.

Worldwide Shortages and the Food Supply Crisis. Shortages and subsequent price increases began to appear in the fall of 1972. The most striking increases in this early period were for construction materials such as lumber, tubular and structural steel, and plastics, and these increases were directly related to the huge demand generated by public works projects under the Tanaka plan. Price increases in lumber also affected related industries such as wood pulp, and textile products rose because of the high prices for raw cotton and wool on the international market. By early 1973, steep increases in prices of daily necessities began to threaten the daily lives of the people. For example, prices for Western-style clothing increased by 40 percent over the previous year, and for men's shirts by 10 percent. Inflation of feed grain prices on the international market caused an explosion in the price of meat. The price of *tōfu* (bean curd) increased 10 percent and *nattō* (fermented soybeans) 70 percent.

The fact that inflation now became linked to shortages in food supplies set off a wave of panic among the Japanese people. A worldwide decline in grain production due to abnormal weather conditions was the basic cause of excessive demand, but speculation on international markets exacerbated shortages and drove prices even higher. The abnormal weather conditions affected soybeans, corn, sorghum, coffee, sugar, and raw cotton. The most dramatic increases, however, were recorded for soybeans and, for the Japanese people, this was particularly alarming. Soybeans tripled in price in the space of one year, from $3 per bushel to

(%)

	1960	1965	1970	1973
Grains	83	61	48	41
(Rice)	102	95	106	101
(Wheat)	38	28	9	4
(Barley, rye)	107	73	34	10
Soybeans	28	11	4	3
Vegetables	100	100	99	88
Fruits	100	90	84	83
Meat	91	89	88	78
Eggs	101	100	97	98
Milk and milk products	89	85	89	83
Feed grains	67	44	33	31

Note: Statistics for meat products do not include whale meat.
Source: Ministry of Agriculture and Forestry.

$11. With a vicious cycle between worldwide shortages in grain supplies and the spread of speculation on international markets, the Nixon administration announced a new set of restrictions on grain exports as part of its anti-inflation policy, prohibiting soybean exports to Japan because of soaring domestic demand. This was a severe blow for Japan, which was dependent on imports for nearly all of its grain supply except rice. Moreover, soybeans, in the form of *tōfu*, *miso* (bean paste), soy sauce, *nattō*, and vegetable oil, constitute a vital source of nutrition for Japanese people. Without the conclusion of the Transactions Stabilization Agreement with America guaranteeing annual shipments of 3 million tons of soybeans and 8 million tons of feed grains, a food supply panic could have spread very quickly.

The term "food supply crisis" began to appear frequently in the media between the spring and summer of 1973 and, while it may have exaggerated the seriousness of the situation, it was based on a rising public consciousness of the following real problems.

1. The basic instability of an economy dependent on imports for more than half its food supply.
2. Shortages in food supply were unpredictable and could occur whenever abnormal weather prevailed.

3. The end of the period of worldwide food surpluses signified a basic shift in the international environment and Japan could not longer depend on cheap supplies of food from abroad.

4. There was a need to rethink the problem of Japan's self-sufficiency in food supplies and the direction of its agricultural policies.

5. The United States held a strategic weapon, should it choose to employ food supplies in international politics

As we have seen, inflation during this period may be seen as the outcome of a combination of three factors: excess liquidity inflation; rapid increases in prices for construction and industrial materials accompanying the overheating of the economy; and worldwide food shortages. Against this background of rampant inflation, hawks in the Diet began to demand an immediate freeze on wages and prices. In March 1973, under strong pressure from Prime Minister Tanaka, the Economic Planning Agency introduced the Law to Prevent Attempts to Corner Markets and Hold Goods Off the Market, designed to restrain speculative activities by private enterprises. In addition, the government adopted a series of policies aimed at providing MITI mediation in transactions involving materials in short supply, restricting financing for real estate deals, as well as imposing emergency countermeasures to secure imports of foodstuffs and price restrictions on individual commodities. However, as none of these policies attacked the basic problems of excess liquidity and excessive demand due to the overheating of the economy, there was little hope that they would be effective in dealing with inflation. During the same period, the Ministry of Finance, under the direction of Kiichi Aichi, drafted a proposal for special measures to stabilize the economy, including the issue of "stabilization bonds" to absorb excess liquidity and a special readjustment tax on exports. Unfortunately, bureaucratic sectionalism and poor timing prevented the bill from being passed in the Diet, and it became known among economic planners as the "phantom economic stabilization law."

Shortages and inflation worsened in the summer of 1973. Industrial accidents occurred one after the other in the petrochemicals industry as producers struggled to increase capacity utilization and meet steadily increasing demand. An unseasonal drought also produced shortages in industrial water and hydroelectric power supplies. Japanese industry was in turmoil as it faced "no plastics," "no electricity," "shortages of record discs," "shortages of steel," and "shortages of nonferrous metals." It was no longer inflation due to rising costs despite an abundance of raw materials as in previous inflationary periods. The problem now was that prices were rising because of shortages in industrial raw materials.[2]

The "Oil Shock" and the Food Panic. In the fall of 1973, there was a temporary decline in the price of vegetables and the pace of inflation seemed to be slowing. By October a number of economic policy makers had begun to predict that the inflation rate would peak once the full impact of the government's stringent monetary policies began to take effect. These naive expectations were destroyed by the "oil shock," which had a profound influence on the raging inflation and on the future of Japan's economic growth.

The "fourth" Middle Eastern war, as the Yom Kippur War is called in Japan, erupted on October 6, 1973. On October 10, an emergency meeting of the oil ministers of the Organization of Arab Petroleum Exporting Countries (OAPEC) agreed to curtail oil production by over 5 percent, the first time that the organization exploited "oil power" in a political conflict. On November 4, the OAPEC ministers cut off oil shipments to the United States and announced further cuts that amounted in total to 25 percent, to be followed by further reductions of 5 percent beginning in December. These announcements were followed by a joint communiqué by the oil ministers of the Organization of Petroleum Exporting Countries (OPEC) saying that the six Persian Gulf states had agreed on a price increase of 2.12 times the new prices established in October.

The impact on the advanced nations was shattering as the Arab countries demonstrated that they could employ the "oil strategy" against the interests of the oil consuming nations and the major international oil companies. Moreover, although the "fourth" Middle Eastern war had provided the ideal environment for this, the oil nations proved that they were able to act collectively through democratically organized groupings such as OAPEC and OPEC. The success of these organizations in influencing events during the war itself carried the implications of the OPEC movement far beyond this single conflict. As the rising tide of democracy swept through the Arab countries, and the movement toward Arab solidarity gained momentum, there seemed to be no end in sight for rapid increases in the price of oil. The term "oil shock," first used by the Japanese press, vividly characterized the panic that gripped the countries of the non-communist world.

Of all the oil consuming nations, Japan felt the greatest shock from the

Figure 13. Impact of the Oil Crisis on High-Speed Growth

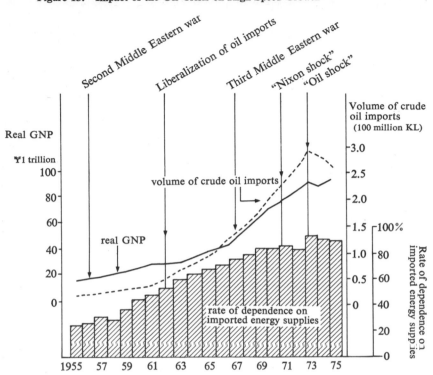

Notes: 1. Rate of dependence on imported energy supplies is given for primary energy supplies.
2. Real GNP is given in 1970 prices.

oil crisis. Despite the fact that Japan was the world's largest oil importer and almost completely dependent on the Middle East for oil, the government was totally unprepared for the emergency and had failed to develop policies or legislation to restrict consumption and restrain speculation. The United States and Western Europe had previous experiences of oil restrictions in the "second" and "third" Middle Eastern wars and, by 1973, these countries maintained sufficient stockpiles for seventy to one hundred days. The Japanese government, naively maintaining that Japan would receive friendly nation treatment until the very end, was caught with stockpiles to last only fifty days. The announcement that oil restrictions would be applied to Japan as well as the other advanced nations, was, to cite a Japanese expression, "like pouring water into the ear of a sleeping child." Japan is dependent on the Middle East for 99.7 percent of

Table 17. Sources of Japan's Oil Imports (1973)

	Million KL	Percent of total
Total	286.7	100.0
Middle East	223.9	78.1
Iran	95.7	33.4
Saudi Arabia	53.7	18.7
Abu Dhabi	26.0	9.1
Kuwait	23.3	8.1
Neutral zone	16.6	5.8
Oman	6.2	2.2
Others	2.4	0.8
Indonesia	42.5	14.8
Brunei	9.3	3.3
Nigeria	5.6	1.9
U.S.S.R.	1.4	0.5
People's Republic of China	1.1	0.4
Others	2.8	1.0

Source: MITI.

its oil supply, which, in turn, comprises 90 percent of its basic energy consumption. The realization that a large portion of its basic energy supply had suddenly disappeared sparked off a wave of panic, with rumors of all kinds of shortages and the certainty of enormous price increases for daily necessities.

The panic was most visible in the public hysteria regarding shortages of toilet paper and synthetic detergents, two very popular supermarket symbols of the mass consumption society. The panic began in Osaka and soon spread throughout the country as housewives rushed to buy up supplies and exhausted the nation's stocks. The government ordered producers to make emergency deliveries, and supermarkets introduced various schemes to ration purchases, but the rush to buy had already created real shortages. The same process soon brought shortages in other commodities, as heating oil, cooking oil, sugar, soy sauce, and salt were subjected to panic-buying. Private taxi owners, in real danger of losing their livelihoods, were forced to form long lines at gasoline stations for daily supplies of gasoline and LP gas.

Thus, the double shock of the oil crisis and food shortages created a psychological atmosphere among consumers that exacerbated the situation. However, a number of private businessmen saw this as the chance of a lifetime and attempted to take advantage of the confusion by holding goods off the market in anticipation of huge price increases. The media gave wide coverage to such cases, evoking a public outcry against private enterprises that were exploiting the crisis in order to reap huge profits. Some idea of the scale of the panic may be suggested by the run on the Toyokawa Credit Association, in Aichi Prefecture, in which depositors withdrew ¥2 billion in one and a half days, forcing the Ministry of Finance and the Bank of Japan to dispatch representatives to assure local residents that their deposits were secure.

Thus, the immediate aftermath of the "oil shock" was this phenomenal disruption, in which each new rumor threatened to spark off another panic. Moreover, this atmosphere pervaded long after the dreams of Shōwa Genroku and the "plan for rebuilding the Japanese archipelago" had been shattered by the oil crisis. Indeed, the spreading panic, and the psychology of "me first," "as long as we're OK," and "if we can just make a profit" suggested to many observers that there had been a collapse of ethics and that Japan had become a society of egoists. However, the most serious problem during this period was still the failure of the government to ward off such a crisis by formulating policies and an administrative framework that would enable it to deal effectively with new domestic problems. In fact, the government did not begin to develop positive countermeasures until the situation had reached critical dimensions.

Finally, in December 1973, MITI began to restrict the consumption of oil-generated electric power in specific industries through administrative guidance. On December 7, 1973, the cabinet submitted two comprehensive laws to deal with shortages and restrain speculation: the Petroleum Supply and Demand Normalization Law and the Emergency Measures Law for the Stabilization of the People's Livelihood. The two laws were promulgated on December 22 after only two weeks of debate in the Diet. The speed of their passage itself, however, reflects just how serious the situation had become in the absence of effective policies. In part, this was due to the sudden death of the minister of finance, Kiichi Aichi, at the peak of the oil crisis, and the period of transition after he was replaced by Takeo Fukuda. In fact, Fukuda quickly announced new policies to deal with the rampant inflation that accompanied large increases in oil prices and the deterioration of the balance of payments situation, which had left Japan with a $1.1 billion deficit in November 1973.

Fukuda's policies called for a strict reduction of aggregate demand through restraints on fiscal spending by the government, on investment outlays by private industry, and on consumer spending. On December 22, interest rates were increased by 2 percent, raising the official discount rate to a postwar high of 9 percent. At the same time, a stringent fiscal budget was drafted for 1974 and Deputy Prime Minister Takeo Miki was dispatched as a special envoy to eight Middle Eastern countries to improve Japan's relations with the oil-producing countries.[3]

2. JAPAN'S RESPONSE TO THE CHANGING INTERNATIONAL ENVIRONMENT

The Period of "Crazy Prices." Despite the new policy initiatives hammered out in December 1973, the state of the Japanese economy after the "oil shock" was far removed from the rosy picture painted by the Tanaka plan. The New Year dawned with large-scale increases in the prices of bread and noodles, and toilet paper and synthetic detergents did not reappear on supermarket shelves until March. It was Fukuda who first referred to this temporary excess demand and abnormal inflation as the "crazy prices" phenomenon. This period peaked in February and March 1974, when wholesale prices increased 37 percent and consumer prices 26 percent over the same period a year earlier. Ultimately, the true nature of the oil crisis was one of an inflation crisis, and Japan suffered most among the advanced countries. Even after the end of the war in the Middle East and the removal of import restrictions, severe inflationary pressures remained due to the large-scale increase in the benchmark price for oil. Both the Diet and the government were under strong pressure to develop solutions to the problem of "crazy prices."

The social frictions created by "crazy prices" were brought into sharp focus in February 1974, when officials of the Fair Trade Commission raided the offices of twelve petroleum-refining and distribution companies and the Petroleum Association of Japan. The commission subsequently charged the companies with operating an illegal price cartel during the oil crisis and turned its evidence to the Tokyo High Prosecutor's Office after publicly warning them to roll back prices. In May, the companies, the Petroleum Association, and seventeen executives were indicted for violations of the Antimonopoly Law. These sensational events were followed by similar raids on offices of detergent producers and general trading companies by officials of MITI. The attack on private industry culminated in a special Diet debate on prices, to which representatives of

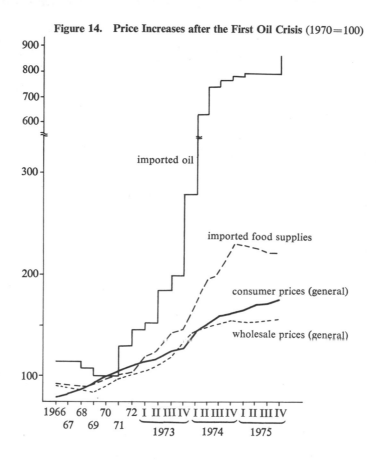

Figure 14. Price Increases after the First Oil Crisis (1970=100)

industries that had recorded particularly high increases were summoned as witnesses. The Diet session occurred during a highly emotional, and often indiscriminate, campaign by the media against the petroleum companies, general trading companies, and big business in general, which were charged with having made enormous profits during the crisis through collusive price-fixing, anticipatory price increases, and holding goods off the market.

There is no denying that a number of companies deserved such harsh criticism and that cases of collusive price-fixing did occur. However, in the rush to censure private industry, a lack of attention was paid to those policies that had caused the crisis. Tanaka's grandiose plan had set the stage for an inflationary crisis even before the "oil shock," and the failure of the government to assess the situation after the "oil shock" was responsible for its devastating impact on the domestic economy. It was with some justification, therefore, that many business leaders began to use the word "scapegoat" in response to public criticism. Nevertheless, on March 31, the Diet passed the Special Temporary Corporate Profits Tax Law, introduced by opposition parties specifically to siphon off the excess profits of large corporations.

"Crazy prices" also spawned the atmosphere for abnormal wage increases. During the spring wage offensive of 1974, workers won increases of 32.9 percent in basic wages, compared to 24.1 percent the previous year. Reflected in these figures is the fact that management had lost the power to resist labor's demands, which were made against a background of widespread criticism of large corporations. Without the traditional spirit of cooperation that characterizes labor–management relations, there was ample reason for concern that an unmoderated wage-price spiral would push inflation rates even higher. Yoshio Kaneko, a specialist in labor–management relations, describes the wage increases of 1974 as follows.

> The mistake made during the spring wage offensive of 1974 by labor and management was that basic wages were increased on the basis of the windfall profits created by "crazy prices." These excess profits should have been converted to public revenues through new tax measures. Even if they could have been redistributed in the form of wages, this should have been dealt with as employee welfare benefits or as a one-time increase. What turned these windfall profits into excessive increases in basic wages was the inflexibility of Japanese-style labor relations and the spring wage offensive system, which had developed during the period of high-speed growth. Thus, the force of habits developed under completely different conditions resulted in an irreversible increase in the level of fixed personnel expenses. This not only exacerbated the problems of management during the subsequent recession but also had serious consequences for the price system. Ultimately a new balance would have to be achieved, and this meant a new price system, at much higher levels, that would be based on the premise of increased labor costs. (Yoshio Kaneko, *"Sengo no chingin kettei"* [Wage settlements in the postwar period] *ESP*, November 1976)

The phenomenon of "crazy prices" put an end to the expansionary policies of the Tanaka cabinet, and the government was finally forced to implement a stringent retrenchment policy aimed at dampening demand and checking inflation. The ¥1.25 trillion of public works expenditures budgeted for 1973 were postponed until the following year, and a target of zero growth in new appropriations was adopted for 1974. Taking into account the phenomenal price increases for construction materials during the period, this amounted to a substantial cut in public works projects. The government also implemented stringent monetary policies. Besides a tightening of window guidance by the Bank of Japan, selective credit restrictions were applied to such "problem" industries as real estate, construction, and general trading companies. The latter policy was designed to reduce the temporary excess demand that had developed in specific industries and to put the brake on inflationary expectations in industries that had become the focus of public outrage over "crazy prices."

The late Kamekichi Takahashi opposed government intervention on the grounds that not only Japan but the entire world was experiencing a revolution in the international price system due to oil. However, given the political situation, it was impossible for the government to ignore public demands for positive measures to deal with inflation. Based on the Emergency Measures Law for the Stabilization of the People's Livelihood, price controls were established for lighting oil, LPG, tissue paper, and toilet paper. In addition, for fifty-nine commodities, including steel materials and vinyl chloride, prior approval of price increases had to be sought in order to prevent opportunistic increases following upward price revisions for petroleum products. This direct intervention by the government on a relatively wide scale was a new development in anti-inflationary policies. The government also took steps to reduce the number of cartels exempted from the restrictions of the Antimonopoly Law and to rationalize the system of resale price maintenance.

In November 1974, Tanaka was forced to resign when a scandal broke over his money-power politics. On December 9, Takeo Miki, known as the "Mr. Clean" of Japanese politics, formed a new cabinet, and Takeo Fukuda was appointed deputy prime minister and director of the Economic Planning Agency. Fukuda publicly promised to give price stabilization top priority and to reduce inflation to below 15 percent in 1974 and below 10 percent in 1975. Prime Minister Miki actively supported a proposal by the Fair Trade Commission to revise the Antimonopoly Law but encountered stiff opposition within the LDP over provisions that would have empowered the commission to split companies that had achieved near-monopoly in their industries. Ultimately, Miki's sponsorship proved inadequate and the bill was squashed in the Upper House.[4]

The Collapse of the Myth of High-Speed Growth. Due largely to the influence of Fukuda, whose authority within the government after the resignation of Tanaka was almost as great as Miki's, strong anti-inflationary measures continued to be the keynote of economic policy in 1974 and 1975. These policies successfully held down consumer price increases to the levels Fukuda had promised, and the period of "crazy prices" was finally brought to an end. The general level of wholesale prices declined in January 1975 for the first time in thirty-six months, and even land prices, which had continued to leap during the period of "crazy prices," began to show a downward tendency. However, this process was accompanied by the deepest and the most prolonged recession in Japan's postwar history.

In the period immediately following OPEC's elimination of restrictions on the oil supply, few observers viewed the economic downturn as a serious problem. Professor Osamu Shimomura's "zero-growth theory" was distinctly a minority opinion, and the opposite view, that the economy was in a "transitory recession," commanded a considerable following. However, the recession lasted much longer and was much more severe than had been anticipated by these optimistic forecasts. In 1974, real GNP declined for the first time in the postwar period. This was a shock to the Japanese, who had grown accustomed to high levels of economic growth even during long periods of recession, and effectively destroyed one of the myths of high-speed growth. Even during the bottom-of-the-pot recession of 1958 or the recession of 1965, economic growth had reached levels of 5 percent to 6 percent, and the negative growth of 1974 transformed Japanese perceptions of the future of the economy. There were large-scale declines in private plant and equipment investment, in private investment in housing construction, and in government investment, while personal consumption increased by only 1 percent. The "oil shock" had brought a permanent end to the "disposables economy," and household budgets displayed a marked tendency toward cutting back. In part, this reflected a rising consciousness among consumers of the need to conserve resources and their wariness after the "crazy prices." Until the end of summer 1974, private enterprises continued to enjoy the inflationary profits that had been produced by shortages and "crazy prices," and their

Table 18. Fiscal and Monetary Policies for Economic Stimulation

FISCAL POLICY	MONETARY POLICY

• First-round measures (decision made Feb. 14, 1975)

(1) Stepping up conclusion and implementation of public works contracts within the framework of appropriations for FY 1974 fourth quarter.

(2) Stepping up execution of FY 1974 fourth quarter programs by organizations receiving appropriations under the fiscal loan and investment program.

• Second-round measures (decision made March 24, 1975)

(1) Ensuring smooth execution of public works projects and other programs in FY 1975 first half.	Official discount rate cut by 0.5% April 16, 1975 (from 9% to 8.5%)

(2) Requesting local public organizations to insure smooth execution of public works programs.

(3) Expanding the framework of local bond issues for FY 1974 (¥177,100 million) and ensuring smooth issuance of local government bonds for FY 1975.

• Third-round measures (decision made June 16, 1975)

(1) Promoting residential construction moving up to FY 1975 first half from second half the loan schedule (equivalent to about 50,000 dwelling units) of Housing Loan Corp. and Okinawa Development Finance Corp. (including only housing loan contracts with individuals).	Rate cut by another 0.5% June 7 (from 8.5% to 8.0%) Rate cut by another 0.5% Aug. 13 (from 8.0% to 7.5%)

(2) Promoting pollution abatement programs and safety countermeasures (expanding the ceiling of development loans from Environmental Pollution Control Service Corp.).

(3) Ensuring smooth execution of public works projects and other programs in FY 1975 first half (target rate of contract signing in the same period set at about 70%).

• Fourth-round measures (decision made Sept. 17, 1975)

(1) Promoting public works and other projects (additional appropriation of ¥867,200 million made; then, the ceiling of local government bond issues raised by ¥206,600 million).	Rate cut by 1% Oct. 24 (from 7.5% to 6.5%) Reserve requirements reduced Nov. 16 Further reduction announced Feb. 1, 1976

(2) Promoting residential construction (raising loan ceilings of Housing Loan Corp. and other lending agencies by ¥260,000 million (equivalent to about 70,000 dwelling units). The amount translates into ¥560,000 million in total value of construction work involved.

(3) Promoting private investment in new plant and equipment, such as pollution abatement investment involving ¥95,000 million in new appropriations (meaning an additional ¥160,000 million in total value of such investment).

Source: Economic White Paper, 1975–76.

expectations for the future remained bullish. Once the temporary demand subsided in fall and winter 1974, however, private industry was faced with declining prices, rapid involuntary increases in inventory, and the necessity of large cutbacks in production.

The sense of recession spread rapidly. Despite simultaneous large increases in raw materials and labor costs, companies now found it impossible to pass these costs onto the consumer in the form of higher prices, and most firms suffered profit declines. Indeed, the number of firms that were forced to liquidate in order to pay off outstanding debts increased rapidly during this period. Faced with deteriorating profit ratios, many firms attempted to cut back on personnel expenses by adopting employment adjustment measures such as reducing overtime allowances, encouraging early retirement, and suspending recruitment of new school graduates. The Employment Security Bureau's effective ratio of job openings to applicants fell drastically. Largely thanks to the Employment Adjustment Subsidy Program, which was launched in January 1975, personnel cutbacks did not reach the high levels of the United States and Western Europe. However, while they were not included in government unemployment statistics, the furloughed workers who received subsidies under this program reach 444,000 at the peak of the recession, representing a new type of "unemployment."

The government announced stimulatory fiscal and monetary policies in February, March, and June 1975, but these, which came to be known as the first, second, and third rounds of Measures for Economic Stimulation, were by no means sufficient to stimulate a recovery. The most important reason for the government's cautious approach in the first three rounds of antirecessionary policies was concern over the outcome of the spring wage offensive. It was feared that a large-scale wage increase in 1975, on top of the 33 percent won by labor in 1974, would result in a reacceleration of the wage-price spiral and that it would therefore be impossible to restrain consumer price increases to levels below the 10 percent promised by Fukuda. In fact, the second reduction of the official discount rate, from 8.5 to 8 percent, was delayed until the third round of antirecessionary measures in June, after the spring wage offensive. However, the government's fears were unfounded as the spring wage offensive ended with an increase of only 13.1 percent in basic wages. Unlike the situation in 1974, there had been a drastic decline in corporate profit ratios and, consequently, in the ability of enterprises to cope with another large-scale increase in personnel costs. Given such conditions, it would have been unthinkable for labor to demand high increases. In fact, those who had warned of a further acceleration of the wage-price spiral after the spring wage offensive had seriously underestimated the flexibility of the Japanese labor relations system.

The result of the government's failure to implement expansive policies more quickly was a worsening of the recession between spring and summer 1975. One out of three major firms listed in the first section of the Tokyo Stock Exchange was reported to have slipped into the red. The number of bankruptcies reported in 1975 was even higher than in 1974, when it had reached a record level for the postwar period, and the manufacturing index declined for the second successive year. Deteriorating profits and production cutbacks also exacerbated fears of a full-fledged unemployment problem. Corporations that had rushed to buy up land during the boom inspired by the Tanaka plan now found they had no buyers, resulting in a further tightening of corporate liquidity.

The industries hardest hit were those that had received the full brunt of massive increases in costs for petroleum and electric power, such industrial materials industries as steel, nonferrous metals, petrochemicals, and textiles. Following the large-scale bankruptcies in these industries in summer 1975, the government finally changed course and in September adopted a fourth round of antirecessionary measures that represented a clear shift to expansionary policies. Fiscal policies included an additional ¥800 billion for public works expenditures and the raising of loan ceilings of the Housing Loan Corporation by ¥260 billion (about 70,000 units). In October the Bank of Japan's official discount rate was lowered by an additional 1 percent along with reductions in deposit reserve requirements. Moreover, the budget for 1976 included a 26.4 percent increase over 1975 for public works projects.

Prolonged Recession and the Explosion of Fiscal Deficits. The prolonged recession produced huge losses in tax revenue in 1975, which declined by 10 percent compared to 1974, falling short of government projections by a hefty ¥3.5 trillion. Moreover, the supplementary budget implemented on November 7, 1975, included the increased fiscal spending measures of the fourth round of antirecessionary policies. In order to make up the losses in tax revenue and pursue its expansionary fiscal policies, the government was forced to issue "special national bonds" (deficit-covering bonds) and construction bonds amounting to ¥2.29 trillion. This represented a huge increase in the government's rate of fiscal dependence on bond issues, from 9.4 percent in 1974 to 26.3 percent in 1975. The most important cause of this large fiscal deficit was the decline in corporate tax revenue due to the fall in profitability, but it was further exacerbated by the stagnation of personal income tax and personal business tax receipts.

The number of local governments experiencing fiscal deficits also increased as direct revenue-sharing transfers from the national government (32 percent of corporate, income, and liquor tax revenues) declined at the same time that personnel costs were skyrocketing. Moreover, local governments were under pressure from the national government to increase public works expenditures as part of the fourth round of anti-recessionary policies. While there was a considerable time lag between appropriations for such projects at the local level, the problem for local administrators was that they were already forced to deal with budget deficits by resorting to such extreme measures as issuing deficit-covering bonds and selling assets. In many cases, the central government's call for even higher levels of spending was met with local protests against reckless welfare spending and the excessive burden on local governments.

At the beginning of 1976, recovery of the economy began to accelerate, due largely to a sharp rise in exports with the rapid economic recovery of the United States. The improved export performance was particularly remarkable in the automobile and home electronics industries, but rising exports in these industries stimulated demand in related industries, and the gloomy business climate seemed finally to be showing signs of life. Unfortunately, the recovery was extremely short-lived, and by summer the economy had once again slipped into recession, although some observers viewed this stagnation as a temporary slowdown. A number of factors may be cited to explain this reversal. Increases in basic wages after the spring wage offensive of 1976, at 8.8 percent, were even lower than for 1975, when they had been held to 13.1 percent. This, together with increases in social security taxes and charges for public services, meant that there was very little increase in disposable real income, resulting in a stagnation of personal consumption. More important, the famous Lockheed scandal involving former Prime Minister Tanaka, and the subsequent political turmoil, acted to disrupt government economic policies for recovery.

On February 4, 1976, the U.S. Senate Subcommittee on Multinational Corporations made public the evidence that Lockheed had bribed Japanese government officials, including Tanaka, in its attempts to sell airliners to All Nippon Airways. The ensuing scandal had an impact on Japanese politics perhaps more profound than the Watergate scandal in

Table 19. Increase of the National Debt

(¥100 millions)

	New issues of national bonds	Amount of deficit-covering bonds	Rate of dependence on national bonds (%)
1965	1,972	0	5.2
1966	6,656	0	14.9
1967	7,094	0	13.8
1968	4,621	0	7.7
1969	4,126	0	5.9
1970	3,472	0	4.2
1971	11,871	0	12.4
1972	19,500	0	16.3
1973	17,662	0	12.9
1974	21,600	0	11.3
1975 (original budget)	20,000	0	9.4
1975 (revised budget)	52,805	20,905	25.3
1976 (original budget)	72,750	37,500	29.9
1976 (revised budget)	71,982	34,732	29.2
1977 (original budget)	84,800	40,500	29.7
1977 (revised budget)	99,850	49,570	34.0
1978 (original budget)	109,860	49,350	32.0

Note: Rate of dependence on national bonds is the percentage of total budgeted expenditures accounted for by new bond issues.

the United States. The Diet session of 1976 convened and closed with an investigation into the roles played by Tanaka, Marubeni Corporation, and All Nippon Airways in the bribery, leading to the arrest of Tanaka and a number of prominent figures. One of the immediate effects of the scandal was to postpone again the Diet debate on the fiscal budget and related legislation.

Factional struggles within the LDP caused by the Lockheed scandal created a political vacuum, with the LDP powerless in the face of opposition demands that discussion of the scandal precede action on the budget. After serving as a provisional budget for forty days, it was finally passed by the Diet in early April 1976, but the government was unable to push through the related legislation during the regular session. As a result, dissatisfaction within the LDP with Miki's administration erupted in intense factional struggles. Finally, an extraordinary Diet session was convened, and the Fiscal Special Measures Law, which provided for the issue of special deficit-covering bonds, was passed on October 15. Legislation approving increases for the Japan National Railways and the Nippon Telegraph and Telephone Public Corporation was passed on November 4. With Upper House elections imminent, the opposition parties took full advantage of the Lockheed scandal to stall passage of the government's fiscal program, opposing the increases for rail and telephone services until the bitter end. The long delay meant that the public works investments envisioned as part of the fourth round of antirecessionary measures also had to be delayed. Construction projects planned by the Japan National Railways and Nippon Telegraph and Telephone were sharply curtailed in real terms, which contributed to the stagnation of economic recovery.

Moreover, the delay in implementing the government's stimulatory policies, together with a severe typhoon and frost damage in Hokkaido and northeastern Japan, created even larger budget deficits. The government's original budget proposal had included a public works reserve fund and had assumed that a midyear supplementary budget should not be necessary for the first time since the war. However, the large increase in public works expenditures due to delays in construction projects made the issue of ¥100 billion new national bonds unavoidable.

The LDP suffered a serious defeat in the Upper House elections on December 5, 1976, and Miki was forced to resign as prime minister and president of the party. Takeo Fukuda won the subsequent party election by only one vote and was appointed prime minister on December 24. However, the overwhelming majority of the LDP in the Diet had been eroded, and the elections had created an unstable political situation in which the ruling LDP and the opposition parties were almost evenly balanced. A supplementary budget for 1976 had already been drafted by the Miki Cabinet, and Fukuda managed to push it through the Diet in January 1977. This called for deficit-covering bonds and construction bonds totaling ¥7.375 trillion, a 33 percent increase over the previous year, increasing the rate of fiscal dependence on bond issues to 29.9 percent. Moreover, the 1977 budget called for an even greater expansion of the national debt. Total bond issues increased to ¥8.48 trillion, and the government's dependence on deficit financing exceeded 30 percent for the first time since the war. This explosion of deficit spending resulted from two contradictory factors. On the one hand, the budget proposals submitted by the Ministry of Finance called for even greater increases in public works expenditures in order to revive the economy. On the other hand, the LDP and opposition parties were gearing up for a general election that would determine whether the LDP could maintain control, and both sides campaigned on the promise of an income tax reduction. Therefore, both expansionary spending policies and the anticipated tax cut were written into the budget for 1977.

Ultimately, the cost of the prolonged recession was a huge increase in the national debt. The total of new bond issues in the three-year period from 1975 to 1977 reached ￥21.34 trillion, and total long-term debt at the end of March 1978 was approximately ￥30 trillion. Moreover, there is little reason to suppose that this high rate of dependence on bond issues can be reduced even if the government pursues an aggressive policy of increasing taxation and the public's burden for social security. In a period when private capital investment and business conditions are stagnant, expansive fiscal policies in the form of deficit spending programs are essential if the domestic economy is to be brought back into balance. Moreover, while the demand of private industry for capital is weak, these huge issues of national bonds can be absorbed by the financial market. However, Japan's financial markets lack a normal interest rates function and, because the issue of national bonds has always been considered an extreme measure, well-defined institutions to regulate bond issues have not yet been established. Given these conditions, unique among advanced countries, there is no guarantee that this huge increase in national debt will not produce severe inflationary pressures and throw financial markets into panic once the economy enters a boom.

Moreover, it is by no means true that the explosion of budget deficits was caused exclusively by the prolonged recession. Despite the fact that the economy is moving out of the period of high-speed growth into a period of moderate or slow growth, projections of fiscal revenues and expenditures continue to be made on the assumption of high-speed growth. This has contributed in no small measure to the rigidity of fiscal administration, as well as to the creation of large deficits. The balanced budget policies of the high-speed growth period, in which all of the tax revenues for a given year were spent in the same year, were valid during the early period of high-speed growth. However, there is no question that tax reductions would have been more effective during periods of recession, or that the government could have responded to fluctuations in the business cycle more effectively if these policies had been revised at an earlier stage in the economic slowdown. For example, the early establishment of a reserve fund to moderate fluctuations in the business cycle would have been desirable. If the national deficit is to be reduced in the future, there is a need for bold adjustments of fiscal policy and administration, as well as a sweeping reformulation of the national tax system.

Japan's Worst Postwar Recession in Retrospect. The first oil crisis had a devastating effect on Japan's economic performance, producing large deficits in the international balance of payments, runaway inflation, and lastly a prolonged recession. In 1973, Japan's deficit in the international balance of payments, $13.4 billion, was the largest in postwar history, but by 1976 it once again enjoyed a healthy trade surplus of $3.2 billion. The period of "crazy prices" reached its peak in 1975, and in 1976, the rise in consumer prices was held to a single-digit increase. While the balance of payments and inflation showed signs of steady improvement, the deflationary effects of the oil crisis continued to be felt until the end of 1978, and it was this aspect of the domestic economy that most clearly revealed the full impact of the oil crisis.

The recession following the first oil shock was the most severe of the postwar period, and recovery from it was exceptionally sluggish. The overall production index for mining and manufacturing industries finally recovered to peak levels of October 1973 in 1978, after five years of stagnation. Even with recovery, the index of lifetime employment in the manufacturing industries was 10 percent below that of 1973. Similarly, private plant and equipment investment and inventory investment, leading indicators of real demand, remained stagnant at 46 percent and 18 percent, respectively, below 1973. Private investment in housing was also significantly below peak levels of 1973.

The bottom of the recession in terms of corporate profitability occurred in the first half of 1975 and, compared to the peak of business upturn in the first half of 1973 just before the oil crisis, profits in all industries had declined by 70 percent. More striking, profits in the manufacturing industries had declined by 84 percent. Indeed, industries such as textiles, steel, nonferrous metals (aluminum and copper), and petrochemicals recorded large deficits in 1975. Even among the firms that managed to avoid slipping into the red, many had done so only by selling assets or eating into capital accumulated during the high-speed growth period. One out of every two major firms listed in the first section of the Tokyo Stock Exchange was reported to be operating in the red in 1975. After 1975, the profit positions of a number of industries began to improve. The automobile and household electric appliance industries were supported by expanding exports, the petroleum-refining industry benefited from increased prices for petroleum products, and a number of other industries were able to improve earnings through reductions in personnel.

However, at the same time, it became clear that many industries had been left with excess capacity and deprived of the foundations for corporate profitability on a long-term basis, the so-called structurally depressed industries. This problem took various forms. For example, the aluminum-refining industry was crippled by the explosion in energy costs while the shipbuilding industry was threatened by a severe decline in international orders following the oil crisis. Textiles and plywood faced a worldwide adjustment problem as firms in these industries met strong competition from developing nations on international markets and a flood of imports at home. Similarly, the chemical fertilizers industry quickly lost its international market due to the ability of the developing nations to supply their own needs. Petrochemicals, once the symbol of high-speed growth, received perhaps the most direct blow from the oil crisis as the explosion in prices for naptha, the basic raw material, quickly undermined profits. Other industries that were eventually designated structurally depressed industries were electric blast furnaces, vinyl chloride resins, soda, cardboard, industrial machinery, sugar refining, and in the nonmanufacturing sector, marine transportation. In the manufacturing sector alone, these structurally depressed industries comprised as much as 15 percent to 20 percent of the overall industrial structure, and their decline in profitability had a serious impact on the problem of declining levels of employment in the industrial sector. In May 1968, the Temporary Measures Law for the Stabilization of Designated Depressed Industries was established for the purpose of promoting a necessary shift in the industrial structure.

Given this background, it is worth asking why the post–oil crisis recession was so serious, and why it lasted so long. This question may be answered both in terms of actual developments worldwide and at home, and from the evaluation of economic policies pursued then. First, from the point of view of economic developments, the post–oil crisis recession was not an ordinary cyclical downturn but was more of what might be called the "end of high-speed economic growth recession." That is, the recession occurred in the process of the economy's shift from long term growth rates of 10 percent a year to much slower growth. The average annual growth rate during the latter half of the 1970s had declined to 5 percent. Until immediately after the oil crisis, private enterprises continued to base investment plans on the expectation of rapid increases in demand, and private plant and equipment investment was designed to expand production by about 10 percent annually.

The changes wrought in the domestic and world economies by the oil crisis resulted in a rapid decline in total effective demand, and Japanese industry was left with the worsening problem of excess capacity. With the precipitous decline of effective demand, it was impossible for private enterprises to reduce plant and equipment capacity rapidly enough to avoid a wide supply–demand gap, and it was for this reason that the period of adjustment in private plant and equipment investment lasted so long. The existence of excess capacity, and the resulting stagnation of demand generated by capital investment, placed severe pressures on the profitability of many private industries and, for the first time in the postwar period, companies in these industries began to devote all their energies to reducing their work force. Against this background, the rate of increase in real wages declined drastically, and the resulting decline in real income reduced the growth rate of real consumer demand to levels less than half those of the period of high-speed growth.

Turning to the second problem, that of evaluating economic policies during this period, it would be difficult to argue that the government's policies were appropriate. Even while the government made a point of emphasizing publicly that the period of high-speed growth had ended, it is now clear that within government itself, and within the ruling LDP, there was a persistent naive confidence in the economy's ability to maintain a pattern of high-speed growth and in private industry's desire to expand capital investment. Moreover, in the rush to stabilize "crazy prices" and bring inflation rates down to one-digit levels, the relaxation of stringent monetary policies and the implementation of stimulative antirecessionary policies were delayed for too long.

Indeed, the government was not able to adopt an effective antirecessionary policy until the fall of 1975, when large fiscal deficits resulting from the decline of tax revenue at the end of the recession emerged as a serious problem. Even then, these government measures fell far short of what was needed to generate a recovery. In January 1976, the Economic Deliberation Council, the prime minister's advisory group on the economy, submitted its "Economic Plan for the First Half of the Shōwa 50s" (1976–80), a scenario for putting the economy on the road to stable growth. This plan called for midterm real annual growth rates of 6 percent and relatively high growth rates in the first three years of the plan (1976–79) in order to close the gap between supply and demand and set the stage for stable growth. However, due to national fiscal considerations, official government projections for 1976, the first year of the plan, called for a growth rate of only 5.7 percent, which was even lower than the midterm annual averages envisioned by the plan, a good indication of the government's passive posture toward stimulating domestic demand. Moreover, as suggested above, the antirecessionary fiscal measures provided for by the national budget for 1976 were delayed by the political turmoil surrounding the Lockheed scandal in early 1976.

The budget was delayed until the end of the year and, with factional struggles within the LDP and the threat that the LDP might lose its majority in the general election, antirecessionary policy was almost completely neglected. Against this background, private enterprises, which were struggling to eke out tiny profits in a stagnant climate, were forced to launch an export drive. Supported by the recovery of the American economy, exports grew steadily and the international balance of payments situation shifted to one of substantial surpluses. Unfortunately, the government's inability to adopt aggressive policies to stimulate the domestic economy, together with the sustained export drive by private industry, invited strident criticism from America and Europe.

Among the advanced nations, the United States recovered most quickly from the worldwide post–oil crisis recession. With the elections in mind, the U.S. administration pursued an aggressive policy to cut unemployment, and the sharp rise in food prices during the food supply crisis had significantly improved the U.S. balance of payments situation and made feasible the pursuit of stimulative policies. However, due to an unexpectedly large increase in oil imports and the time lag between America's recovery and that of other advanced countries, the U.S. balance of payments situation deteriorated after 1976, and the subsequent fall of the dollar against other international currencies once again threatened to disrupt world economy. In contrast to U.S. economic policy, which was too expansionary too soon, the shift of Japanese economic policy to measures designed to stimulate the economy and restore internal-external equilibrium was too late.

Against this background, the focus of high-level international conferences turned to the policies Japan should pursue to reduce international economic and trade frictions. In negotiations between Japan and the United States at the end of 1977, Japan's economic growth rate for 1978 became the subject of an international agreement. Subsequently, during

Prime Minister Fukuda's visit to America in May 1978 and at the Bonn Summit in June, attention focused on whether Japan would be able to achieve 7 percent growth that year. The United States and Britain were pursuing expansionary policies designed to deal with their unemployment problems while Japan and West Germany were placing more emphasis on stabilizing prices. As a result, Japan and West Germany were recording larger trade surpluses while the United States and Britain were suffering larger deficits. Japan, in particular, was strongly requested to raise its exchange rate, increase economic growth, stimulate domestic demand, and open its markets to imports.

In this international environment, the exchange rate for the yen rose dramatically against the dollar: from ¥290 at the beginning of 1977 to ¥240 at the end of the year, and from ¥220 in spring of 1978 to ¥180 in the fall. Ultimately, the growth rate of the Japanese economy reached only 5.7 percent in 1978, substantially below the 7 percent demanded by the other advanced nations at the Bonn Summit. However, the rise in the value of the yen contributed significantly to a reduction in Japan's trade surplus and helped to ameliorate trade imbalances with the other advanced nations.

The Problem of Reduced Oil Supplies: Differences between the First and Second Oil Crises. By fall 1978, the domestic economy finally seemed to be on the road to a healthy recovery. The earnings position of private industry was improving and there was a visible increase in both plant and equipment investment and inventory investment. Moreover, with the stabilization in prices, real private consumption began to recover its momentum and the economy was finally growing on the basis of domestic demand. The employment situation improved and in 1979, unemployment actually declined. Just as these favorable developments were taking place in the domestic economy, the second "oil shock" was sparked by the Iranian revolution. Discussion at the Tokyo Summit, held in June 1979 at the height of the crisis, centered on an agreement among major oil-consuming nations to curtail oil imports.

In the turmoil of the revolution, Iranian oil production dropped to 500,000 barrels a day, and the subsequent shortages and OPEC surcharges resulted in a huge increase in the benchmark price of oil, which once again threw Japan's balance of payments into a deficit and produced severe inflationary pressures. However, Japan's response to the second "oil shock" stands in vivid contrast to the panic that followed the first one.

Table 20. Key Economic Indicators after the Oil Crises

	Overall balance of payments ($100 millions)	Increases in wholesale prices	Increases in consumer prices	Growth in real GNP	Increases in manufacturing production	Totally unemployed (10 thousands)
1972 FY	29.6	3.2%	4.5%	10.4%	10.2%	70
1973	−134.0	22.6	11.7	6.5	13.5	68
1974	−33.9	23.4	24.5	−0.0	−9.4	80
1975	−17.7	1.9	10.4	3.2	−4.4	104
1976	32.5	5.5	9.4	5.9	10.8	106
1977	121.5	0.4	6.7	5.8	3.2	113
1978	−23.0	−2.3	3.4	5.7	7.0	122
1979	−189.5	12.9	4.8	6.1	9.3	114

Table 21. Post–"Oil Shock" Decline of Profitability of Firms in Manufacturing Industries

	First half of 1975	First half of 1977
All Industries	30.5	00.3
Non-manufacturing industries	69.5	125.7
Manufacturing industries	15.7	73.5
Textiles	−58.7	−29.2
Steel	−23.3	7.2
Non-ferrous metals	−93.3	−13.5
General machinery	83.3	66.5
Electrical machinery	48.5	111.8
Shipbuilding	59.4	73.0
Automobiles	121.2	257.3
Chemicals	17.6	85.6
Oil refining	−205.5	190.1
Ceramics	8.0	61.0
Paper pulp	−69.3	51.5
Processed foods	33.0	128.7

Note: − indicates deficit.

Source: Bank of Japan, *Shuyō kigyō tanki keizai kansoku* (Short-term economic outlook of major enterprises), based on a survey of 384 large firms.

Both the government and private industry responded to the crisis with relative calm and, ultimately, displayed a high degree of creativity. Indeed, it is no exaggeration to say that Japan's effectiveness in responding to the second oil crisis was responsible for the strong position Japan enjoys today in the world economy. It is thus worth examining the domestic and international conditions that made it possible for Japan to recover so quickly from the crisis and restructure its economy to deal with the new international environment.

The first significant difference between the first "oil shock" and the second was that the government had increased oil stockpiles from a fifty-day to a hundred-day supply, an indication that the government had learned its lesson well. Indeed, one of the most important developments since the first oil crisis was that Japan's international economic policy became much more sophisticated. Immediately before the first oil crisis, the government had responded to the problem of excess liquidity inflation with the wrong kind of policy. Despite the existence of severe inflationary pressures, Tanaka had pushed ahead with his grandiose plan, insuring that the inflationary psychology would spread throughout the economy. These pressures exploded after the first oil crisis and, faced with "crazy prices," the government had no choice but to give priority to curbing the abnormal inflation at the cost of plunging the economy into the deepest and most prolonged recession of the postwar period. Policy makers had learned from this experience, and mushrooming fiscal deficits had created a growing realization that there would be severe limitations on the sources of revenues needed to fuel a recovery if the economy were allowed to slip into another recession.

Therefore, after the second oil crisis, the government pursued a policy that it called "keeping an eye on both inflation and the business cycle." That is, economic policy would not be allowed to become slanted too much in the direction of restraining inflation, and careful consideration would be given to the task of maintaining economic growth. Moreover, the government recognized the necessity of allowing private enterprises to pass on increased energy costs to consumers in the form of higher prices and refrained from intervening as it had done after the previous oil crisis. Despite this, private industry exercised restraint in raising prices and played a major role in preventing the sudden rise of oil prices from creating an inflationary spiral in the domestic economy. As I will discuss in more detail below, private industry also played an important role in reducing inflationary pressures by implementing ambitious investment programs

Table 22. Comparison on the Depths of Postwar Recessions

	Mining–manu-facturing production	Producers' inventory ratios	Capacity utilization ratios	Lifetime employment in all industries
1954 recession	−5.1%	+31.5%	....	−1.3%
1958 recession	−9.4	+58.2	−19.9%	−0.2
1962 recession	−3.3	+33.7	−10.7	−1.4
1965 recession	−2.9	+13.3	−8.2	−1.2
1971 recession	−2.7	+27.8	−8.8	−1.4
"Oil shock" recession	−20.2	+78.1	−24.0	−4.0

Note: Figures represent percentage changes in seasonal-adjusted monthly statistics from the peak to the bottom of each recession.

Table 23. Comparison of Changes in Demand in Major Postwar Recessions

	Bottom-of-the-pot recession (1958)	Structural recession (1965)	"Oil shocks" 1974	"Oil shocks" 1977/1973
Real GNP	6.0%	5.7%	−0.2%	12.8%(3.0%)
Real personal consumption	4.8	5.5	3.2	16.2(3.8)
Real private housing investment	14.8	17.1	−14.4	−1.3(−0.3)
Real private investment in plant and equipment	−6.6	−9.1	−14.5	−17.5(−4.1)
Real government investment	3.8	15.1	2.2	16.6(3.9)
Real private inventory investment	−89.4	0.2	−25.0	−45.9(−9.9)
Real exports	8.4	18.8	23.5	63.3(13.0)
Real imports	−8.0	7.8	4.9	13.7(3.2)
Mining–manufacturing production	3.4	3.1	−8.5	−1.4
Lifetime employment (manufacturing industries)	3.9	1.5	−0.4	−9.9

Note: 1977/1973 figures compare fiscal 1977 to fiscal 1973. Figures in parentheses are yearly averages.

to conserve energy and, in particular, to reduce their dependence on oil.

The monetary policies pursued by the Bank of Japan were also much more effective than in the previous oil crisis. Tight money policies were implemented at an early stage and a much more cautious approach was adopted in managing the growth of money supply. These early preventative measures were highly effective in checking an inflationary psychology among private enterprises and consumers. The exchange rate policy also contributed to the success of these monetary policies. As in the previous crisis, the yen declined sharply after the oil crisis of 1979 but shifted much more quickly to a higher rate against the dollar than in the previous one. That served to dampen the impact of higher oil prices on the domestic economy. All these factors worked together to keep inflation below levels experienced after the first oil crisis, providing ample evidence that the government, private industry, and consumers had learned valuable lessons from the 1973 "oil shock."

The deflationary effect of the second oil crisis was also much less severe than in the previous crisis. A stagnation of personal consumption and private investment in housing was unavoidable, and there was a sharp reduction in public works expenditure by the government. However, private investment in plant and equipment, principally by large firms in the manufacturing industries, continued to expand at a healthy pace, supporting the continued growth of the economy and relatively high levels of employment. The resilience of private capital investment in the aftermath of the second oil crisis may be explained by the fact that private industry had been engaged, since 1973, in a transformation of the industrial structure. In the industrial materials industries, which had provided the basis for previous economic growth, investment in new plant and equipment was aimed at introducing new technology to reduce energy costs. For example, New Japan Steel, Japan's largest steel producer, reduced the average quantity of petroleum required to process one ton of raw steel from 128 kiloliters in 1973 to 86 kiloliters in 1979, and predicts that this average may be further reduced to 60 kiloliters by 1985. Similar energy conservation plans were introduced in the chemicals, cement, petroleum-refining, and paper pulp industries, and aggressive plant and equipment investment programs were required to support these efforts to restructure existing production systems. The automobile and household electric appliance industries are representative of those industries in which capital investment was aimed at producing new product lines that emphasize energy conservation.

A second major factor in the strength of private capital investment was the rapid expansion of the new industries that would lead the way to a new knowledge-intensive, high-technology industrial structure. The rapid development of semiconductor technology and new applications of electronics technology sparked huge increases in capital investment in both existing industries and new ones. For example, new products that combined existing technologies of mechanical and electrical engineering were introduced in the camera and watch industries. New industries, such as industrial robots and microcomputers, are rapidly replacing the traditional heavy and chemicals industries as the key industries in future economic growth. In both traditional sectors and new industries, private enterprises have staked their future on expanding research and development in new technologies in order to survive in the new global environment of reduced oil supplies. The degree to which Japan will be able to meet the challenges posed by reduced supplies of raw materials and higher costs will depend largely on the continuation of efforts by private industry to expand investment in new technologies.

EPILOGUE

THE POSTWAR ECONOMY IN RETROSPECT AND PROSPECTS FOR THE FUTURE

The Postwar Transformation of the Economy. In the nearly forty years since its beginnings amidst the total destruction of World War II, the postwar economy has undergone constant and multidimensional change. As we have seen in the preceding chapters, the solution of one problem has been followed by the immediate appearance of another. After a difficult period of reconstruction, Japan confronted new problems posed by the technological revolution, high-speed economic growth, and the full employment society. After successfully dealing with these problems and achieving economic independence, mounting pressure from abroad forced the country to grapple with problems of trade and capital liberalization. After overcoming chronic trade deficits, Japan now found itself with large recurring surpluses, and this disequilibrium in its balance of payments with other countries led to the "Nixon shock," the yen revaluation, and the collapse of the Smithsonian Agreement. Close on the heels of these developments followed the first oil crisis, "crazy prices," and the deepest and most prolonged recession of the postwar period. Just when the economy was finally recovering from the recession, it was hit by a second oil crisis. As I will suggest below, Japan dealt with the two oil crises more effectively perhaps than other advanced nations. Nevertheless, these solutions have themselves created new problems, and the pattern of convulsive changes in the global economy demanding new and creative responses from Japan has not come to an end.

It is important to recognize, however, that Japan has accomplished a great deal in the postwar period. Even while plagued by kaleidoscopic changes in the world economy, and new challenges both at home and abroad, Japan has joined the ranks of the advanced industrial nations as a nonmilitary, economic superpower. This was never achieved during the long period of Westernization and modernization that began with the Meiji Restoration in 1868 and lasted until Japan's defeat in World War II. Before 1945, Japan could boast that it had achieved "great power" status only in terms of military might, for the lives of its people remained far below the standards of the truly advanced nations. Both its economy and its people were constantly attacked by poverty, disease, insecurity, and unemployment. Enforced poverty led to overwork and malnutrition, which in turn led to tuberculosis. When the head of a household or other family members succumbed to the disease, the family was reduced to even greater poverty. Children of poor families, forced to work in order to supplement their families' incomes, were seldom able to maintain regular attendance even at the elementary school level. Furthermore, frequent depressions and economic crises constantly threatened the meager livelihoods that factory workers and farm families were able to maintain even in the best of times. The rigid class system enforced by the power elite was based on an extremely unequal division of wealth, and there was little hope for improvement for the average worker or shopkeeper. As a result, the domestic market was extremely constricted, and Japan was frequently attacked for social dumping, or an export system based on cheap labor. The absence of a well-developed domestic market was also one of the major factors that drove Japan to its invasion of China.

The development of the postwar economy may be said to have been completely different in character from this prewar pattern. After defeat in World War II, the "peace constitution," with its complete renunciation of military solutions to international problems, allowed Japan to pursue a policy based on the principles of insuring its existence and promoting its development through the expansion of its economy. Radical reforms during the Occupation put a permanent end to the prewar class system and, during the same period, land reform, democratization of labor, dissolution of the *zaibatsu*, and antimonopoly reforms were implemented. These reforms of the basic institutions of the political, economic, and social systems, which were carried out with the chief aim of destroying militaristic elements in these institutions, had a much greater effect than either the Occupation authorities or the Japanese government could have predicted. From a long-range perspective, they also had an enormous effect in improving the division of wealth and income and in expanding the domestic market. Without this kind of reform at the very beginning of Japan's postwar history, the basic framework of the political and social systems would be much more rigid than it is today, and it is highly unlikely that the Japanese "economic miracle" could have taken place.

Economic democratization began in the immediate postwar period and proved to be a major factor in the technological and consumer revolutions that transformed the economy in the period between 1955 and 1975, setting the stage for an unprecedented period of sustained high-speed economic growth. The promotion of the heavy and chemicals industries and infant growth industries such as automobiles and computers became the cornerstone of economic policy, and policies designed to provide incentives for private plant and equipment investment, including low interest rates and preferential taxation measures, served to spur on aggressive investment behavior by private industry. Despite initial fears, trade and capital liberalization policies also functioned as major factors in stimulating active competition among private enterprises in promoting investment for modernization. The unprecedented expansion of private plant and equipment investment had an enormous inducement effect on personal incomes and private consumption, and the period of rapid economic growth witnessed the formation of a mass consumption society and a rapid expansion of the domestic market, phenomena that would have been unthinkable in the prewar period, or even during the period of reconstruction. After a certain time lag, Japanese exports also began to expand rapidly. Improvements in quality due to aggressive investment in modern technology and new economies of scale made possible by the expansion of the domestic market led to improvements in quality, which strengthened Japan's international competitiveness.

Achievements of the Postwar Economy. In broad statistical terms, the achievements of the postwar economy may be summarized as follows. A comparison of 1980 and 1946 yields the following data. Real GNP has increased by fifteen times, real per capita personal consumption has increased by thirteen times, mining and manufacturing production has increased by fifty-two times, and the volume of exports has increased by two hundred and twenty times. Considering the fact that 1946 represents the lowest point in Japan's economic activity, it would perhaps be more appropriate to compare 1980 to the 1934–36 period, often used during the period of reconstruction as the yardstick of postwar recovery. Such a

Table 24. The Expansion of the Postwar Economy

	1980 compared to 1946	1980 compared to prewar (average for 1934–36)
Real GNP	15.1 times	9.1 times
Real personal consumption	13.3	8.3
Real private fixed capital formation	28.0	25.7
Real government fixed capital formation	25.2	48.3
Mining–manufacturing production	52.1	17.9
Consumer durables	721.5	192.4
Consumer nondurables	23.4	6.4
Capital goods	128.8	59.8
Steel	138.5	30.1
Agricultural, forestry, and marine production	2.4	1.9
Rice	1.2	1.1
Eggs	70.8	12.5
Milk	40.7	23.4
Total volume of exports	217.1*	16.0
Total volume of imports	48.8*	9.8
Volume of crude oil imports	649.1	64.8
Volume of wheat imports	16.7	13.7
Volume of soybean imports	1,467.0	7.6
Total population	1.6	1.7
Total employment	3.3**	2.9***
Nominal wages in manufacturing industries	532.1	4,808.4
Consumer prices	26.9	1,359.7
Wholesale prices	50.6	825.1

Notes: 1. All figures are for fiscal years.
2. * indicates comparison to 1948.
3. ** indicates comparison to 1947.
4. *** indicates comparison to 1950.

comparison yields the following. Real GNP has increased by nine times, real per capita personal consumption by eight times, real fixed capital formation (private plant and equipment investment plus private housing investment) by twenty-six times, government fixed capital formation by forty-eight times, mining and manufacturing production by eighteen times, and the volume of exports by sixteen times. During the same period, nominal wages have increased by four thousand eight hundred times, and real wages by 3.5 times. The number of persons employed in nontraditional industries has increased by 1.7 times. Among industrial products, consumer durables, led by household electric appliances and automobiles, have shown amazing increases of one hundred and ninety times (nondurables have increased by only six times). Production of capital (or producer's) products, which are related to private capital investment demand, has also increased by a staggering sixty times. Production of agricultural, forestry, and marine products has increased at a much slower pace as substantial increases in beef, eggs, and other products that reflect a Westernization of Japanese tastes have been offset by declining demand for such traditional products as rice.

Increases in the country's ability to supply increasing demand cannot be explained solely in terms of increased domestic production. The total volume of imports has expanded by ten times compared to the postwar figure, with oil imports increasing sixty-five times and imports of wheat fourteen times. What has made this growth in imports possible is the enormous increase in exports. Indeed, it is precisely the remarkable rise of Japan's ability to import supplies of needed commodities that has made it possible for this small, resource-poor nation to emerge as an economic superpower.

The rather lengthy list of statistics presented above demonstrates that Japan has indeed reached the level of an economic superpower, and suggests the extent to which Japan has become a materially wealthy country. However, the achievements of the nearly forty years since the war have not been limited to increases in material prosperity. There have also been other remarkable improvements. The Shinkansen trains, the network of freeways, and the development of domestic and international air routes have vastly reduced the time and expense of transportation, while the development of new communications systems has ushered in an age of direct dialing, telexes, computers, high-speed copying, and automated banking. High-speed economic growth has eliminated the problem of overpopulation, long considered insoluble, and by the early 1960s,

Japan had become a full employment society. Moreover, Japanese unemployment levels are low in comparison to the United States and Europe, indicating that Japan has been able to maintain its unique labor–management relations system, in which male lifetime employees can expect to keep their jobs until retirement. Perhaps more important is the emergence of equal opportunity in postwar Japanese society. As suggested above, the reforms of the immediate postwar period were highly significant in ending traditional class discrimination, but the expansion of the economy as a whole, and the rise of personal incomes in the subsequent period of economic growth, also played an important role in the development of an equal opportunity society. As we have seen, employment opportunies increased enormously during the thirty years of high-speed growth, and freedom in choosing one's place of work grew accordingly. Similarly, compared to the postwar period in which only the select few were able to go to high school or college, the number of Japanese children who are now able to continue higher education has reached the levels of other advanced nations, in many cases surpassing them. The expansion of employment and education opportunities also reflects the effectiveness of regional development policies in reducing income disparities between regions and between economic sectors. Finally, improvements in nutrition and medical services that accompanied increases in overall per capita incomes have produced a stronger, healthier population. The height and weight of today's third graders is approximately the same as those of sixth graders before the war, and average life expectancies have increased from forty-seven for men and fifty for women before the war to seventy-three for men and seventy-nine for women.

Postwar economic development has vastly improved the lives of the Japanese, and we can say with some pride that Japan has become one of the most sophisticated societies in the postwar world. The Japanese people were quick to recognize the problem of industrial pollution during the late 1960s, and strong public pressure forced the government to adopt strict environmental standards and private industry to pursue aggressive antipollution programs. Similarly, Japan responded quickly to the two oil crises, and has become a leader in the development of a new knowledge-intensive industrial structure. In the following section, I would like to review some of the reasons for Japan's remarkable success in the postwar period.

The Mechanisms and Institutions of High-Speed Growth. The growth of the postwar global economy up to the first oil crisis was about 4 to 5 percent a year, double the annual growth of 2 percent before the end of World War II. During the same period, however, the Japanese economy grew more than twice as fast, at 10 percent a year (compared to about 4 percent a year before the war). What accounts for this rapid growth of Japan's postwar economy?

First, at a purely economic level, one may point to the high rate of personal savings which supported a high level of plant and equipment investment. On the one hand, Japan was fortunate to have a relatively young labor force, in many cases from agricultural families, eager to master the skills of industrial employment and easily trained in new technologies. These workers not only contributed to rapid increases in productivity but were also the principle source of the large capital supply that flowed into capital markets in the form of savings deposits. On the other hand, the competitive spirit of private enterprises, and their aggressive attitude toward technological innovation, contributed to the rapid introduction of technology from abroad during the "catching-up" period. These private enterprises made effective use of the large capital supply provided by the high rates of saving by individual households. It is no exaggeration to say that this balance between high rates of personal savings by individual households and the high rates of plant and equipment investment by private industry was the most important factor in Japan's rapid economic growth. In this sense, Japan's postwar experience stands in sharp contrast to the recent stagnation of the American economy due to low rates of personal savings and the decline of net investment in new plant and equipment by private industry, not to mention President Reagan's emphasis on "supply-side economics."

What has attracted the most attention among both domestic and foreign observers of Japan's rapid economic growth is the existence of unique institutions in the Japanese economy, particularly in the management practices of large Japanese companies. Increasingly, attention has become focused on the dynamism and flexibility of labor–management relations in the group-oriented societies of these large enterprises. The unique features of Japanese-style labor–management relations may be summarized as follows.

1. The Lifetime Employment System. In principle, a new school graduate's employment is guaranteed until his retirement. Such workers constitute an elite within large companies. Temporary workers,

even though they may stay in a single company until retirement, and may have much more seniority than younger lifetime employees, have no such guarantees and usually receive lower levels of compensation.

2. The Seniority Wage System. This system, which, in principle, is limited to lifetime employees, guarantees that wages and non-wage benefits will increase steadily from the time a new school graduate enters the company.

3. The Enterprise Union System. Unions are not organized by industry or craft but by individual enterprises. As a result, strike activities are conducted by the workers of an individual enterprise, even though overall labor activity may occur on a concerted basis, as in the annual spring wage offensive. Needless to say, the enterprise union system plays a large role in strengthening the individual worker's ties to the company that employs him.

4. The Bonus System. Bonuses, which are paid twice annually, directly reflect the individual company's performance during the year that they are paid, not the worker's productivity or performance. Again, this serves to strengthen the worker's awareness of his stake in the company's success or failure. Moreover, recent research suggests that the system of paying a large percentage of employees' compensation in the form of periodic bonuses is the most significant factor in the high rate of personal savings.

Together, these features comprise what is widely known as the lifetime employment system. The employment of workers who have left other companies is extremely small, and the demand for new school graduates is overwhelmingly large. This, together with the fact that the seniority wage system makes it extremely unprofitable for employees to leave the company before retirement, enables companies to guarantee their labor force of lifetime employees, and to pursue aggressive on-the-job-training programs without fear that the employee with take his training, and perhaps company secrets, to another company in the same industry. Moreover, the lifetime employment system is supported by a general societal belief that employees who change jobs frequently lack ability or moral character, and most workers are committed not only to staying with a company as long as their employment is guaranteed but also to the long-term goals and interests of that company.

Thus, the individual worker's commitment to his company is not simply a passive willingness to stay with the company unless he is fired, but a positive ethos, a "my company spirit" that may imply accepting reduced wage increases during an economic downturn. Furthermore, wage settlements are conducted on a basis quite different from the three-year wage contracts common in the United States. New wage agreements are signed each year, and agreements on bonus payments are settled twice each year, directly reflecting the overall performance of the company. These practices serve to make the individual aware of the short-term fluctuations in the company's profitability through the direct medium of increases and decreases in his own income. The entire system is supported by the enterprise union system, which not only forces workers to adjust their wage demands to the economic position of their own company, thus enabling the company to avoid sudden increases in fixed labor costs, but also smooths the process of transfers and contributes to a relatively high degree of labor mobility within the company. In fact, after the first oil crisis, labor and management within individual companies collaborated in developing strategies for the survival of their companies in opposition to government policies aimed at rationalization and industrial reorganization. Based on cooperation between management and enterprise union representatives, job transfers were handled with a minimum of difficulty. Labor itself took the lead in establishing quality-control, or QC circles, and labor cost reductions were achieved while holding down layoffs to levels considered impossible by government industrial planners. In this sense, it cannot be denied that the unique institutions of Japanese-style labor–management relations have been highly effective in comparison with their counterparts in the West.

The commitment of individual workers to their companies, the worker's identification of his private life with his company, the group-orientation of Japanese companies, these have all contributed to the flexibility of private enterprises in the face of rapid change. It should also be noted that the highly developed sense of competition for promotion among middle-level managers has served to enhance overall morale within individual companies and has contributed to the maintenance of discipline in the labor force. This has become an increasingly important factor in the comparatively high levels of organizational efficiency in Japanese companies.

I would like to point out, however, that this group-orientation phenomenon of Japanese-style management, especially in large enterprises, has not always received high praise during the postwar period. Until 1954, when Japan was still a poor country after the destruction of World War II, industrial labor unions were under the influence of extreme left-wing ideologies, and labor conflicts were characterized by levels of violence that are difficult to imagine today. Today, many intellectuals continue to be extremely critical of Japanese-style management, partly because of their inferiority complex toward the West, and view group-orientation as a remnant of Japan's feudal past. During the period of public furor over the problem of pollution, many of these intellectuals took the extreme position that the roots of the pollution problem could be traced to Japanese-style management. It was not until the aftermath of the first oil crisis that Japanese intellectuals began to recognize the strong points of the group-orientation of Japanese society and the effectiveness of Japanese-style management.

It also required a good deal of time before the Japanese recognized the growth potential of their economy, and this has been a major source of international frictions. Long after the period of reconstruction, it was widely believed that the growth of the economy would soon slip back to prewar rates. The targets for economic growth established by the Economic Deliberation Council, the body of academics charged with advising the government on drafting national economic plans, have consistently underestimated real growth rates. Indeed, contrary to the image of Japan Inc., the actual development of the postwar economy has been largely a trial-and-error process. However, the Japanese people and private enterprise, much more quickly than economic planners, recognized high-speed growth as a fact, and it became a built-in factor in their expectations for the future. Based on this expectation, private enterprise planned business so as to induce the next stage of high-speed growth as, for example, during the period when the phrase "investment begets investment" became popular. While high-speed growth may also have been responsible for such problems as industrial pollution, it has produced a number of positive benefits: enormous increases in real incomes and improvements in standards of living; a modern society characterized by abundance and convenience; elimination of the pressures of overpopulation and the achievement of a full employment society; an equitable distribution of wealth from an increasingly larger pie; and a strong competitive international position due to expansion of the domestic market and active investment in new technologies. From the government's point of view, rapid growth has contributed to the creation of a political environment in which there are very few serious social tensions and in which public opinion has supported the policies of the several LDP governments since the end of the war. Moreover, each stage of rapid economic growth has provided new lessons for the next stage, and the effectiveness of continued development in solving economic problems has firmly implanted an ethos of economic "growthmanship" among the Japanese people.

However, it would be a serious exaggeration to say that Japan's "economic miracle" was the result solely of the strength of the Japanese or of domestic conditions. Japan's rapid economic growth was possible precisely because of a number of favorable conditions in the international economic environment. The long period of Pax Americana, the expansion of world trade under the principle of free trade, and the free transfer of technology from the United States and Europe were essential conditions for Japan's "economic miracle." Moreover, given the fact that Japan's ability to supply its own raw materials is extremely low, the availability of cheap raw materials from the developing nations was extremely important for the development of modern industries. This was especially true of imported petroleum, which comprises a larger share of Japan's primary energy sources than for any other of the advanced nations. Until the first oil crisis, for example, the average price Japan paid for imported oil was just over one dollar a barrel. Needless to say, these favorable conditions are changing at an incredible tempo.

Japan's Responses to the Two Oil Crises. As suggested in Chapter Six, the first oil crisis had an immense effect on the Japanese economy, and it was in Japan that the term "oil shock" was used for the first time. Many observers, both here and abroad, concluded that "Japan is finished." Totally dependent on imports for its oil supplies there is no question that Japan was hardest hit by OPEC's large-scale price increases. These observers predicted that the prices of Japanese products would become extremely high on international markets, and that the subsequent decline in exports would throw Japan's balance of international payments into a huge deficit from which it would be impossible to recover. This would lead in turn to rapid declines in production and an enormous unemployment problem. However, these dire predictions did not materialize. It is true that the first oil crisis put a permanent end to high-speed economic growth. Nevertheless, as indicated by the statistics in Table 25, while Japan's growth rate did decline to an average of 5 percent a year during the period 1975 to 1979, it still remained high compared to the United States and to Europe. Both inflation and unemployment rates have remained low

Table 25. Japan's Postwar Economic Growth

1945–55	9.1%
1955–65	10.0
1965–75	8.3
1965–70	11.0
1970–75	4.4
1975	3.6
1976	5.1
1977	5.3
1978	5.2
1979	5.5
1980	3.7

Table 26. Comparison of Prewar and Postwar Growth Rates

	Prewar	Postwar (to 1975)
World	2%	4–5%
Japan	4%	10%

compared to the other advanced nations and, while large deficits were experienced initially in the balance of international payments, recovery has been remarkably rapid. In terms of the so-called economic fundamentals, the economy has performed exceptionally well.

What are the reasons for Japan's success in dealing with the first oil crisis? The most important is the fact that the reduction of energy consumption in the industrial sector proceeded at a much more rapid pace than anyone had predicted. This was due both to direct investment in energy conservation technologies in existing industries and the rapid shift of the industrial structure away from relatively high-energy consumption industries, such as the materials industries, toward the more knowledge-intensive processing industries. These two factors underlie a substantial reduction in the amount of investment in oil supplies necessary for economic growth. Real GNP has increased by 30 percent since 1973, the year of the first oil crisis, while during the same period imports of crude oil declined by 10 percent, one indication of the rapid shift in patterns of investment and industrial structure that occurred during the period. The rapid-growth industries of the post–oil crisis economy are VTRs, audio systems, automobiles, cameras, watches, NC lathes, industrial robots, and computers. What these industries share in common is the systemization of new technologies that unite the techniques of electrical and mechanical engineering by exploiting rapid advances in semiconductor technology: integrated circuits, large-scale integration (LSI), very large-scale integration (VLSI), and so on. These new products, developed during the period of industrial readjustment following the first oil crisis, have paved the way for a new technological revolution. This is not to say that Japan has overcome the effects of the two oil crises and can look forward to a rosy future of stable development. Rather, it seems inevitable that the long period of rapid change, the constant recurrence of new problems, and the need to deal with new challenges both at home and abroad will continue. A number of important issues confront the economy, and it is still plagued by structural weaknesses that must be overcome if it is to continue to develop.

Issues for the Domestic Economy. The following problems have become the subject of most discussion as conditions for Japan's survival and continued development within the global economy. First, how should Japan deal with worldwide reduced oil supplies? The problem of securing energy supplies will have a major effect on the Japanese economy well into the twenty-first century. Beginning with the immediate problems of securing oil and maintaining strategic stockpiles, the issue of supplying domestic energy needs has wide-ranging implications. It has brought into sharp focus the necessity of promoting alternate sources of energy and expanding research and development investment aimed at the development of new types of energy. It has also been the most important fact in the rapid reorganization of the industrial structure in the direction of more effective utilization of natural resources and energy conservation, as well as the active promotion of energy conservation by consumers. Second, a related problem is how to exploit, to the utmost, the vitality of the private economy within the framework of the free market system in order to achieve a creative transformation of the industrial structure. A good deal has been accomplished already, but further development of an industrial structure that is both energy- and resources-efficient and knowledge-intensive is essential if we are to take full advantage of the new employment structure of a society that is increasingly characterized by high levels of educational training.

Third, both economically and socially, Japan confronts an important turning point in terms of the composition of its population, a problem that will increase in importance into the next century. The relatively low average age has been one of the major factors in Japan's rapid postwar growth, but the gradual aging of the population has created new problems. If Japan fails to deal effectively with its aging population, the vitality of the economy could very easily be sapped, both in terms of its labor force and the increased social costs of higher expenditures for pensions and health care. The system of early retirement, at fifty-seven or fifty-eight, must be revised, and we must come to grips with the question of what is the appropriate age for national pension payments.

Fourth, Japan must discover how to improve "living space and living time," the sector of the welfare system that remains far behind the other advanced nations. The rapid increases in ownership of consumer durables that accompanied high-speed economic growth has only thrown into sharper relief the cramped conditions of residential housing. An excessively laissez-faire land policy has resulted in insufficient land for housing, and increases in prices have made it virtually impossible for the average worker to own his own home. At the same time, while the industriousness of Japanese workers was a significant factor in rapid economic growth, excessively long working hours now present major problems. With the rapid development of industrial robots and office automation, Japan may be faced once again with the problem of excess labor and increasing unemployment. It is essential that immediate steps be taken to reduce overtime, encourage workers to take advantage of the system of yearly paid vacations (twenty days), which up to now has existed in name only, and to insure the adoption of the five-day week. This is not only to respond to criticism from abroad that the Japanese are "workaholics living in rabbit hutches," but also to demonstrate Japan's international competitiveness on an equal footing.

Japan is also standing at an important crossroads now that the time has come for a basic reexamination of public choices. This issue is closely related to the problems of the explosion of fiscal deficits and the recent debate over the rehabilitation of national finances. After peaking in 1979, when the rate of dependence on national bonds issues reached 35 percent in the revised budget, fiscal deficits seem superficially to have been steadily reduced. However, the current outstanding balance of national bonds is ¥100 trillion, much higher than the combined national debts of the United Kingdom, West Germany, France, and Canada, and is equivalent to nearly 40 percent of the GNP. Moreover, debt service costs at the end of fiscal 1981 had reached ¥8.2 billion, and the cost of interest payments on

Table 27. Further Increases in the National Debt

(¥100 millions)

	New issues of national bonds	Percent of deficit-covering bonds	Rate of dependence on national bond issues
1965	1,972	0	5.2
1975 (original budget)	20,000	0	9.4
1975 (revised budget)	52,806	20,905	25.3
1976 (original budget)	72,750	37,500	29.9
1976 (revised budget)	71,982	34,732	29.2
1977 (original budget)	84,800	40,500	29.7
1977 (revised budget)	99,850	49,570	34.0
1978 (original budget)	109,860	49,350	32.0
1978 (revised budget)	112,850	49,550	32.8
1979 (original budget)	152,700	80,550	39.6
1979 (revised budget)	140,500	69,170	35.4
1980 (original budget)	142,700	74,850	33.5
1980 (revised budget)	142,700	73,150	32.7
1981 (original budget)	122,700	54,850	26.2
1981 (revised budget)	129,000	58,600	27.4
1982 (original budget)	104,400	39,240	21.0

Note: Rate of dependence on national bond issues is the percentage of total budgeted expenditures accounted for by new bond issues.

national bonds itself has now become a significant factor in fiscal deficits. Debt-servicing expenses will grow to an estimated ¥13 trillion by 1986, a situation in which all the revenues from new annual bond sales at the current level would be barely sufficient to cover interest charges on previous bond issues and pay up on maturing bonds. The expansion of the national debt has also disrupted financial markets, competing with private demand for capital and serving to increase interest rates. As I suggested earlier, the stimulative fiscal policies adopted after the two oil crises were only partly responsible for the expansion of the national debt. The most important cause of large fiscal deficits was the fact that fiscal expenditures, the administration of the government, and societal expectations continue to be based on the high-speed growth period even though that period has clearly ended.

It is undeniable that the existence of inefficient and often self-righteous public corporations, the expansion of subsidies to agriculture due to overprotective policies, the inefficient national health care system, excessive administration intervention by the government in private enterprise, the proliferation of government-related institutions, an unclear division of responsibilities between the public and private sectors, and an unclear definition of the roles of the central government and local governments have combined to create swollen fiscal budgets and an enormous government bureaucracy. While the private sector economy has developed on the basis of intense competition among a large number of enterprises, politically Japan has remained, since 1868, a country characterized by strongly centrist political institutions and a strong sectionalist bureaucracy. The high level of national tax revenues during the period of high-speed growth served to conceal the contradictions in this system. However, as the economy moved into a more mature stage of development, and the values of the Japanese became more diverse, the tide of public opinion has turned against this excessive centralization toward a call for greater decentralization. Against this background, a fundamental reassessment of public choices and the need for administrative reforms designed to drastically reduce the scale of fiscal spending and the size of the government's bureaucracy have become topics of general public concern.

Japan's Role in the Global Economy. The most important task confronting the Japanese economy is the problem of mounting trade frictions with the United States and Europe, and the related problem of working for the further development of its own economy while making a positive contribution to world peace and international development. Economic policy in the postwar period has been extremely effective in creating the environment for Japan to increase its ability to supply its domestic needs, to strengthen its international competitive position, and to catch up with the United States and Europe. On the other hand, however, Japan's economic policies toward other countries has reflected a lack of aggressive leadership in the international arena. The clearest symptom of this problem is the fact that economic policies toward other countries have almost always been characterized by a pattern of reacting to pressure from abroad. This has been true of Japan's reaction to all the major developments in the global economy: trade and capital liberalization; upward revaluation of the yen; expansion of economic assistance to developing nations; and disequilibrium in Japan's balance of payments with other countries. Without substantial pressure from abroad, it has been virtually impossible for the government to marshall a new consensus of public opinion for new policies. Moreover, the responses of the people and policy makers to changes abroad have often had the character of overreactions, resulting in wild shifts of policy. This kind of overreaction was responsible for the panic surrounding upward evaluation of the yen, the first oil crisis, and the subsequent period of "crazy prices." It also cannot be denied that the tendency of the Japanese media to give wide coverage to often groundless reports of impending disaster has been a negative factor in preparing the public to respond to new international developments.

Another major problem is that the political and economic policy makers have become too accustomed to taking world peace for granted as a premise of policy, in part due to the long period of peace after 1945. Recently, this has meant that the government found itself completely defenseless in the face of wars abroad. Consequently, it has been forced to implement emergency measures to cope with their effects on Japan, contributing to the disruption and confusion of the public and private industry. The ideal of every country conducting its military and economic policies with the aim of promoting peace for mankind is extremely important, but it is also essential that each country pay its share of the cost for preserving such a system. The Japanese need to become more aware that even if Japan escapes involvement in another war, it is more than possible that the eruption of war abroad will have serious repercussions on Japan that may threaten its very existence.

The first oil crisis remains a vivid memory. After OPEC's imposition of measures banning exports, the government was forced to push through emergency legislation to provide a framework for controls on oil consumption and other scarce products. Both the delay in implementing measures and the subsequent shock of the controls themselves produced unnecessarily severe effects on the public and on private enterprises. This failure to anticipate a serious international problem was largely responsible for the severity of the "oil shock" and the subsequent period of "crazy prices." More recently, the problem of a new economic and security pact with the United States, including U.S. demands that Japan assume a greater share of the burden for its own defense, has become a widely debated public issue.

Japan's passive approach to the formulation of economic policies toward other countries has become a subject of rising criticism from abroad. However, it is extremely dangerous to ascribe this passive stance in international affairs to some special quality of Japanese culture, the approach taken by those who advocate the so-called *Nihonjin-ron*. It is all too easy for this approach to lead to the conclusion that the consciousness, the attitudes, and the modes of behavior that the Japanese have displayed up to now in defining their role in the international order are absolute, unchangeable, and therefore a permanent feature of Japan's foreign relations. Such a conclusion, in turn, offers little hope for solutions to the problems Japan has in dealing with other countries, including the increasingly serious one of trade frictions. My own view of the problem is that the passive attitude of the Japanese in dealing with international economic problems must be explained against the historical background of the postwar period and that it reflects basic contradictions in domestic political and economic institutions, the lack of reliable information concerning international developments, and the consequent inability of policy makers to base policies on accurate judgments of the overall situation. Moreover, all these factors have combined in complex ways to impede the development of international economic policies appropriate to Japan's position as a major economic power.

The historical background may be understood in terms of a significant time lag between the actual development of the economy and Japanese perceptions. As we have seen, the unprecedented high-speed growth of the economy propelled Japan into the position of an economic superpower almost overnight. It is hardly surprising, therefore, that there was a considerable time lag before the Japanese began to perceive Japan as one of the advanced nations and became aware of the new kinds of behavior and new responsibilities that such a recognition implies. Indeed, we have experienced this time lag a number of times during the postwar period. It was several years after the period of reconstruction was over before the public, and policy makers as well, became conscious of it. Similarly, even after Japan became a GNP superpower, it was several years before the Japanese threw off the "small-country complex" that created so much conflict with other countries.

A second aspect of the historical background is the fact that the Japanese traditionally have shied away from the unknown. One of the unfortunate remains of the long period of war before Japan's defeat in 1945, a much longer period than many foreigners realize, is that the Japanese have had little contact with foreigners and consider themselves extremely unskilled in communicating with them. Japan is under increasing pressure to recognize its position and to accept its responsibilities as one of the leading economic powers, but the Japanese people have had no experience of such a role. Japan has never been a world leader, or even an influential opinion leader. Demands that Japan make a contribution to mankind or to the global society produce reactions of confusion and hesitation.

Against this historical background, Japan is also confronted with many contradictions in its political culture and its political and economic institutions. Unlike the advanced nations of the West, which share a common Christian culture, Japanese democracy is not yet firmly grounded on any well-defined world view. Moreover, there is a conspicuous lack, among Japanese party politicians, of the kind of leadership that would enable the government to balance the various internal interest groups in order to establish the consensus needed for a clear position for Japan in the international political and economic systems. More important perhaps in Japan's strongly bureaucratic state is that the sectionalism of the bureaucracy, and the strength of narrow principles of national self-interest, have impeded the development of a normal foreign policy. Finally, the lack of information necessary to formulate timely and accurate readings of changes in the international situation has made it diffiuclt for policy makers to make accurate judgments of new situations, undermining the ability of the government, private industry, and the public to respond appropriately.

Based on this analysis, I believe that what is most essential if Japan is to adapt to the new global economic order is a shift toward a new paradigm more appropriate to its international position, and a new program for its domestic economy. Recently, the Economic Planning Agency, in which I received most of my training as an economist and spent the greatest part of my career, has published a report on the long-term prospects for Japan's economy. This report predicts that by the year 2000 Japan's per capita GNP will have surpassed that of the United States. My own view is that such a prediction is absolutely meaningless. Indeed, I wonder if the present members of the Economic Planning Agency are not suffering from precisely the kind of lag in perceptions discussed above; (if they are not under the anachronistic illusion that the foundation of economic policy should continue to be one of stirring up the spirit of catching up with the West). What is most vital is that we turn all our thoughts to the question of how Japan, as a country that has achieved the status of an economic superpower despite its lack of natural resources, can contribute to the global economy while insuring its own existence and its continued development.

During the process of rapid economic growth, the Japanese economy has undergone vast changes, including several transformations of its overall industrial structure. One thing that has not changed, however, is its basic orientation toward economic growth based on exports of industrial commodities. Japan's leading exports have shifted from labor-intensive ones such as textiles, to capital-intensive products, and finally to knowledge-intensive products, and there is no question that the expansion of exports based on high levels of private capital investment in new technologies and production systems has played an extremely important role in growth. Moreover, as a country that possesses virtually no natural resources of its own, it is inevitable that the structure of Japan's foreign trade will continue to be characterized by what economists call "vertical international specialization." That is, Japan must expand exports in order to import energy supplies and industrial raw materials and, as in the past, it will continue to emphasize exports of finished products and imports of raw materials. However, Japan has relied far too much on exports as the basis of its economic growth and, unless we attempt to achieve a better balance between our own interests and those of foreign countries in pursuing future development, it is highly likely that problems with the United States and Europe over trade frictions and the disequilibrium in Japan's balance of payments will intensify.

Two factors may be cited to explain the fact that the intensification of economic frictions has centered on criticism of Japan. First, whether consciously or unconsciously, Japan has continued to pursue economic policies heavily slanted toward expansion of exports. There is ample room for expansion of domestic demand through increases in social capital expenditures, an area in which Japan lags far behind the other advanced nations. In any case, unless Japan takes appropriate steps to achieve more balanced economic growth in terms of its relative reliance on domestic demand and exports, the disequilibrium in its balance of trade with the United States and Europe cannot be easily alleviated. The concept of an international division of labor, or international specialization, which is based on the principle of relative superiority in specific industries, has been extremely effective in promoting worldwide free trade during the postwar period. Even more in the present, it may seem to be highly advantageous to Japan, which holds a strong position in many of the international growth industries.

However, both the theory of international specialization and the principle of free international trade were formulated on the premises of relatively equal competitive strength among the major members of the trading community, or at least the absence of serious differences, and moderation in the promotion of exports. The latter implies the absence of a large concentration of one country's exports in the markets of another. If these premises are not fulfilled, the foundations of the free trade system may be badly shaken. Moreover, while international economic theory is concerned with the international balance of payments on a global scale, when the trade imbalance between two countries becomes so serious that it presents political problems for the country with a large trade deficit, it is impossible to deal with the resulting friction by merely waving the banner of free trade. In short, the essential task for economic planners is not to make assertions about Japan's superior competitive position, either in the present or the future, but to take immediate steps to develop a solid policy line that will enable Japan to maintain a healthy level of economic growth without depending on excessive export expansion, a policy line based on a clear recognition of the need to balance economic growth and Japan's balance of trade with other countries.

The second major factor in the intensification of trade frictions, and the one that is most often subject to criticism abroad, is the fact that while Japan is extremely aggressive in promoting exports it maintains a highly defensive, closed posture toward imports. As the U.S.–Japan Wise Men's Group reported at the beginning of 1981, "There is a need for Japan to make much greater efforts to open its domestic markets to the inflow of goods, services, and capital to a degree equal to that of the United States." If Japan is to solve the problem of trade frictions, maintain its partnership with the other advanced countries, and continue to develop on the basis of mutual coexistence within the international community, the opening of its domestic markets is unavoidable.

One major obstacle to providing greater access to Japanese markets is the system of import licensing and inspection, the most notorious of the so-called nontariff trade barriers and one that has a bad reputation even among the Japanese. Requirements for reinspection of imported products that have already passed inspections in the exporting country extend to a wide range of key industrial products, including pharmaceuticals, cosmetics, processed foods, electric appliances, apparel, and automobiles. Moreover, the system has created a proliferation of standards, requirements, and import procedures that are incredibly complicated for some products. In many cases, criticism is deserved for there is no objective, rational basis for the continuation of these practices.

A second obstacle to more open markets is the government's protectionist agricultural policy, which attempts to maintain a large number of exceptions to the principle of import liberalization. This has not only served to intensify trade frictions but also worked to the detriment of Japanese consumers. The price of white rice, for example, is extremely high by international standards, and there is a rising public demand for import liberalization of such agricultural products as beef, oranges, and tobacco, since foreign products are of higher quality and less expensive than Japanese ones. This is related to the problem of tariffs. Foreign criticism that Japan maintains tariff barriers in order to protect domestic industries is no longer justified by an international comparison of customs schedules except in the case of a number of processed food items, such as biscuits and cookies. This reflects the high domestic prices of such raw materials as wheat and sugar, and the protectionist policies of the government toward agriculture. These protective tariffs should be lowered rapidly, with a view to exposing agriculture to the impact of international competition, leading eventually to an overall improvement in the agricultural system.

In addition, a number of other steps should be taken to provide greater access to Japanese markets. Opportunities should be expanded for foreign enterprises to participate in bidding to supply procurement demands of public corporations and government agencies. Foreign companies should also be given the same rights enjoyed by Japanese firms in other countries to hold stock in and participate in the management of Japanese firms. A related problem is that of further liberalization and internationalization of the banking system and financial markets. Recently, the problem of providing greater access to new technologies developed by Japanese enterprises has received increasing attention. The list could be expanded indefinitely, but what is clear is that rapid steps must be taken to answer the demands of the United States and Europe for more access to the Japanese market.

The need for Japan to play an active role in promoting world peace and development is not limited to the problems of alleviating trade frictions and expanding cooperation with advanced industrial nations. Indeed, from the point of view of making a contribution to mankind, it is even more important for Japan to play a greater role in dealing with the North–South problem. Japan's foreign assistance policy has been notoriously passive, and the development of a clear commitment to international cooperation with the developing countries and a positive program for concrete action is long overdue. The developing countries, particularly those in the Asian region, are at various stages of development, and Japan must formulate a clear vision of what role it can play in providing capital and technological cooperation.

More than twenty years have passed sinced Hayato Ikeda moved toward an open economy as a major policy objective. At that time, the meaning of "opening the economy" was trade and capital liberalization, and the aim of the policy was to enable Japan to join the elite industrial nations. Today, the principle of the open economy has much broader significance. It means that Japan must accept its obligations as one of the leading economic superpowers and assume a positive role in preserving and promoting the global system of free and peaceful trade and economic activity on the basis of true reciprocity and mutual understanding. It implies a metamorphosis of national economic policy from emphasis on quantity to emphasis on quality. The period when Japan could occupy its little corner of Asia and devote all its efforts to strengthening its own economy in order to catch up with the West has now become something of the past. Japan now has the third largest economy in the world, and its influence on the global economy is enormous. Japan must discard the inferiority complex and the autistic behavior of the past. In an age of deepening mutual interdependence, it must become aware that its own future is inextricably bound up with the future of the global economy.

NOTES

INTRODUCTION

1. The Potsdam Declaration

The essential points of the Potsdam Declaration, announced by the leaders of the Allied powers (Truman, Churchill, and Chiang Kai-shek) on July 25, 1945, may be summarized as follows.

1. Japan's unconditional surrender.
2. The purge of militarists.
3. Occupation of Japan by the Allied powers.
4. Limitation of Japanese sovereignty to territories held before the Russo-Japanese War (1905).
5. Complete disarmament and demobilization of Japanese military forces.
6. Punishment of war criminals and the introduction of democratization.
7. Maintainence of industries necessary to sustain the economy but not those that would enable it to rearm for war.
8. Withdrawal of Occupation forces after the establishment of a government based on the free wishes of the Japanese people.

The Japanese foreign ministry received a draft of this declaration on July 28, after it had been picked up on a radio broadcast. The first atomic bomb was dropped on Hiroshima on August 6, and another was dropped on Nagasaki on August 9. On the same day, the Soviet Union announced its intention to enter the Pacific War on the side of the Allied powers. On August 14, 1945, the cabinet met with the emperor, and at this meeting it was decided that Japan would accept the terms of unconditional surrender set forth in the Postdam Declaration.

2. Damage to the World Economy during World War II

"Economic losses resulting from World War II were approximately five times greater than those incurred during World War I, even if only direct military expenditures are considered. It is estimated that total losses to the world economy due to direct military expenditures reached $1.099 trillion. In Europe alone, damage to cities, factories, and cultural institutions reached $260 billion. War casualties, including civilians, are estimated to have claimed 56 million victims. It has been said that the number of lives lost during World War I exceeded the number of people killed in the entire one-thousand-year history of warfare up to that time. Yet the victims of World War II were seven times that of World War I." (Kakuten Hara, *Sekai keizai no henkaku to hatten* [Revolution and development in the world economy], Shin Hyōron-sha.)

3. The Altered Aspect of the Postwar World
After the end of World War II, the world began to grope toward a new order based on the following conditions.

> 1. The United States had escaped almost unscathed from the war and possessed enormous industrial strength and a huge ability to produce food supplies. This enabled it to assume a strong position of leadership in the postwar international political system, the world economy, and diplomacy. In contrast, the major industrial powers of Europe, exhausted by the long war, were suffering from shortages of dollars and other foreign reserves, and were forced to rely on the United States for massive aid in reconstructing their battered economies. Germany and Japan, once leading industrial powers, were both occupied by the victorious Allied powers and were forbidden to participate in world trade for some time after the end of the war.
> 2. The Soviet Union emerged from the war as a superpower second only to America. Seizing the opportunity presented by victory, the Soviet Union quickly expanded its sphere of influence to include Eastern Europe and northwest Asia. This expansion was based on two facts: the Soviet Union had finally joined the Allied powers in the war against fascism; and local communist parties had played the leading roles in liberating countries occupied by the Axis powers, thus creating a foundation for new Soviet spheres of influence. Moreover, the Soviet Union aggressively pursued expansionist policies in an effort to exploit the resources and productive capacities of the new countries in the communist bloc in rebuilding its damaged economy.
> 3. With the defeat of the Axis powers and the decline of the political and economic power of Western Europe came the disintegration of the colonial system, and self-determination movements gained strength rapidly in the colonized nations. In the immediate postwar period, the center of the self-determination movement was in South and Southeast Asia, and one after the other Korea, Indochina, Malaya, Burma, India, Pakistan, and Indonesia achieved independence. At the same time, the communist revolution in China was moving forward.

4. A Japanese Vision of Economic Reconstruction
The shock of defeat and the realization that Japan was about to be occupied by

its former enemies threw the government into a state of total chaos. However, even as it floundered in a political vacuum, a group of academics and young bureaucrats was discussing the problem of Japan's postwar reconstruction. This group, which had been formed on August 16, 1945, one day after the end of the war, was the Special Investigation Committee of the Ministry of Foreign Affairs (originally the Ministry of Greater East Asia). Its members included Professor Hyōe Ōuchi, Hiromi Arisawa, Ichirō Nakayama, Harvard-educated economist Shigeto Tsuru, and Hidezō Inaba, author of Japan's first Economic White Paper. Its general secretaries were Saburō Ōkita and Yonosuke Gotō, who would later be dispatched from the Ministry of Foreign Affairs to play a major role in creating the Economic Planning Agency (EPA). The group met more than forty times and, in March 1946, submitted its findings to the Diet and GHQ in a report entitled *Basic Problems in the Reconstruction of the Japanese Economy*. The major points of this report may be summarized as follows.

1. Economic reconstruction should take as its premise Japan's participation in the world economy within the framework of the IMF system.
2. In order to promote the principles of economic democratization, Japan should not rely on the agricultural sector to absorb excess population but should participate in the international division of labor by strengthening and modernizing its industrial structure through technological development.
3. Despite the prevailing extreme pessimism concerning the reconstruction of the economy and its future development, there were a number of factors that would work in Japan's favor, and the Japanese people should not give up but should prepare themselves to work hard for economic recovery.

The report pointed out that, despite the destruction of the war, the Japanese economy still had the basic industrial structure and technology to enable it to produce heavy industrial commodities and eventually supply its own needs. Moreover, the defeat had eliminated the economic burdens of supplying the military and maintaining an enormous colonial empire. Finally, while the report acknowledged that sudden democratization would create temporary confusion, ultimately, democratization would free the energies of the domestic population and result in a significant increase in productive potential.

In retrospect, this report was amazingly prophetic, and it was highly significant that such a long-term view could be taken during this period of political and social chaos. Moreover, it became the initial basis upon which negotiations were carried out with GHQ on the future of the Japanese economy. However, at this early stage in the Occupation, the Allied powers and GHQ took a completely negative view of any proposal to make heavy industrialization the basis of Japan's postwar economic reconstruction. In fact, the Allied powers were determined to reduce Japan to the level of an agricultural economy with only light industries. It was to take almost three years of persistent negotiations and repeated setbacks for the Japanese government before any changes in Occupation policy took place.

CHAPTER 1

1. The Food Supply Crisis and U.S. Relief Aid

Immediately after the Occupation, the Japanese government made the first of several appeals to GHQ for emergency imports of 4.62 million tons of food supplies by the end of 1945. GHQ took an extremely cool attitude toward these requests. Occupation authorities doubted the validity of statistics projecting an impending food crisis, and took the position that a crisis could be averted if the government took the obvious steps of searching out the food supplies hoarded by the army and navy and return them to official rationing channels and of taking stricter measures to insure the delivery of food supplies by private farmers. GHQ's attitude was influenced by the fact that the United States was finding itself hard pressed to meet growing demands for food relief. The world food supply situation had deteriorated badly, and there were massive crop failures between 1945 and 1947 in every part of the world except the United States and South America. Confronted with the threat of starvation in countries that had been its allies during the war, as well as in the liberated territories under its jurisdiction, there was little room for the United States to give high priority to the appeals of a defeated enemy. From August 15 to December 31, 1945, Japan was unable to secure any imports of food and received only meager relief in the form of food supply releases under the jurisdiction of GHQ.

With the implementation of the Emergency Economic Policy, the government appealed once again to GHQ for intervention with the U.S. government. Between March and May of 1946, GHQ did this strongly on Japan's behalf, arguing that monthly imports of at least 100,000 tons of grain and rice substitutes were essential to maintain a minimum intake of 900 calories a day. However, actual U.S. food relief amounted to only 700,000 tons for 1946, less than one-fourth of the amount requested by GHQ. Once again, the clamor for food relief raised by defeated and victorious countries alike presented the Far Eastern Commission with the difficult task of assigning priorities, and Japan ranked very low indeed.

Nevertheless, the anticipated mass starvation did not materialize, despite the dire predictions of the government and the press. One result of this lucky miscalculation was that MacArthur severely chastised Prime Minister Yoshida for the inaccuracy of the Ministry of Agriculture and Forestry projections. There is no question that the quality of statistics available to the Japanese government up to this time had been extremely low, and one legacy of the Occupation was a thorough reform of the system of gathering and analyzing statistics.

However, the food supply situation remained critical until the end of 1948, and emergency relief imports reached a level of more than half of Japan's total imports. Much of these imported supplies consisted of wheat, wheat flour, corn, soybean flour, skim milk, dried beans, canned goods, and other substitutes that had never been a part of the traditional Japanese diet. It was during this period that the dietary habits of the Japanese began to shift toward bread, noodles, and other foods based on a variety of flours that remain popular today.

2. The Origins of the Economic White Paper

In February 1947, at the same time that the Japanese government published its first Economic White Paper, the Labour Party cabinet of Britain's Prime Minister Clement Attlee published Britain's first White Paper on the Economy. The origin of the term "white paper" may be traced to the fact that official documents in the U.K. have white covers, and the Japanese borrowed the British custom of referring to these documents as "white papers." In the same year, the U.S. government published its first Economic White Paper, "Report on the State of the Economy", based on the provisions of the New Employment Law. Saburō Ōkita has traced the development of economic white papers in the United States as follows.

> With the end of the war approaching, the problems of how to prevent a disastrous recession and severe unemployment became the subjects of serious discussion in the capitalist countries. A full employment law was presented in the U.S. Congress in the spring of 1945, even before the war had ended, and after several amendments was finally passed as the Employment Law in 1946. This law, which took the form of a resolution, stated that it was the perpetual responsibility of the United States government to maintain maximum employment, maximum production, and maximum purchasing power, and made it clear that the government must use every available means to fulfill that responsibility. On the basis of this law, the president's Council of Economic Advisers and similar bodies in both houses of the legislature were formed to consider the various problems of overall economic policy, particularly those of countercyclical policies and economic growth. The Employment Law also established the basis for regular annual reports by the president to the legislature on the state of the economy. (Saburō Ōkita, *Nihon no keizai seisaku* [Japan's economic policies], Yūki Shobō.)

It is interesting that the practice of preparing annual white papers was established during the same year in the United States, England, and Japan. Subsequently, however, they lost their importance in England and are no longer published every year. Today, the publication of annual white papers on the economy is continued only in the United States and Japan.

3. The Revival of Publishing

Even in the immediate postwar period, when daily life for most people was the struggle to find enough to eat, the publishing industry recoverd with amazing speed. Magazines that had been forced out of publication, either because of censorship regulations or shortages of paper, reappeared one after the other, and were joined by a number of new publications that competed for survival. It was a period during which anything published would sell, reflecting the fact that the highly literate Japanese had long been without access to the printed word and that Occupation reforms had established freedom of speech and thought for the first time in Japan's history. Among the early best-sellers were books that revealed some of the behind-the-scenes history of the war and facts concealed from the people during the war years. Other books that described the social conditions of the immediate postwar period won wide popularity for their outspoken criticisms of Japanese society and culture or for dealing with hitherto banned subjects. Somewhat later, traditional book lenders also began to resume their prewar vitality.

What supported this recovery during a period of massive shortages was the use of a low-quality paper called *senkashi*, or "thousand flowers paper," produced by recycling old newspapers and other scrap paper. This paper fell outside the rationing and price controls restrictions, and was produced in large quantities by small manufacturers and sold to publishers at a premium. The availability of this paper was so significant in the recovery of publishing that the literary culture of the immediate postwar period came to be called the "thousand flowers paper culture." It was not until 1955 that the quality of Japanese publications began to approach prewar levels.

4. The West German Currency Reform

Plagued by rampant inflation throughout the war, the countries of Western Europe were already drafting policies to contain inflation through currency measures by its end. In the case of occupied Germany, the military government of the Allied Occupation moved quickly to institute a currency reform. There was considerable fear that a vicious cycle of severe declines in production, inflation, a black market, starvation, and unemployment would create the same kind of economic instability that, in fact, did occur in Japan. In May 1946, Joseph Dodge, then chief of the Fiscal Affairs Department of the military government, submitted a proposal for currency reform based on much the same principles that would subsequently provide the basis for his policies in Japan.

Based on the premise of abolishing the influence of fiscal policies pursued by the Nazis during the war, the proposal called for the following five measures.

1. A freeze on bank deposits accompanied by the issue of a new currency one-tenth the value of the old deutschmark.
2. Cancellation of the debts of the Nazi government.
3. Implementation of a graduated estate tax.
4. Implementation of a fixed assets tax aimed at redistributing income.
5. Establishment of a fixed exchange rate for the new deutschmark.

It was drastic plan, designed to work together with the proposed discontinuation of military scrip issues to attack inflation at its roots. Interestingly, with the exception of the proposal for a downward denomination of the mark, it bears a close resemblance to the Emergency Monetary Measures Ordinance that had been drafted by the Japanese government only a few months earlier in February 1946.

The proposal encountered strong opposition from the Soviet Union, which had set out to establish complete control of the German economy by flooding it with military scrip, and it was not until June 1948 that a currency reform was finally accomplished without the participation of the Soviet Union. The currency reform carried out in the sectors controlled by the United States, France, and England closely followed Dodge's original proposal (the new deutschmark was denominated at 0.65 to 10 against the old mark, and the fixed assets tax levy was postponed due to the technical difficulty of implementing it). The Soviet Union retaliated by instituting the Berlin blockade and carried out its own currency reform in the East German sector.

The currency reform in the West German sector was amazingly effective, leading Dodge to boast that "it brought about an almost unbelievable change in the German economy." In fact, within six months after its implementation, inflation had been checked, manufacturing production had begun an upswing, and trade had begun to expand. In this sense, it is no exaggeration to say that the currency reform provided the springboard for launching the West German economic miracle.

Slightly before the currency reform, in April 1948, a fixed exchange rate had been established for the mark at US thirty cents to one mark. The decision to fix the exchange rate at this rather high level was based on the policy of giving precedence to promoting imports essential to the recovery of industrial production. In response to the devaluation of the pound in 1949, however, the mark was reduced to twenty-three point eight cents (a 20.6 percent devaluation), and this, together with the rapid pace of recovery, led to a sustained expansion of exports.

The currency reform was viewed as essential for the effective implementation of the Marshall Plan, but it also caused considerable confusion in East Germany, where both the new West German deutschmark and the Soviet-sponsored currency were current. This situation continued until the establishment of the Federal Republic of Germany (West Germany) on September 7, 1949 and the German Democratic Republic (East Germany) on October 7, 1949.

5. The Marshall Plan and the Formation of the EEC

During the same period that the Economic Rehabilitation Plan was being implemented in Japan, the Marshall Plan was beginning to produce concrete results in Western Europe. As suggested above, with the exception of the United States, Canada, and a few other countries, World War II inflicted enormous damage on the economies of most of the world's nations. For these countries, regardless of whether they were on the losing or the winning side, the reconstruction of their economies and eventual economic independence would have been virtually impossible without aid from the United States. The highly industrialized countries of Western Europe were by no means an exception.

Moreover, in the period from the end of 1946 through the first half of 1947, Western Europe suffered through an unusually long winter followed by an early frost, and the resulting poor harvest, together with a severe shortage of fuel for industry and transportation, dealt heavy blows to economic reconstruction. Production declines in both agriculture and manufacturing made unavoidable expansion of imports from the U.S., but the accumulation of liabilities during this period of sustained adverse trade balances had already badly eroded the dollar reserves of the European countries, and they found themselves confronted with an increasingly serious dollar shortage. The IMF and the World Bank, which had just been established, did not yet have the resources to supply the dollar funds required by these countries.

The social instability created by the uncertainties of daily life presented excellent opportunities for communist forces in the European countries, and they made rapid advances. Against this background, Secretary of State George C. Marshall proposed the concept of an aid plan for the reconstruction of Europe in June 1947. This proposal became the basis for the American relief program that came to be called the Marshall Plan. In response to the proposal, sixteen European countries joined in establishing the Organization for European Economic Co-operation (OEEC) as the institution responsible for administering American aid funds and, in March 1948, the U.S. Congress passed the Economic Cooperation Law. The Marshall Plan eventually pumped more than $10 billion into Europe, and its effects far exceeded the expectations of its creator.

By 1951, the plan's target year, the overall level of the European economy was 60 percent higher than prewar levels (1938). Without the Marshall Plan, the recession in Europe, which continued from 1948 until the outbreak of the Korean War, would have had a much graver impact on the world's capitalist countries.

The process of economic recovery under the Marshall Plan brought into high relief the growing rift between the United States and the Soviet Union in Europe, and in 1949 the Soviet Union and the East European countries in its sphere of influence established the Council for Mutual Economic Assistance (COMECON) to promote economic reconstruction and the expansion of trade among the communist countries.

In 1961, the OEEC was reorganized and, with the addition of the United States and Canada, replaced by the Organization for Economic Co-operation and Development (OECD) as the principle organization for economic cooperation among the advanced nations of the free world. Japan was admitted to the OECD in April 1964.

6. The Denouement of the Law for the Elimination of Excessive Economic Concentration

Application of the Law for the Elimination of Excessive Economic Concentration aroused much debate both in Japan and abroad. Conceived by SCAP as the last stage of *zaibatsu* dissolution, the law was designed to break up gigantic monopolistic enterprises and, as we have seen, three hundred and twenty-five large enterprises were designated for dissolution by the Holding Companies Liquidation Commission. However, these companies comprised the bulk of Japan's key enterprises, and such a radical dismemberment of such firms would have dealt a serious blow to the economy. Many argued that full implementation of the law would imperil Japan's smooth reconstruction.

In May 1948, the Elimination of Excessive Economic Concentration Commission (also called the "Five-Man Commission") was sent to Japan to advise MacArthur on the actual implementation of the deconcentration program. This commission, composed of five American businessmen, had the greatest effect in relaxing the application of the law. After a four-month-long investigation of the problem of excessive concentration in the Japanese economy, it published a set of basic principles recommending that the law be applied only "in cases where enterprises clearly obstruct competition." By July of the same year, the Holding Companies Liquidation Commission had reexamined the documents submitted by the original three hundred and twenty-five companies designated for dissolution in February and reduced the number to one hundred.

In fact, by the time the application of the law was suspended in March 1950, only eighteen companies remained designated for dissolution. In addition, ten electric power companies were reorganized into nine regional public utilities under the jurisdiction of the Public Utilities Commission.

7. The Midterm Stabilization Concept

In early 1948, when industrial production had begun to show signs of a steady recovery, domestic opinion on policies to curb inflation were sharply divided between those who advocated immediate stabilization and those who called for midterm stabilization. Advocates of the former argued that the principle cause of inflation was the runaway money supply, and called for the rapid implementation of tight fiscal and monetary policies to cut inflation at its roots. The proponents of midterm stabilization argued that such harsh policies at a time when production remained at low levels would result in inevitable large-scale unemployment and large numbers of bankruptcies. Moreover, the resulting stabilization panic would exacerbate social and economic unrest. Rather, they argued, anti-inflationary policies should be implemented at a stage when production had gained higher levels.

The midterm stabilization thesis was particularly strong among economic planners of the Economic Stabilization Board and the Ministry of Finance, who were pushing ahead with economic reconstruction plans under the Ashida Cabinet and viewed high levels of domestic capital investment as essential to these plans.

The midterm stabilization concept was given concrete form in a proposal submitted to the cabinet on March 14, 1948, by the Economic Planning Agency. Called the "Midterm Economic Stabilization Plan," its principle points may be summarized as follows.

1. Preparatory Stage (June–October 1948). Establish a basic preparatory structure for the implementation of midterm stabilization measures, including minimum necessary revisions of the price system and minimum

necessary investment for the reconstruction of enterprises, and, within these limits, reduce capital investment from the fiscal budget as much as possible.

2. First Period of Economic Stabilization (nine months to one year beginning November 1948). Eliminate wage-price spiral, increase production and reduce costs through concentrated production, and improve the international balance of payments through export expansion.

3. Second Period of Economic Stabilization (to end no later than March 1950). Establish a temporary fixed exchange rate, revise prices to bring domestic prices in line with international prices, revise custom schedules and relax trade restrictions to promote the acquisition of foreign currency, and continue to expand exports.

Of course, with the publication of SCAP's Nine-Point Economic Stabilization Plan for Japan and the Dodge Line, the Midterm Economic Stabilization Plan was abandoned, and subsequent policies gave precedence to halting inflation over reconstruction, resulting in the stabilization panic.

8. Hidden Trade Subsidies

From the beginning of the Occupation to the implementation of the Dodge Line, Japan's trade was conducted on the basis of a highly unusual arrangement between the government and GHQ. For exports, the government purchased products at domestic prices and these were, in turn, exported by GHQ at international market prices. Similarly, imported products were purchased by GHQ and then sold by the government at domestic prices. The exchange rate system was extremely complex, with different rates for each product and periodic fluctuations in each of these rates. Moreover, transactions in foreign currencies and in yen were controlled separately, with GHQ handling foreign reserves and the government handling yen transactions through its Special Account for Trade Funds.

Because of the high level of imports in this period, including relief aid from the United States, this unusual system would have produced a substantial surplus in the Special Account for Trade Funds if there had been a normal link between receipts and expenditures in foreign currencies and yen, and if appropriate exchange rates had been established. In fact, however, the account consistently posted large deficits which had to be made up from the general budget and covered by Bank of Japan bonds.

This may be explained by the fact that the special account was actually paying large subsidies for both imports and exports that did not appear in government statistics, the "hidden subsidies" referred to in Dodge's recommendations. In order to maintain the official price system, imported products were being sold domestically at prices below their actual costs and, similarly, in order to expand exports, exchange rates were fixed at levels that made domestic products less expensive in international prices than in yen. In 1948 alone, these kinds of hidden subsidies amounted to about ¥100 billion.

The early establishment of a fixed exchange rate for the yen proposed by the Dodge Line was designed to normalize the economy by eliminating these hidden subsidies and their effect as a factor in further swelling the money supply. Similarly, in order to provide a more rational system for administering relief aid capital from the GARIOA and EROA accounts, GHQ established the U.S. Counterpart Fund for Relief Aid to Japan on January 1, 1949, eliminating the complex system of administering foreign trade.

9. The Behind-the-Scenes History of the ¥360 Exchange Rate

From about the middle of 1948 to spring of the following year, extensive planning was being carried out at various levels of the government on the possibility of establishing a fixed exchange rate and the probable effects of a variety of exchange rates on economic reconstruction. In fact, however, the final authority to establish a fixed exchange rate rested with the United States.

On June 12, 1948, Professor Leif Young, head of the Special Mission Concerning Yen Rate Policy, filed his report on the conclusions of the mission, which had conducted extensive investigations of government and GHQ documents after arriving in Japan in April. The Young Report was classified "top secret" until the end of 1970, and the report was finally made public in August 1972.

The Young Report recommended that a fixed exchange rate should be established by October 1, 1948, and that it should be ¥300 to the dollar. It also would have given GHQ the authority to make adjustments of 10 percent either way depending on changes in the situation between the submission of the report and implementation (i.e., ranging between ¥270 to ¥330). The report met with stiff opposition from GHQ, which argued that the establishment of a fixed exchange rate for the yen should be put off until production and trade had recovered to postwar levels. Reflecting this opposition, the National Advisory Council on International Monetary and Financial Problems, which convened on June 28, accepted the recommendations of the Young Report but left the timing of its implementation to GHQ by including the phrase "as soon as administratively possible" in its decision. In effect, the council gave GHQ free rein to ignore the October 1 target date.

By early 1949, however, Dodge was in Tokyo to implement the Nine-Point Economic Stabilization Plan. Determined to establish a fixed exchange rate at the level of ¥330, on March 23, he requested approval in MacArthur's name for establishing the new rate on April 1. In response to this request, the council, in a meeting on March 29, agreed to strongly recommend an upward revision of the rate to ¥360. The council argued that the progress of inflation since the Young Report and Japan's unfavorable balance of payments on the eve of the first sterling devaluation had made the ¥330 rate an unrealistic evaluation of the yen's actual strength. Finally, after a month of negotiation, GHQ and Dodge accepted the council's recommendation, and it was announced on April 23 that the ¥360 rate would go into effect on April 25.

CHAPTER 2

1. The Intensification of East-West Confrontation in Asia

The international situation in the months before the outbreak of the Korean War was characterized by an intensification of the confrontation between the United States and the Soviet Union due to the establishment of the People's Republic of China in October 1949 and the Soviet Union's successful test of a nuclear weapon in September of the same year. However, the formation of NATO in April 1949 and the lifting of the Berlin blockade in April of the same year had served to stabilize the situation in Europe, and the focal point of the Cold War shifted quickly to Asia.

Confrontation was most serious in three regions: the thirty-eighth parallel of the Korean Peninsula; the Taiwan Straits; and Indochina (Vietnam). In Korea, as we have seen, the Republic of Korea was established in the south in August 1948, immediately followed by the establishment of the Democratic People's Republic of Korea in the north in September. The United States and the Soviet Union had withdrawn their troops from both areas, but political instability continued, especially along the thirty-eighth parallel, where sporadic skirmishes between North and South Korea threatened to touch off war at any moment.

The Taiwan Straits had become a dangerous area of confrontation because the United States feared that the Chinese communists would attempt to follow up their victory on the mainland by pursuing the Nationalists across the straits into Taiwan. In Indochina, the Soviet Union and the People's Republic of China recognized the government of Ho Chi Minh in January 1950, and the United States, still smarting from its loss of China, immediately recognized the government of Bao Dai and began direct military assistance to the French army, thus beginning the long history of American intervention in Southeast Asia.

2. The Scope of American Relief Aid to Japan

Aid to Japan from the United States ended in mid-1951, more than one year before the government, GHQ, and the Department of the Army estimated that Japan's international payments could achieve balance. In fact, however, the improvements in the economy after the beginning of special procurements had made further reliance unnecessary.

U.S. assistance had taken the form of supplying Japan with imported commodities, and a significant share of this relief aid had been handled in the form of loans, which were repaid after the signing of the San Francisco Peace Treaty. Relief aid from the United States totaled somewhat less than $2 billion (the United States set the figure at $1.95 billion and the Japanese Foreign Ministry's figure was $1.8 billion). If this figure is compared to the $40 billion in total American foreign aid during this period, or to the $12.8 billion to finance the Marshall Plan, it is clear that Japan was not given priority (economic aid to Germany by the Allied powers during this period reached $4.4 billion). However, the role of American aid in covering the extreme shortages of materials and food, and in promoting economic recovery, must not be underestimated.

Overall, 60 percent of total relief aid was in the form of food supplies and 40 percent was accounted for by petroleum, fertilizers, raw cotton, and other raw materials essential for recovery and the expansion of manufactured exports. In 1946 and 1947, when the country was in the midst of a food crisis, nearly 80 percent of relief was food products, but in the subsequent period imports of industrial raw materials gradually rose.

The relative shares of GARIOA and EROA funds in total economic aid to Japan were not clearly distinguished, and it is meaningless to attempt to distinguish them in Japan's case.

3. The Problem of Japan's Remilitarization

In the talks conducted between Japan and the United States from January to August 1951, there were few points of disagreement except on the issue of the security pact, which in fact boiled down to the problem of Japan's remilitarization. Yoshida stated that if the United States stationed forces in Japan, any anticipated direct or indirect attacks could be repelled, and argued for a policy of holding down Japanese military capabilities to the minimum level of a self-defense force (or a national police reserve) necessary to preserve domestic order. Even Dulles, who wanted Japan to establish a modern army, navy, and air force, and to form in both name and fact a mutual defense pact with the United States, was forced to bow to Yoshida's stubborn opposition, in which he made full use of domestic and international public opinion. In the end, the preamble to the U.S.–Japan Security Treaty merely stated that "Japanese remilitarization is anticipated at some time in the future." Yoshida, in his *Nihon o kettei shita hyakunen* (The hundred years that determined Japan's history), stated the following.

> I opposed Dulles's advocacy of remilitarization directly. . . . A modern military requires ridiculous amounts of money. Therefore, if we built a force that would do any good, the Japanese economy would collapse, and if we didn't build a force that would ruin the economy, it would not do any good. Moreover, the psychological foundation that would have supported remilitarization had been lost. For the Japanese, who had been forced into a war without a cause, the scars of defeat still remained. And if Japan were to remilitarize, it might provoke the neighboring countries in Asia. I opposed remilitarization for all these reasons, and I still think I was right to do so.

4. The International Economy after the Korean War

One difficulty in understanding the Yoshida deflation is the fact that despite the cyclical downturns in the economies of Europe and the United States after the Korean ceasefire, Japan's economy continued to boom as special procurements demand supported strong domestic demand. The booming domestic situation, however, concealed the fact that Japan's balance of international payments was rapidly falling into the red.

Cyclical downturns in the major economies after the peak period of the Korean War were characterized by a one-year gap between Europe, the United States, and Japan. In Western Europe, the downturn began shortly after the peak of fighting in Korea in 1952, while the downswing of the American economy did not begin until spring 1953, after the signing of the ceasefire. Stringent monetary policies were imposed in Japan in October 1953, but a clear downswing was not perceptible until spring 1954. While there was this one-year gap in the post–Korean War boom downturns in Europe, the United States, and Japan, they were all created by precisely the same factors.

If Japan's economy had its present strength, other countries would have welcomed the continuation of stimulative policies after Japan's economic downturn had set in. However, criticism of these policies from abroad was severe in the post–Korean War period. Foreign observers spoke of the Japanese economy at this time as a "fool's paradise," or "skating on thin ice." This was an objective view, perhaps best stated by the World Bank's response to the government's request for a loan: "It is impossible to supply credit to a country that is on the brink of serious inflation." Such reactions from abroad provided the strongest motive for Prime Minister Yoshida's imposition of deflationary policies.

CHAPTER 3

1. The Cold War Thaw

With the death of Stalin, tensions relaxed between the Eastern and Western blocs. The Korean War was brought to an end both in name and fact, and the Geneva Convention on peace in Indochina was signed. In October 1956, the Hatoyama Cabinet succeeded in negotiating the restoration of diplomatic relations between Japan and the Soviet Union, and in December Japan was finally admitted to the UN (Japan's admission had previously been vetoed by the Soviet Union).

Strangely enough, this relaxation of tensions had the effect of subtly stirring up Japan's drive toward economic development. Part and parcel of the communist bloc's shift toward peaceful coexistence was the joint communiqué issued by Soviet and Chinese leaders to compete economically with the West. Coming at a time when Japan had launched itself into a program of high-speed economic growth, this communiqué served to strengthen Japan's consciousness of the rift between the capitalist countries and the communist bloc.

In November 1957, on the anniversary of the Russian revolution, Premier Khrushchev boasted that in fifteen years the Soviet Union would catch up with and surpass the United States in manufacturing production. Similarly, launching the Second Five-Year Plan in April 1958, Chinese Vice-Premier Li Fu-ch'un forecast that in fifteen years the People's Republic would surpass England in manufacturing steel and other major industrial products.

2. The Middle Eastern Oil Boom and the Cheap Oil Revolution

Before World War II, Iran and Iraq were the main producers of oil in the Middle East. In 1938, Iran (10 million tons), Iraq (4.3 million tons), Bahrain, and Egypt produced a total of only 15.5 million tons, or 5.5 percent of world production. In 1946, immediately after the end of the war, these four countries, together with Saudi Arabia and Kuwait, produced 35.4 million tons of oil, accounting for 9.4 percent of world production.

With the huge increase in demand for oil after the war, these figures continued to climb at an amazing pace: 100 million tons in 1952, 300 million tons in 1962, and 900 million tons in 1972 (the eve of the "oil shock"). If Libya and Algeria are included, the figure had reached 1.07 billion by 1972, accounting for 41.4 percent of total world production (2.59 billion tons). World demand for petroleum increased 7 percent after World War II, while oil production in the Middle East grew by an annual 12.6 percent, and it is this fact that ushered in the era of cheap oil.

These enormous increases in production were achieved by rapid advances in the technology of exploration, leading to the discovery of vast oil reserves in Saudi Arabia, Kuwait, Iran, Algeria, and Libya. This development of Middle Eastern oil reserves was perhaps the greatest factor in shaping postwar industrial development in Japan and throughout the world. Cheap oil not only fueled heavy industry but also offered the possibility of exploitation in such new industries as petrochemicals.

3. The Introduction of Foreign Capital and the World Bank

As we have seen, one of the special features of Japan's postwar economic growth was that, while there was an aggressive introduction of foreign technology and high rates of growth, the introduction of foreign capital was extremely small. There were two principle reasons for this. First, for a long period, the government actively suppressed the introduction of capital from powerful foreign enterprises. While foreign capital that promised to promote the modernization of industry was welcomed, in general the government allowed foreign investment only on a highly selective basis. In fact, this was a clear government policy based on the Foreign Capital Law established in 1950. Ultimately, the capital for rapid economic growth was supplied through the mechanism of overloans.

Despite the relatively small figures involved, however, foreign capital was extremely important throughout the period of high-speed growth from 1955 to 1965, during which the balance of international payments was almost constantly in the red, and foreign capital was essential to achieving an overall balance. The most important source of funds in the period immediately after independence was the World Bank, which made its first large-scale loan to Japan in December 1953 to three large public utilities corporations. Such loans to public corporations were handled through the Japan Development Bank, with the government as the guarantor. Moreover, by 1960, the World Bank had made loans to private enterprises amounting to $310 million, and the borrowers represented Japan's top-ranking enterprises. After 1960, the World Bank steadily shifted its attention to developing countries, and the primary source of foreign capital became the issue of foreign bonds.

CHAPTER 4

1. A Behind-the-Scenes History of the National Income-Doubling Plan

"When Ikeda became prime minister, the violence surrounding the *Anpo* demonstrations had still not disappeared. Something was needed to calm this atmosphere and turn people's energies in a more constructive direction. In short, what was needed more than anything else was the announcement of a new policy." Osamu Shimomura, economic experts from Ikeda's faction, and the important agency chiefs and ministers of the Economic Planning Agency, the Ministry of Finance, and MITI gathered at Hakone to hammer out such a policy. The biggest problem was the projection of growth rates to be targeted by the plan. The policy committee of Ikeda's faction advocated 7.2 percent a year, which would have doubled GNP in ten years. Shimomura and other members of Ikeda's brain trust called for 11 percent. Ikeda finally settled on a policy that called for 9 percent growth in the first three years of the plan starting in 1961. The final report of the Hakone group reads thus.

> In view of the past performance of the economy, average growth rates of 9 percent are possible in the three years beginning in 1961. That is, per capita income should increase from ¥120,000 in 1961 to ¥150,000 in 1963. If the proper steps are taken to achieve this goal, national income should double in ten years' time.

The report established nine conditions for achieving the goals of the National Income-Doubling Plan, among which were: parliamentary politics with open discussion between the ruling and opposition parties; peaceful foreign relations; a plan for rapid economic growth; reform of education; policies for women and young people. Government policies were to be divided into those for the economy and those for education and welfare. Economic policy was to provide for high-speed growth without inflation. The three pillars of the plan were to be increased public investment, reduced taxes, and social security. Internationally, the government would promote the principles of free trade; domestically, it would devise policies to expand employment, promote labor mobility, and devise plans for the modernization of agriculture and small business. (*See* Masaya Itō, *Ikeda Hayato, sono sei to shi* [Hayato Ikeda, his life and death], Shiseidō.)

2. Osamu Shimomura's Theory of a Historic Period of Renaissance

"The Japanese economy has already entered a historic period of renaissance. The driving force of this historical upsurge is the liberation of the creative powers of the Japanese people. The fact that the Japanese economy achieved a growth rate of 17 percent in 1959 and the fact that despite this huge expansion the economy developed in a stable condition are proof of its basic strength. The rationalization, modernization, and increased productivity of private entrepreneurs, managers, technicians, and workers has already produced the amazing results described above. To the extent that we do not fail to further nurture and strengthen this determination toward more improvements, there is no doubt that this high-speed growth will continue. I believe that in the next ten years it is possible not only to double our GNP but to increase it by 2.5 or even 3 times. There is no doubt that such high-speed economic growth will bring revolutionary changes in every aspect of economic life." (Osamu Shimomura, "Seichō seisaku no kihon mondai" [Basic issues in the high-speed growth policy], *Kinyū zaisei jijō* [The present situation in monetary and fiscal policy], November 7, 1960.)

3. The European Shift To Currency Convertibility and the Establishment of the EEC

By 1951, the countries of the Organization for European Economic Co-operation, aided by the Marshall Plan, had achieved economic recovery. Their gold and dollar reserves had increased from $8.8 billion in 1950 to $14.5 billion in 1957, and the severe dollar shortages of the postwar years had become a thing of the past. In 1958, under strong pressure from the United States, most of the OEEC countries were beginning to shift toward full currency convertibility, removing the restrictions they had placed on external payments in their own currencies, and toward reductions in or elimination of the discriminatory restrictions on American imports they had imposed during the period of dollar shortages.

Besides demands from the United States, one of the major reasons that Japanese policy makers were in such a hurry to liberalize trade and exchange controls was their awareness that the failure to do so would invite discriminatory restrictions on Japanese imports into Europe. Moreover, Japan could not afford to lag behind its trading partners and competitors in Europe if it hoped to be treated as an equal member of the community of advanced nations.

Also in 1958, France, West Germany, Italy, Belgium, Holland, and Luxembourg formed the European Economic Community (EEC, or Common Market). The EEC countries reduced tariffs among member countries, adopted uniform tariffs on imports from outside the community, liberalized restrictions on internal capital and labor flows, and adopted common policies on monetary and fiscal issues and agriculture. The EEC attracted a great deal of attention from other countries and, indeed, its effectiveness during the 1960s merited this attention.

In order to compete with the EEC, a group of seven European countries established the European Free Trade Association in 1960. In 1973—after a period of intense debate over Britain's membership—Britain, Ireland, and Denmark were admitted into the EEC, and the organization's name was changed to the European Community (EC). In no small part because of the similarity between Japan's position and that of the EC countries as smaller countries caught up in the confrontation between the United States and the Soviet Union, Japanese economic planners were highly interested in the EEC, and during Ikeda's administration there were frequent trips to Europe by Ministry of Finance and MITI officials.

4. A Chronology of "Defense of the Dollar" Policies

Due to increased foreign involvement of the United States and the process of "catching up" in Europe and Japan, the economic superiority of the United States and the dollar shortages of the postwar period had disappeared by the early 1950s. Despite its burgeoning balance of payments deficits and the increasing outflow of dollars, the United States was unwilling to impose stringent policies at home and, instead, attempted to maintain the prestige of the dollar and its stability as an international currency by implementing a series of "defense of the dollar" policies. As we have seen, each of these policies had a major impact on the Japanese economy. The following is a chronology of these policies.

> November 16, 1960 (Eisenhower). Reduction of foreign expenditures for supplies for foreign aid and special procurements, reduction of dollar payments by U.S. forces stationed overseas, and priority for the purchase of U.S. products for aid programs ("Ship American"). Its goal was the reduction of the balance of payments deficit by $1 billion. The policy was accompanied by strong demands for the elimination of European and Japanese discriminatory tariffs against the U.S. and for the promotion of import liberalization.

> July 19, 1963 (Kennedy). For the Kennedy administration, which had campaigned on a platform of rapid growth, the large balance of payments deficit was a constant problem. In order to reduce the effect of the Euro-dollar system, an interest rate equalization tax was established and restrictions on foreign credit were tightened. The goal of the policy was a reduction in the payments deficit of $2 billion by the end of 1964. The policy resulted in substantial reductions in the inflow of foreign currency into Japan and Europe and a sharp decline in stock prices (the "Kennedy shock").

> February 10, 1965 (Johnson). Implemented after the second devaluation of the pound and the subsequent attack on the dollar, the policy called for strengthening all the measures outlined above. At the same time, demands were stepped up toward Japan and Europe for the elimination of remaining import restrictions and nontariff trade barriers. In March 1968, Johnson announced the suspension of bombing over North Vietnam, and in April the implementation of a double price system for gold.

> August 14, 1971 (Nixon). A 10 percent surcharge on imports and suspension of the convertibility of the dollar into gold, the "Nixon shock." Nixon's

New Economic Plan also froze domestic wages and prices and was accompanied by demands for upward revaluations of foreign currencies against the dollar. After a second devaluation of the dollar in February 1973, and substantial price increases for agricultural products, the U.S. balance of payments improved substantially and Nixon's "defense of the dollar" policy was discontinued on January 30, 1974.

5. The Kennedy Administration and the New Economics
Half a year after the establishment of the Ikeda Cabinet in Japan, John F. Kennedy was elected president of the United States. While the Ikeda Cabinet held aloft the banner of high-speed economic growth, the new Kennedy administration campaigned on the realization of full employment through the promotion of economic growth. Kennedy called for annual growth rates of 5 percent in order to reduce unemployment to 4 percent. After the conservative policies of Eisenhower, which had resulted in low levels of growth and high unemployment, Kennedy's ambitious economic policy had broad appeal and succeeded in producing the most active peacetime economy in the postwar period.

The activist theories proposed by the economists of Kennedy's brain trust were labeled the "new economics." The basic approach of the new economics was based on the Keynesian principles of demand creating policies to promote full employment and rapid economic growth. Its basic framework may be outlined as follows.

1. Full employment budgets. The concept of full employment budgets was based on the idea that even if tax cuts produced temporary fiscal deficits in the long run, the realization of full employment would increase tax revenues and the budget would naturally shift to surpluses.
2. A relaxation of monetary policies.
3. A price stabilization policy based on price guidelines and presidential jawboning directed at major oligopolistic enterprises.
4. The whole range of welfare policies that have come to be known as the "great society."

Kennedy's international economic policies were based on the same principles as the new economics at home. A fervent advocate of rapid development of the world economy and the principles of free trade, Kennedy called for large-scale reductions of existing tariffs by all the advanced countries. The target set by the so-called Kennedy round was an across-the-board reduction of tariffs by 50 percent. Also at Kennedy's initiative, the UN General Assembly in 1961 proclaimed the 1960s to be the decade of UN development, and adopted a policy that called for advanced countries to set a target of 1 percent of GNP for economic aid to developing nations.

The aspirations evoked by the Kennedy administration were short-lived, but during that period the world witnessed a period of economic development and expansion of free trade that is unparalleled in postwar economic history.

6. A Relaxation of East-West Tensions and the Emergence of the North-South Problem

Before World War II, there were only some fifty countries in the world. With the collapse of the colonial system and the rapid advance of national independence movements, that number had increased, by 1976, to one hundred and forty-seven countries in the UN alone, and the number of newly independent countries continues to increase today. Because most of these countries are in Asia, Africa, and Latin America, they have come to be called the countries of the South, in opposition to the industrialized countries of the North.

The phrase "North-South problem" began to be widely used in 1959, but the movement among the newly independent countries of Asia and Africa to join hands in their drive for economic independence had begun long before. The Bandung Conference in 1955, which was attended by twenty-nine countries including Japan and the People's Republic of China, raised the call for regional cooperation and strengthened the consciousness of solidarity among countries of the South. It also became a major factor in broadening the competition between the United States and the Soviet Union to expand their influence through foreign aid to these regions. This was also the period in which relations between the United States and the Soviet Union were shifting from Cold War to peaceful coexistence. The monolithic communist bloc was being split apart by the rift between the Soviet Union and China. The United States, saddled with enormous balance of payments deficits due to massive military aid expenditures during the Cold War period, was beginning to shift its foreign aid program to loans rather than outright grants, and was demanding that Europe share more of the burden.

Against this background, the Kennedy adminstration called for a massive expansion of economic assistance to the developing countries. In proposing his concept of a "decade of UN development" to the UN General Assembly in 1961, Kennedy called for a goal of increasing the annual growth rates of the developing countries to 5 percent (from 2.5 percent during the 1950s). Kennedy's proposal was adopted unanimously. On the basis of this agreement, the focus of subsequent aid to the developing nations shifted from unilateral foreign aid programs to one of UN assistance.

The first meeting of the United Nations Conference on Trade and Development (UNCTAD) was held in Geneva from March to June 1964, attended by one hundred and twenty countries from the North (including the communist bloc) and the South. One result of this meeting was a report entitled "In Search of a New Trade Policy," which called for greater efforts by the advanced nations to promote import liberalization, a system of general preferential tariffs for the developing nations, and the establishment of an international body to oversee this system.

The North-South problem remains as one of the most important, and most difficult, problems of the postwar global economy. The current global financial crisis, due to the enormous debt burdens of the developing nations and high interest rates in the advanced nations, is ample evidence of the enormity of the problem and of the difficulty of finding solutions. Nevertheless, international organizations such as UNCTAD have played a vital role in improving the level and quality of economic cooperation between the North and the South.

CHAPTER 5

1. Repercussions of the Second Sterling Devaluation
In November 1967, England was forced to devalue the pound by 14.3 percent. As in the case of the first pound devaluation in 1947 (*see* Chapter 1), this second devaluation had major consequences for the world economy.

The immediate cause of the devaluation was the precipitous decline in England's balance of payments situation after the "third" Middle Eastern War and the closing of the Suez Canal. However, the pound crisis had by then already reached such proportions that it was impossible to avoid a devaluation by borrowing from the IMF or securing emergency loans from other countries. England's accumulation of long-term debts since World War II already had seriously eroded the pound even before the war in the Middle East.

Under the IMF system, the dollar and the pound had been designated the two key currencies with convertibility into gold. The fact that England had been forced to devalue the pound set off a wave of international speculation, with frantic sales of pounds creating an unprecedented rush on gold. Moreover, the devaluation of the pound aroused fears that the dollar would be next, reflecting the sharp decline in the dollar's prestige due to the huge balance of payments deficits the United States had incurred in its escalation of the Vietnam War. To make matters worse, De Gaulle chose this moment to launch an attack on the dollar, throwing the international monetary system into an extremely dangerous situation.

It was against this background that Johnson instituted the third "defense of the dollar" policy and appealed to Europe and Japan for cooperation in January 1968. In February, after the United States had been hit by the third wave of the gold rush, Johnson announced the double pricing system for gold, which distinguished the price of gold for currency conversion and the price of gold on the open market. Gold outflow from public reserves was prohibited. In March, the IMF adopted the system of Special Drawing Rights (SDRs) to serve as an international standard (1 SDR = $1 = 0.888671 mg. of gold fine), to increase international liquidity, and, in the future, to serve as a new international currency.

The establishment of SDRs once again raised the issue of large international payments deficits in the United States and England. If equilibrium could not be established in the balance of payments of these two key economies, the conditions for the effective functioning of the SDR system could not be created. The most important issue at this time was the United States' overinvolvement in the Vietnam War, and there was strong pressure for de-escalation. On March 31, shortly after the IMF conference in Stockholm, Johnson called for a peace settlement in Vietnam and announced that he would not seek a second term. The government of North Vietnam accepted this proposal on April 3, and arrangements began for the Paris Peace Conference.

2. The "Economic Miracle" as Seen from Abroad

Until the late 1950s, the Japanese economy received very little attention from abroad and was scarcely mentioned in foreign newspapers and magazines. Japan was still seen as a country exporting cheap labor that had somehow managed, with the help of American special procurements, to reconstruct its manufacturing industries. This attitude changed quickly as Japan continued to post growth rates of 10 percent even after its admission to IMF and GATT.

Shortly before Prime Minister Ikeda's trip to Europe, *The Economist* published a special issue on Japan for the first time in September 1962. Entitled "Consider Japan," the special issue gave high marks to Japan's high-speed growth and, indeed, many of the articles read like success stories of a late arrival. They also contained heavy implications of a general critique of the low growth rates of the British economy and, indirectly, provided strong support for Japan's admission to the OECD. Another special issue of *The Economist* in 1967, entitled "The Risen Sun," created an immense stir in Japan because it argued that Japan must now be counted as one of the six leaders of the advanced nations.

Also in 1967, Herman Kahn published his book, *The Year 2000*, in which he argued that by the end of the twentieth century or the beginning of the twenty-first, Japan could quite possibly surpass the United States in per capita GNP to become the top GNP superpower. Published in Japan under the title *Nijū-isseiki wa Nihon no seiki da* (The twenty-first century is Japan's century), the book was enormously successful and started a great deal of discussion in the media. Perhaps more than any other book published during this period, Kahn's *The Emerging Japanese Superstate: Challenge and Response* supported the rising consciousness both in Japan and abroad that Japan had become a GNP superpower.

On the other hand, future secretary of state Zbigniew Brzezinski's *The Fragile Blossom: Crisis and Change in Japan*, published in 1972, argued that of the twenty factors supporting Japanese economic growth, only four could be maintained in the future, and that in the near future Japan would face increasingly severe economic conditions. Considering actual events since 1972, Brzezinski's predictions were unusually farsighted.

In any event, these foreign observers of the Japanese economy had a significant influence in creating among the Japanese a more objective view of Japan's economic strength and the potential of its economy. They were also influential in reducing the inferiority complex of the Japanese, casting doubt on facile Marxist analyses of the economy, and exposing the groundless nature of many of the excuses Japanese negotiators were putting forward to explain Japan's failure to assume an international role that would be more appropriate to its position.

3. The New Comprehensive National Development Plan

The Comprehensive National Development Plan, established in 1962, called for restraining industrial concentration in overpopulated areas and established special areas for industrial facilities investments in each region of the country. Unfortunately, its vision of large-scale regional development remained largely a vision. Rather, in the period of high-speed economic growth during the late 1960s, the contradictory problems of overcrowding in major urban areas and depopulation of outlying regions reached staggering dimensions. In the Tokyo–Yokohama area, the concentration of population proceeded at an alarming rate, exacerbating the inflation of land prices, housing shortages, and the inadequacy of transportation and communication facilities. At the same time, the already serious outflow of population, and especially of young workers, from rural areas and outlying islands proceeded at a correspondingly rapid rate. The problem of depopulation became an increasingly serious social problem as more and more rural areas found it impossible to maintain regional finances and living conditions. Moreover, the rapid displacement of coal by petroleum had left many coal mining districts with vast numbers of unemployed workers, who quickly left for major urban areas.

Against this background, the New Comprehensive National Development Plan was established in May 1969 to replace the old Comprehensive National Development Plan. A long-range development plan, it called for a massive regional development program with a target date of 1985. This was the period in which the fad for futurology had reached its peak, and the conception of the plan clearly reflected this trend. Essentially it proposed large-scale public investment in the establishment of a national transportation and communications network, industrial parks, agricultural parks, distribution centers, tourist parks, residential cities, and so on. Like the earlier plan, it designated specific key areas for regional development, and regional governments and private industry quickly made plans for taking advantage of these designations.

The new plan was established at the peak of the period of high-speed growth, but its popular appeal was relatively short-lived. Growing awareness of the pollution problem gave rise to citizens' movements against development projects and, later, the inevitable association of the plan with Tanaka's plan for rebuilding the Japanese archipelago seriously damaged its prestige.

4. The Kumagai Report of 1972 on Incomes Policies

As the advanced capitalist countries began to achieve full employment, employment rates began to increase at alarming rates. Tight labor markets and higher wage settlements set the stage for higher costs, and the appearance of multinationals and oligopolistic enterprises strengthened the system of managed prices, making it easier for companies to pass on higher labor costs to consumers by raising prices. Against this background, there was increasing interest in the concept of incomes policies, which would enable the government to intervene in some form in fixing wages, prices, and profits.

The idea of an incomes policy began to be widely discussed in Japan after 1965, when the advent of full employment presented the dilemma of an accelerating wage–price spiral. In July 1967, the Economic Deliberation Council established the Research Committee on Prices, Wages, and Productivity, and appointed Professor Hisao Kumagai as its head. In September 1968, the committee presented its report under the title "Price Stabilization and Incomes Policies" (the report came to be known as the "Kumagai Committee Report"). The report argued that there was an inherent trade-off between economic growth and price stability, rejected the concept of price stabilization, and called for policies that would, as much as possible, give equal emphasis to both. Basing its conclusions on concrete case studies of incomes policies abroad, the committee's conclusions on the applicability of such policies to Japan were largely negative. They may be summarized as follows.

1. There is no evidence to support the conclusion that the formation of an oligopolistic price structure is a major cause of inflation in Japan.
2. There is no immediate need to adopt an incomes policy in Japan.
3. The policies that should be given top priority in stabilizing prices are the existing overall demand management policies, centering on fiscal and monetary policy and the promotion of competition. These policies should be appropriately and actively pursued.
4. Unrealistic expectations should not be attached to the concept of incomes policies, and strict conditions should be imposed on their implementation as policy options.

These conclusions were restated in the Kumagai Report of 1972.

5. The Secret "Operation Alpha" on Yen Revaluation
It is widely held that Japanese economic planners were unanimously opposed to an upward revaluation of the yen and that they held out until the very last minute even after the "Nixon shock." In fact, however, in November and December 1969, twenty months before the "Nixon shock," chief policy makers in the Ministry of Finance were conducting top-secret preparations for a yen revaluation, code name "Operation Alpha." According to the recollections of Daizō Hayashi, chief of the Research and Planning Section of the ministry's secretariat at that time, the proceeding of these meetings were as follows.

In order to form a consensus among leading ministry officials, top-secret meetings were held on November 12, November 22, and December 15. These meetings progressed to the point of drafting a public statement for delivery by the finance minister in the event of a revaluation, and gathering materials for consideration of a redenomination of the yen. Three arguments were raised against devaluation: 1) criticism of the basic premise for revaluation, which was that balance of payments surpluses were now a permanent feature of the economy; 2) tampering with the ¥360 rate, which had been in existence for more than thirty years, would make it impossible to conduct future economic policy

("the ¥360 rate is sacred" argument); 3) yen revaluation was politically un-
feasible.

In the third meeting on December 15, Finance Minister Takeo Fukuda
delivered his judgment and declared that the first two counterarguments were
based on simple preconceived ideas, but that the political situation was not such
as to permit such a drastic policy decision. He concluded that "Operation Alpha"
should be tabled until after the general election (December 27) and taken up
again after the New Year. Unfortunately, the political situation after the elections made it even less likely that a yen revaluation could be carried out. The
election had left grave doubts as to the smooth succession from Satō to Fukuda,
and relations between the minister of finance and the prime minister became
extremely tense. Given the split in the LDP over the succession, and Fukuda's
eclipse, the political conditions for a yen revaluation were totally nonexistent
(Daizō Hayashi, "En seisaku kaiko-roku" [Recollections on yen policy], *Kinyū
zaisei jijō* [The present situation in monetary and fiscal policy], February 1977,
No. 7.)

CHAPTER 6

1. Tanaka's Plan for Rebuilding the Japanese Achipelago

Tanaka's ambitious plan envisioned a "Shōwa Restoration" on the centenary
of the Meiji Restoration, suggesting the grandiose nature of the plan. Its three
pillars were industrial relocation, new regional cities of 250,000 people, and the
construction of a vast network of freeways and Shinkansen trains linking the
four islands of the archipelago. It is worthwhile to point out the differences
between this plan and the ill-fated New Comprehensive National Development
Plan (*see* Chapter 5, note 3).

Both plans emphasized the necessity of a radical reconstruction of the archipelago in order to solve the dilemma of overcrowding in industrial centers and
depopulation in rural and outlying areas. However, while the earlier plan had
given priority to responding to the advent of an "information society" through
the formation of a new transportation and communications network, the Tanaka
plan gave highest priority to industrial relocation. Similarly, both plans emphasized establishing new regional cities with populations of around 250,000.
However, Tanaka's plan developed this concept in much more concrete detail.

Perhaps the most important difference between the two plans was in their
respective expectations for the future growth of the economy. The shift to slower
growth was a basic premise of the earlier plan, and it forecast economic growth
rates of 7.5 percent and a GNP of ¥200 trillion in 1985 (at prices in 1970).
Tanaka's plan was based on growth rates of 10 percent a year, and a GNP of
¥300 trillion by 1985. In fact, Tanaka's plan wildly overestimated the ability of
the economy to expand industrial production, mass transportation, and social
overhead investment.

Finally, while the earlier plan deferred to regional governments in conceiving concrete development projects, and was based on the expectation of creative development proposals by local governments, Tanaka's plan designated specific grant lands throughout the country and outlined concrete development concepts for each region. Needless to say, this aspect of the plan met with an angry response from local governments.

Indeed, Tanaka's plan became the subject of loud local complaints almost from the date of its publication in late 1972. Land prices in designated areas exploded; inflation soared. In October 1973, the oil crisis put a permanent end to this wildly unrealistic plan. Moreover, about one year after the oil crisis, Tanaka was caught in the Lockheed scandal and the scandal surrounding his money-power politics and was forced to resign in favor of Takeo Miki (*see* Hiromi Arisawa, *Shōwa keizai shi* [An economic history of the Shōwa period], Nihon Keizai Shimbun-sha.)

2. The "Phantom Economic Stabilization Law"

This law has received little attention in research up to now, but it was one of those policy proposals to which I was referring in the Preface when I said that the fact that they were not adopted, or abandoned in midstream, had a substantial impact on future events. After the budget for 1973 had passed the Diet, Michio Takeuchi (chief of the secretariat) and Takehiro Sagami (chief of the Research and Planning Section), under directions from Finance Minister Aichi, hurriedly drafted a proposal for the law entitled the "Special Measures Law Concerning Fiscal and Monetary Policies for the Promotion of Economic Stabilization." The speed with which the proposal was drafted suggests the extent to which Finance Ministry officials felt that the failure to put forward a policy for restraining inflation would amount to an intolerable loss of face for the ministry. The measures put forward by the draft proposal may be summarized as follows.

1. The absorption and freezing of excess liquidity through the issue of so-called stabilization bonds.
2. A temporary increase in corporate tax levies as a countercyclical measure.
3. Reductions and relaxations of tariffs on imports of products related to daily life aimed at stabilizing the domestic prices of these products.
4. A uniform readjustment of tariff schedules aimed at the promotion or suppression of specific imports.
5. Specification of measures to suppress exports designed to eliminate the chronic disequilibrium in the balance of payments.
6. Introduction of the system of reserve requirements on loan capital designed to supplement and strengthen the existing deposit reserve system.

Ultimately, due to the failure to reach a consensus among all the related ministries and agencies, and because of the turmoil over shortages and "crazy prices," the draft proposal was never presented to the Diet. While this "phantom economic stabilization law," as it came to be called, may be criticized for having been basically a measure designed to avoid an upward revaluation of the yen, it was important in the sense that it recognized that the existing framework of monetary and fiscal policies was not sufficient to respond effectively to rapid changes in the domestic or international economic situation. Moreover, it had great historical significance in the sense that its first and second proposals attempted to develop and establish innovative economic policy measures (many of these measures were borrowed from West Germany's Law for Economic Stabilization and the Promotion of Economic Growth). Had the principle points of this law been enacted, subsequent monetary and fiscal policies could have been implemented much more effectively. Moreover, it represented an attempt to formulate economic stabilization measures during a period when some of the momentum of high-speed growth still remained. Unfortunately, the myth of high-speed growth continued to dominate economic policy long after that period had ended.

3. OPEC, OAPEC, and the Oil-Producing Countries

OPEC was established in September 1960 by Iran, Iraq, Saudi Arabia, Kuwait, and Venezuela, but quickly expanded to include Qatar, Indonesia, Libya, Abu Dhabi, Algeria, Nigeria, the United Arab Emirates, and Gabon. OAPEC (Organization of Arab Petroleum Exporting Countries) was formed in 1968 by Saudi Arabia, Kuwait, and Libya in opposition to OPEC's total ban on petroleum exports after the "third" Middle Eastern War in 1967. Subsequently, it devoted its efforts primarily to protecting the profits of the Arab oil-producing countries. By the time of the oil crisis of 1973, it had ten members.

OPEC's original purpose was to resist arbitrary oil price reductions by the majors (international petroleum countries) during a period of worldwide overproduction, and to maintain and expand oil income for producing countries. It was a period in which Venezuela found its position threatened by the enormous increases in Middle Eastern production, while Iran and other countries in the Middle East were going through a period of intense nationalism, in which there were rising demands for nationalization of Iranian oil companies.

The first blow to the overwhelmingly superior position of the majors and the oil-consuming nations came in September 1970, when Libya succeeded in an across-the-board increase in official prices by threatening to nationalize oil companies in its territory. The other OPEC countries immediately followed suit (the leapfrog effect dreaded by the oil companies).

The twenty-first general meeting of OPEC in Caracas in the same year and the Tehran Agreement in 1971 effectively put an end to the era of low energy costs. The Tehran Agreement raised the official price of oil by thirty-eight cents a barrel (from $1.80 to $2.18) and introduced the system of indexation to compensate for declines in the dollar. On August 15, with the "Nixon shock" and the international shift to the float system, OPEC raised the official price of oil once again to compensate for the loss of real income due to the devaluation of the dollar and instituted the system of quarterly price readjustments to respond to currency fluctuations resulting from the floating exchange rates.

In the New Geneva Accord, signed in 1973 (the year of the "oil shock"), an extremely complicated system of measures was instituted to insure that the oil-producing countries would not suffer losses due to fluctuations in exchange rates or the value of the dollar. These measures constituted a mechanism by which oil prices would increase almost automatically in response to any changes in the international economic situation.

OPEC did not stop with increasing prices but developed common policies for the promotion of participation (enterprise-level participation in oil profits) and actively supported nationalization of oil companies. The New York Agreement of 1972 between the six Persian Gulf states and twenty-three international oil companies established the principle of long-term, gradual increases in the oil-producing countries' participation ratios until a level of 51 percent participation had been reached in 1983. Needless to say, OPEC's recognition of its power to influence international political events was already apparent in June 1967.

4. The Scale of "Crazy Prices"

The phenomenon of "crazy prices" seemed to be a re-creation of the rampant inflation of the immediate postwar period. Consumer prices in Tokyo in February 1974 had increased by 24 percent over those only a year earlier, the highest inflation rate since June 1949 (24.8 percent). Moreover, this figure disguises the fact that the prices of daily necessities were increasing at much higher rates. The following are some examples of price increases over 50 percent: cabbage (over 400 percent); sweet potatoes, nails (300 to 400 percent); spinach, onions, lettuce, carrots, turnips, cauliflowers, sewage construction, toilet paper (200 to 300 percent); *udon* (noodles), potatoes, radishes, mackerel, alarm clocks, thread, letter paper, scrubbing brushes, wall construction (80 percent to 200 percent); sweet bean paste, flowers, instant noodles, *miso* (bean paste), salmon, squid, shellfish, Chinese cabbages, cookies, rice crackers, cement, sugar, glassware, tea kettles, light bulbs, school uniforms, men's shirts, dictionaries (50 to 75 percent).

APPENDIX: Cabinets from 1945 to 1983

Prince Naruhiko Higashikuni
    Aug.–Oct. 1945
Kijūrō Shidehara
    Oct. 1945–May 1946
Shigeru Yoshida
    (1) May 1946–May 1947
Tetsu Katayama
    May 1947–March 1948
Hitoshi Ashida
    March–Oct. 1948
Shigeru Yoshida
    (2) Oct. 1948–Jan. 1949
    (3) Feb. 1949–Sept. 1952
    (4) Oct. 1952–May 1953
    (5) May 1953–Dec. 1954
Ichirō Hatoyama
    (1) Dec. 1954–March 1955
    (2) March 1955–Nov. 1955
    (3) Nov. 1955–Dec. 1956
Tanzan Ishibashi
    Dec. 1956–Feb. 1957
Nobusuke Kishi
    (1) Feb. 1957–June 1958
    (2) June 1958–July 1960

Hayato Ikeda
    (1) July 1960–Nov. 1960
    (2) Dec. 1960–Dec. 1963
    (3) Dec. 1963–Oct. 1964
Eisaku Satō
    (1) Nov. 1964–Feb. 1967
    (2) Feb. 1967–Jan. 1970
    (3) Jan. 1970–July 1972
Kakuei Tanaka
    (1) July 1972–Dec. 1972
    (2) Dec. 1972–Dec. 1974
Takeo Miki
    Dec. 1974–Dec. 1976
Takeo Fukuda
    Dec. 1976–Nov. 1978
Masayoshi Ōhira
    (1) Dec. 1978–Oct. 1979
    (2) Nov. 1979–June 1980
Zenkō Suzuki
    July 1980–Nov. 1982
Yasuhiro Nakasone
    Nov. 1982–

INDEX

"one group, one set," 126. *See also* keiretsu.
Organization for Economic Co-operation and Development (OECD), 120, 174, 193
Organization of Arab Petroleum Exporting Countries (OAPEC), 201
Organization of Petroleum Exporting Countries (OPEC), 201, 209, 221, 237
Ōta, Kaoru, 133
Ōuchi, Hyōe, 31, 50
overloans, 54, 78, 80, 96, 100, 102, 127, 143

Pacific Belt Region Concept, 115
Pauley, Edwin W., 24
Pauley Report, 24, 46
petrochemicals industry, 91, 93, 125, 126, 218
Petroleum Association of Japan, 205
petroleum industry, *see* oil
Petroleum Industry Law, 119
Petroleum Supply and Demand Normalization Law, 204
Philippines, the, 67
Pioneer, 128
Plan for Rebuilding the Japanese Archipelago (Tanaka), 190, 192
plant and equipment boom, 69–73
pollution, 115, 164–69, 232, 236
Pollution Countermeasures Basic Law, 167, 168
postwar period, chronology of, 12
Potsdam Declaration, 13, 18
price controls, *see* wage and price systems, rationing
Priority Production Concept, 36, 41–44, 52, 69
productivity differentials inflation, 141, 170
Public Housing Corporation, 106
"public–private cooperation," 119
Purge of Public Officials Law, 63

rationing, 27–29, 32, 34, 38–41, 52–53
raw materials, 18, 36, 40, 60, 62, 76, 93, 98, 118, 119, 143, 145, 164, 170–71
readjustment inflation theory, 194
Reagan, Ronald, 233
recessions, (1951; post–Korean War) 64, 68, 69, 99; (1954) 78, 79, 143, 147; (1958; bottom-of-the-pot) 102–4, 143, 147, 209; (1965) 146–50, 151, 209 (*see also* structural recession theory); (1971; yen revaluation) 189; (1974; post–oil shock) 209–20
Reconstruction Finance Bank, 35, 37, 43, 48, 49, 50, 62
Reconversion Finance Bank, *see* Reconstruction Finance Bank
relief aid, 37, 46, 43

reparations, 23, 24, 46, 66, 67
Report on Actual Conditions in the Economy, 39
reserve funds system, 65, 66
Revised Agricultural Lands Adjustment Law, 20
Ridgway, Matthew B., 63

Sadanori Shimoyama incident, 53
salary-doubling theory, 113, 114
San Francisco Peace Treaty, 56, 62, 63, 65, 66, 109
Sankyō Seiki, 128
Sanwa Bank, 64
Satō, Eisaku, 149, 156, 163, 164, 169, 175, 176, 177, 188, 189
Schiller, Karl, 181
Second-Period Plan for the Petrochemicals Industry, 91
Second Rationalization Plan, *see* steel industry
Sharp, 71
Shibusawa, Keizō, 31
Shidehara Cabinet, 19, 31
Shimomura, Osamu, 38, 99, 114, 140, 209
Shinchōsha Publishing Company, 107
Shinohara, Miyohei, 147, 148, 183
shipbuilding industry, 15, 70, 91
Shōwa Economic History (Arisawa), 194
Shōwa Electric scandal, 48
Sino-Japanese Trade Agreement, 189
Six-Year General Economic Plan, *see* Five-Year Plan for Economic Independence
Small and Medium Enterprises Finance Corporation, 137
Small and Medium Enterprises Modernization Financial Assistance Law, 137
Small and Medium Enterprises Modernization Promotion Law, 137
Small and Medium Enterprises Organizations Law, 138
Smaller Business Finance Corporation, 66
Smithsonian Agreement, 12, 186–87, 192–96
social dumping, 73, 86, 87, 113
social overhead investment, 66, 97, 98, 99
Sony, 71, 127, 138
Southeast Asia, 16, 53, 61, 62, 67, 75, 76, 77
Soviet Union, 46, 79, 109
Special Account for Provisional Military Expenses, 30
Special Account for Trade Funds, 50
Special Finance Law, 150
Special Foreign Exchange Account, 58, 60, 62
Special Measures for Pollution-Related Damage to Health Law, 167
Special Measures Law for the Establish-

ment of Owner-Cultivators, 20
Special Measures Law for the Promotion
of Designated Industries, 119, 120
special procurements, 56–61, 68, 75, 76,
77, 81
Special Tax Measures Law, 65
Special Temporary Corporate Profits Tax
Law, 207
stabilization panic, 52, 53
Stans, Maurice, 177
steel industry, 36, 37, 39, 61, 69, 70, 79,
89, 97, 125, 127, 225; First Rationalization Plan, 70, 89; Second Rationalization Plan, 89–90
stock market, 61
Strike Reparations Report, 48
structural recession theory, 147–148
Suez Canal crisis ("second" Middle Eastern War), 96, 99, 101
Sumitomo group, 22; Bank 64; Chemicals, 91
Suzuki Cabinet, 19
synthetic fibers industry, 71, 90, 106, 123

Taiwan, 18, 36
Takahashi, Kamekichi, 208
Tanaka, Kakuei, 178, 189–96 passim, 198,
200, 205, 206, 208, 213–14, 223
Tate, Ryūichirō, 141
taxes, 35, 114, 212–13; capital accumula-
tion system, 66; cut, 76, 104, 111, 186,
216; exemptions, 65; land, 34, 164
technology revolution, 12, 83, 86, 89, 93
Temporary Measures Law for the Stabilization of Designated Depressed Industries, 218
Ten-Year Plan for Residential Construc-
tion, 106
textile industry, 61, 68, 73, 76, 85, 122–23,
140, 177, 178, 218
third yen policy, 194
Thirty-Year History of the Economic
Planning Agency (Arita), 191
Tōshiba, 71
Toyokawa Credit Association, 204
Tōyō Rayon, 71
Toyota, 71, 91, 126, 158
Trade Control Law, 194
trade frictions, 117–18, 157, 173–79, 181–
82, 193–94, 220–21, 242–49
trade liberalization, 111, 116–20, 121, 125,
126, 177, 178, 179
Trade Union Law, 21
Transactions Stabilization Agreement, 199
Truman, Harry S., 56
Tsuru, Shigeto, 38, 39, 44, 45

"Tsuru White Paper," 39

Uchida, Tadao, 153, 183
unemployment, 39, 52, 53, 87, 211, 212,
232, 241; decline of, 129, 221
Unemployment Insurance Law, 21
United Nations, 55, 56, 57
United States, 46, 220–221; currency
crisis, 153, 155, 192–96; economic
policy, 220–21; food crisis, 199–200;
Japan's growth compared, 157, 160;
–Japan trade relations, 117, 119, 176–
87; Korean War boom, 55, 56, 62, 75;
military in Japan, 63, 109–10; oil crisis,
201, 202; recession, 79, 104
Upward Revaluation of the Yen: What
Will Happen When It Comes?, 176
U.S. Economic Cooperation Administra-
tion, 61
U.S.–Japan Security Treaty, 63, 67, 109–
10, 164

Vietnam, 67
Vietnam War, 155, 180, 196
Volcker, Paul, 195

Wada, Hiroo, 38, 40, 43, 45
wage and price systems, 27–39, 41, 42, 43,
52. See also rationing.
wage increases, 61, 87, 113, 122, 131–33,
137, 141, 142, 159, 160, 162, 170, 207,
211, 213, 219, 231
war indemnities, 30–35
War Indemnity Special Measures Law, 35
West Germany, 113, 157, 160, 173, 178,
181, 182, 195, 221
window guidance, 78, 99, 100, 102, 143
World Bank, 63, 70, 82, 145

Yamaichi Securities, 146
Yamamoto, Takayuki, 38
Yasuda group, 22
Yawata Steel, 70, 90, 153
yen revaluation, 175–76, 179–87, 194, 195,
196
Yokkaichi petrochemical complex, 98
Yom Kippur War, 201
Yoshida Manufacturing, 128
Yoshida, Shigeru, 36, 37, 45, 52, 78, 79,
81, 82, 109, 111
Yoshida Cabinet (first), 31, 35, 41;
(second), 48, 51

zaibatsu (financial combine), 19, 21–23,
64, 65
Zaibatsu Dissolution Law, 64

定価3,500円
in Japan

Economic Fluctuations in response to Major Events in the Postwar Period

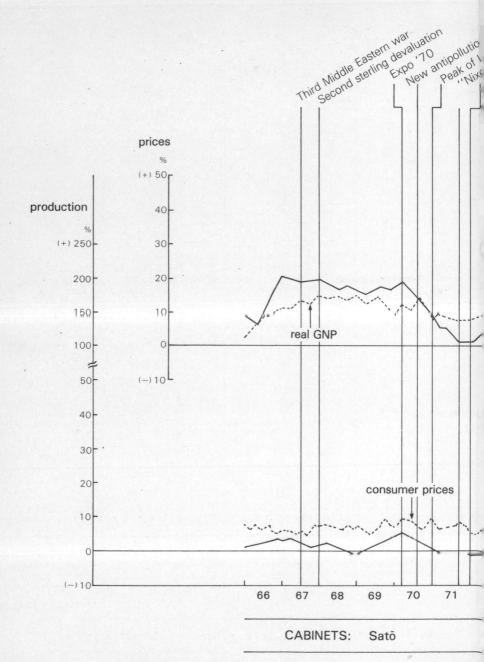

Third Middle Eastern war
Second sterling devaluation
Expo '70
New antipollutio[n]
Peak of I[
"Nix[on

prices

%

(+) 50

40

30

20

10

0

(−) 10

production

%

(+) 250

200

150

100

50

40

30

20

10

0

(−) 10

real GNP

consumer prices

66   67   68   69   70   71

CABINETS: Satō